BECOMING QUALITATIVE RESEARCHERS

BECOMING QUALITATIVE RESEARCHERS

An Introduction

SECOND EDITION

Corrine Glesne
University of Vermont

An imprint of Addison Wesley Longman, Inc.

New York • Reading, Massachusetts • Menlo Park, California • Harlow, England
Don Mills, Ontario • Sydney • Mexico City • Madrid • Amsterdam

Acquisitions Editor: Art Pomponio
Associate Editor: Arianne Weber
Marketing Manager: Renée Ortbals
Project Editor: Donna DeBenedictis
Design Manager/Cover Designer: Rubina Yeh
Electronic Production Specialist: Joanne Del Ben
Prepress Services Supervisor: Valerie Vargas
Print Buyer: Denise Sandler
Electronic Page Makeup: Joanne Del Ben
Printer and Binder: The Maple-Vail Book Manufacturing Group
Cover Printer: Coral Graphic Services, Inc.

Library of Congress Cataloging-in-Publication Data

Glesne, Corrine.
    Becoming qualitative researchers : an introduction / Corrine
Glesne. — 2nd ed.
        p.   cm.
    Includes bibliographical references and index.
    ISBN 0-8013-1633-2 (pbk.)
    1. Social sciences—Methodology.   I. Title.
H61.G555   1998
300′.1—dc21   98-48121
                                                           CIP

ISBN 0-8013-1633-2

    5678910—MA—02

Contents

Chapter 8

Writing Your Story: What Your Data Say   155

Chapter 9

Improvising a Song of the World: Language and Representation   175

Chapter 10

The Continuing Search   193

List of Exhibits

Introduction:
A Sense of Things to Come

The second edition of *Becoming Qualitative Researchers* has been a long time coming. For a while, I resisted requests from the publishers for an update. Eventually, colleagues convinced me to develop a second edition that would better reflect recent qualitative research conversations. In the seven years since the first edition, qualitative texts have proliferated and discussions have expanded in scope. I decided to accept the challenge of incorporating more of these perspectives into the text, without losing its accessibility for the intended audience—those of you who are new to qualitative research.

Writing the second edition has allowed me to see how I have changed in my perspectives and understanding of qualitative research over the last decade. As foreshadowed at the end of the last edition, I have continued to be interested in and partial to inquiry approaches that involve research participants more fully in the work as in action research and often in feminist and critical research. I believe that inquiry-based practice, accompanied with critical reflection, can contribute to making society more humane and equitable. I therefore include more discussion of such approaches in this edition. Nonetheless, I keep the focus on traditional ethnographic techniques as the means for the novice researcher to begin to understand the practice of qualitative inquiry.

In the years between first and second editions, I also have been drawn to thinking about how and for whom qualitative researchers write up their work. In particular, I have become interested in creative and experimental forms of writing qualitative research. Chapter 9, subtitled *Language and Representation,* is a new addition to the text and reflects this interest. I also discuss influences of postmodern thought on the practice of qualitative inquiry (Chapters 1 and 9) since postmodernity is a guiding intellectual viewpoint of this time. Throughout the book, I provide more examples, update references, and recommend sources for further information. Because of requests concerning the kinds of activities I do with my classes, I have also developed end-of-chapter exercises for those of you who find these helpful. Some of the exercises are meant to be carried out individually, while others are to be engaged in collaboratively and build upon previous group exercises as the course proceeds.

In qualitative research, face-to-face interactions are the predominant distinctive feature and also the basis for its most common problems. Through researchers' involvement with the people they study, lives become entwined, with all the accompanying challenges and opportunities that such closeness brings. The prominence of face-to-face interactions necessitates the discussion of rapport, subjectivity, and ethical issues. The chapters on rapport and subjectivity (Chapter 5) and ethics (Chapter 6) involve matters that must be considered throughout the research process but which are often less fully addressed in other introductory texts. This edition includes discussions of reflexivity and intersubjectivity, as well as examples of students monitoring their own subjective lenses.

The significance of the relationship between the researcher and the researched even affects how we refer to those from whom we want to learn. In quantitative studies, those researched are commonly called *subjects*. Qualitative researchers tend to be uncomfortable with the term *subject* because it implies the *acting on* rather than the *interacting with* that at best characterizes qualitative inquiry. Therefore, I use the following terms somewhat interchangeably throughout the book: *research participants, respondents, interviewees,* and *researched,* as well as the term *others* as suggested by postmodernists.

Chapters tend to compartmentalize thoughts, giving the impression that data collection, for example, is distinct from data analysis. Although the activities of qualitative inquiry tend to be ongoing and overlapping, I use chapters to focus upon one research aspect at a time. My guiding principle throughout these pages has been to create a book I would want to use as a primary text to help students begin to conduct qualitative research. The book therefore guides you through the research process, with separate chapters on research design (Chapter 2), participant observation (Chapter 3), interviewing (Chapter 4), data analysis (Chapter 7), and writing (Chapters 8 and 9). Along the way it raises issues, questions, and quandaries with which my students and I have struggled. As students in my classes have noted, my most frequent answer to questions raised by qualitative inquiry is, "It depends." In class discussions and in this book, I provide no solutions, find no truths. My goal is to raise questions, thereby indicating what is problematic, and suggest guidelines for developing your own judgment in order to learn from and manage the complex issues you may encounter. To become competent researchers, you must acquire the general lore associated with research processes and learn how, in light of your personal qualities and the research situation, you can best conduct your inquiry.

Since many of you will be working on theses or dissertations, I periodically address some of the particular problems that you might encounter. Many of the text examples are drawn from educational settings, but the book is not limited to the context of schools or to the needs of scholars of education. The sources of examples are the experiences of students, my own inquiries, the research of Alan Peshkin (he was co-author of the first edition), and published works. I am most indebted to students at the University of Vermont*; they have taught me much about

---

*Some examples in the text are drawn from students at the University of Illinois, noted by Alan Peshkin in the 1992 edition.

qualitative inquiry. With permission, I identify their examples by their first names, or, for some, by pseudonyms.

From my perspective, acquiring the skill and understanding for conducting qualitative inquiry has three dimensions: reading, reflecting, and doing. Preferably, all three are done simultaneously so that the outcomes of each continually interact. Read widely and deeply about your topic *and* about the conduct of inquiry throughout the research process. Practice qualitative research techniques on problems of significance to you as you read about doing qualitative research. Ideally, the course is occasion for supervised pilot studies for theses and dissertations. Reflect before and after each step in your research journey (from developing your research statement to completing your research report) through keeping a field journal and through discussions with peers, supervisors, and research participants.

Keeping a field journal that describes your practices and, no less important, your critical reflections on these practices is crucial to doing good research. I cannot emphasize it enough. The field journal, in effect, becomes not only an *audit trail* of the research process, but also a personal methods book that contains the insights that result from the interaction of reading, reflecting, and doing research. Learning to reflect on your behavior and thoughts, as well as on the phenomenon under study, creates a means for continuously becoming a better researcher. *Becoming* a better researcher captures the dynamic nature of the process. Conducting research, like teaching or dancing, can be improved; it cannot be mastered.

In my late teens and early twenties, I spent summers teaching swimming lessons. Communicating the process of qualitative inquiry provides me some of the same kinds of rewards that teaching swimming did. At the end of a semester (or better two semesters), students no longer fear to jump in, nor are they at risk of drowning in data. With careful, sure strokes, they stride through data collection, analysis, and writing—albeit, not without the occasional stormy day. Students gain a useful skill that can serve them beyond the thesis and dissertation stages. In return, I learn much from students about both the process of doing qualitative research and their topical area. They educate me, for example, about the social construction of developmental disabilities or about the workings of effective partner team-teaching in middle schools. I believe that qualitative research can provide a forum for reflection and communication that results in better programs, gives voice to those who have been marginalized, and assists researchers, participants, and readers to see the world in new ways. For comments, suggestions, or questions, please contact me at cglesne@zoo.uvm.edu.

CORRINE GLESNE

Acknowledgments

Alan Peshkin, who joined me in writing the first edition, chose not be part of the revised edition. Examples from his work and many of his contributions to the first edition persist. I remain grateful to him as well as to others whose examples in the first edition continue to serve and to Naomi Silverman, whose urging and guidance was responsible for the development of the book in the first place.

For this edition, my appreciation goes to Penny Bishop, who worked with me much of one semester, contributing insights, writing, and editing skills as well as examples from her own work; to Marleen Pugach and Phil Smith, who allowed me to use excerpts from their work and who readily and critically read chapters I sent their way; and to Carolyne White, whose example always pushes me to consider other ways of thinking about qualitative research. Thanks too to many other students and colleagues whose work or support contributed to the text; particularly, Kelly Clark, Rebecca Esch, Katie Furney, Pam Kay, Yvette Pigeon, my writing group (Rob and Jill Tarule, Michael Strauss, Toby and Laura Fulwiler, Mary Jane Dickerson, and Glenda Bissex), and the 1998 Reading and Writing Ethnography Class. I am also grateful to the readers (one professor asked her whole class to critique the first edition) and Longman reviewers who made suggestions that helped guide me in my work. These thanks go to

Nancy Dana, Pennsylvania State University
Gail C. Furman, Washington State University
Jan Gamradt, University of New Mexico
Harold G. Levine, University of California, Los Angeles
Sandra Mathison, State University of New York, Albany
Jamie Meyers, Pennsylvania State University
Flora Ida Ortiz, University of California, Riverside
Carolyn Payne, Iowa State University
Timothy Reagan, University of Connecticut
Bob Stake, University of Illinois
William M. Stallings, Georgia State University

Finally, thanks to editor Arianne Weber for her persistence and assistance.

C. G.

Chapter 1

Meeting Qualitative Inquiry

Beginnings

Sofie knew and taught me that everyone had some story, every house held a life that could be penetrated and known, if one took the trouble. Stories told to oneself or others could transform the world. Waiting for others to tell their stories, even helping them do so, meant no one could be regarded as completely dull, no place people lived in was without some hope of redemption, achieved by paying attention. (Myerhoff 1979, 240)

Anthropologist Barbara Myerhoff was talking about the grandmother who raised her and who, through her love of stories, perhaps set the course for Myerhoff's life. Learning to listen well to others' stories and to interpret and retell the accounts is part of the qualitative researcher's trade.

Since qualitative researchers seek to make sense of personal stories and the ways in which they intersect, I begin with a personal narrative of my connections to research. If you know something about my story, you may more fully understand and interpret my perspective in the text that follows.

I do not remember "discovering" qualitative inquiry. Where or when I first heard the term escapes me. The process, however, is one with which I have been familiar for some time. I grew up in a small, rural, Midwestern town where most everyone went to church (no synagogues) and most everyone had European ancestry (predominantly German). I was always interested in people who were culturally different from me and my neighbors. I read each month's *National Geographic* and filled my nights with folk tales from around the world. Books such as *Arctic Wild* (Crisler 1958) and *No Room in the Ark* (Moorehead 1959) from my parents' bookshelves supplemented library books about travelers, explorers, and adventurers from Genghis Khan to Amelia Earhart.

I gravitated toward anthropology as an undergraduate, which allowed me to continue learning about the many different ways people live. I wrote papers on land tenure in Madagascar and kinship in Sarawak, traced the development of the Chinese novel, and researched the effects of colonialism on the Maori. The more I read, the more I wanted to see for myself. For anthropologists, fieldwork—being present in others' lives—is *the* way to learn about another culture.

Thus began a postgraduate trek in which I traveled and worked from Wales to Afghanistan. On a kibbutz in Israel, I pollinated date palms, pruned banana plants, picked grapefruit, and grew increasingly interested in tropical agriculture. Later, I lived in Jerusalem and joined a team of archaeologists for a year. Herodian walls, Roman baths, Byzantine mosaics, and Crusader arches remain vivid images for me because I carefully measured and drew to scale these uncovered structures. I continued with archaeological work in northern Kenya. I camped in dry riverbeds and walked over the tracks of rhinos and lions as I helped to trace the southern migration of people away from the Nile 10,000 years ago. Throughout this period, I kept journals. As I read them now, I am struck by my joy about what I was learning, and my frustration about how to make use of all I experienced. Constantly stimulated by different ways of doing things and multiple ways of understanding them, I was restless and eager to put it all together. Such desires led me to graduate school with plans to apply anthropology through education.

In graduate school, I took classes in anthropology, international agriculture, and education. I ventured into research courses. The word sounded hard, formal, abstract. Several courses taught me about experimental and quasi-experimental design and helped me to understand control groups and dependent and independent variables. I took statistics and worked with computers on analysis programs. It seemed like a game, but I could not link this approach to what I had learned about people in my travels. Then I took a course in cognitive anthropology followed by one on in-depth interviewing. The courses focused on question development, interviewing strangers, keeping field logs, and making sense of it all. They provided theory and structure for what I had been doing more haphazardly on my own.

My first qualitative research project (my master's thesis) was an interview and archival study of Illinois rural women who worked the land. Then, as a doctoral student, I was asked by Alan Peshkin to be one of two research assistants in an ethnography of a fundamentalist Christian school. Peshkin moved to the community. The other assistant and I spent two days a week at the school for the academic year. For a semester we observed from the back of classrooms, keeping detailed field notes. During the second semester, we conducted multiple-session interviews with teachers and students.

Before beginning my dissertation research, I worked for nearly a year under the direction of Michael Quinn Patton as an action researcher in Saint Vincent and the Grenadines as part of a multiple-nation Caribbean Agricultural Extension Project. My primary role was to work with representatives of various private agencies, governmental groups, and farmers organizations to create a national agricultural extension plan that was passed by the Vincentian parliament. I returned to Saint Vincent to do a traditional ethnography in one rural village, focusing on young people, agriculture, and education. It was at this time in particular that I sought out the literature that helped me to make more sense of the lives of others as well as my own—texts and tales on qualitative inquiry. Since then, I have been involved in a number of qualitative evaluation projects, a life history project, and another action research project (as described later in this chapter).

Through my qualitative research experiences and through reading the work of other scholars, I have become particularly sensitive to and interested in interactions and relationships between researchers and study participants. I perceive much research as grounded in an ethical commitment to a "greater good," rather than to the people involved. I readily acknowledge a need for inquiry that does not set out to serve research participants, but I am personally inclined toward research that contributes to the lives of the participants. This position aligns me more closely with philosophies of action, feminist, and critical research. Nonetheless, this book presents a fairly traditional approach to doing ethnography, the basics, in a sense, used by people doing many kinds of qualitative research.

I use a quotation from *The Tao of Painting* (Sze and Wang 1963/1701) in my qualitative research syllabus that represents my perspective on learning to do qualitative inquiry:

> Some set great value on method, while others pride themselves on dispensing with method. To be without method is deplorable, but to depend on method entirely is worse. You must first learn to observe the rules faithfully; afterwards, modify them according to your intelligence and capacity. (17)

Learning to do qualitative research is like learning to paint. Study the masters, learn techniques and methods, practice them faithfully, and then adapt them to your own persuasions when you know enough to describe the work of those who have influenced you and the ways in which you are contributing new perspectives.

Searching

Dictionaries define research as a careful and diligent search. We have all been engaged in a variety of careful and diligent searches without necessarily labeling the process research, let alone a particular type of research. For example, my mother became interested in our family's genealogy. In her search to develop the family tree, she asked questions of great aunts and second cousins; requested that they and other relatives share letters and photo albums; wandered in cemeteries in towns where ancestors had lived; and sent for documents from hospitals, town clerks, and churches. From the formal and informal documents and the words of relatives, she carefully and diligently traced our family's history, recording both the dates of significant events (births, marriages, deaths) and the stories she heard.

As students some of you may have conducted searches without having been assigned to do so. For example, perhaps when you were undergraduates living in a residence hall, you and your friends became increasingly dissatisfied with the selection of food provided by the food service. You complained, but nothing changed. Over a particularly unsatisfactory meal, you and your friends decided to develop a survey for residents. The survey took shape as a series of statements followed by a five-point scale that ranged from strongly agree to strongly disagree. You typed it up, discussed it at a hall meeting, and got the resident hall adviser to make copies, which were distributed via mailboxes. Respondents were asked to deposit the survey in a box outside the dining hall by a certain date. On that date, you and your friends collected the surveys and began to tally the numbers. By the end of a long evening, you knew what proportion of residents responded and how those residents felt about certain aspects of the food service. Armed with your facts in the form of a written summary, you distributed a copy to the school newspaper, the university president, and the food service.

As professionals, you may have continued to conduct searches. A middle school English teacher was struck each September by a pattern of frightened, uncertain new students. She had a hunch that teachers, administrators, and older students could do something to ease the transition, but she was not sure what. So she asked her sixth-, seventh-, and eighth-grade classes to write essays about how they felt during their first few days as sixth graders, what made the experience good, what made the experience bad, and what could be changed to make it better. Then, working with the students, the teacher prepared a report for presentation to staff and administration, suggesting steps that the school could take.

In all three of these examples, people are engaged in research. They deliberately set out to collect data for specified purposes. In all three cases data might have been collected more carefully, but the point is that people do carry out research of sorts in their everyday lives—even though they may not name the approach they use or be aware of how to improve the process so the results are more trustworthy and, thereby, of greater use. This book is meant to help you improve your approach to qualitative research so that your results are both trustworthy and useful.

Some of you may have been conditioned to think of research as a process that uses an instrument such as a survey, involves a large number of people, and is analyzed by reducing the data to numbers. This mode of inquiry, as demonstrated by the food survey, is termed *quantitative* research. The middle school example and parts of the genealogical search show the researcher gathering words by talking with a small number of people, collecting a variety of documents, and, in the middle school example, observing behavior. Both of these cases use *qualitative* approaches.

The two modes of inquiry are frequently contrasted. Quantitative and qualitative researchers, however, use similar elements in their work. They state a purpose, pose a problem or raise a question, define a research population, develop a time frame, collect and analyze data, and present outcomes. They also rely (explicitly or implicitly) on theory and are concerned with rigor. Nonetheless, how researchers go about putting these elements together makes for distinctive differences in both the research process and final product.

Ways of Knowing

The research methods you choose say something about your views on what qualifies as valuable knowledge and your perspective on the nature of reality or *ontology*. "Ontology is the concern about whether the world exists, and if so, in what form. . . . Because we cannot experience the world directly (unfiltered through our senses), we will never know for sure what the world really is. . . . It is a matter of belief . . ." (Potter 1996, 36). Quantitative methods are, in general, supported by the *positivist*[1] paradigm, which characterizes the world as made up of observable, measurable facts. Positivists assume a fixed, measurable reality exists external to people. In contrast, qualitative methods are generally supported by the *interpretivist* (also referred to as *constructivist*) paradigm, which portrays a world in which reality is socially constructed, complex, and ever changing. The ontological belief for interpretivists, therefore, is that social realities are constructed by the participants in those social settings. To understand the nature of constructed realities, qualitative researchers interact and talk with participants about their perceptions. The researchers seek out the variety of perspectives; they do not try to reduce the multiple interpretations to a norm.

"Paradigms are frameworks that function as maps or guides for scientific communities, determining important problems or issues for its members to address and defining acceptable theories or explanations, methods and techniques to solve defined problems" (R. Usher 1996, 15). The concept of research paradigms grew out of work by Thomas Kuhn, who published *The Structure of Scientific Revolutions* in 1962. Kuhn, trained as a theoretical physicist, also had a strong interest in philosophy. While a doctoral candidate, he became intrigued with how history informed the philosophy of science (Loving 1997, 430). The book that resulted from this exploration began a philosophical revolution in the practice of science. From Kuhn and others came the argument that "data and observations are theory-led, that theory is paradigm-led, and that paradigms are historically and culturally located" (R. Usher 1997, 16).

Research paradigms determine not only the approach or research methods used, but also the purpose of the research and the roles of the researcher (Firestone 1987). Positivists seek explanations and predictions that will generalize to other persons and places. They use primarily quantitative methods with careful sampling strategies and experimental designs that help them produce generalizable results. The researcher's role is to observe and measure, and care is taken to keep the researcher from affecting the data through personal involvement with research subjects. Researcher "objectivity" is of utmost concern.

Meanwhile, since interpretivists assume that they deal with multiple, socially constructed realities or "qualities" that are complex and indivisible into discrete variables, they regard their research task as coming to understand and interpret how the various participants in a social setting construct the world around them. To make their interpretations, the researchers must gain access to the multiple perspectives of the participants. Their qualitative study designs, therefore, generally focus on in-depth, long-term interaction with relevant people in one or several sites. The researcher becomes the main research instrument as he or she observes, asks questions, and interacts with research participants. The concern with researcher objectivity is replaced by a focus on the role of subjectivity in the research process.

Exhibit 1.1 compares some of the assumptions, purposes, approaches, and researcher roles associated with positivist and interpretivist paradigms. These should not be taken as hard and fast distinctions, but rather as predispositions of the different inquiry approaches. For more discussion on research paradigms and qualitative-quantitative differences, see Eisner 1981; Guba and Lincoln 1994; Howe 1988; Lincoln and Guba 1985; Rist 1977; Schwandt 1989, 1990; Scott and Usher 1996.

—————————————— EXHIBIT 1.1 ——————————————
Predispositions of Positivist and Interpretivist Modes of Inquiry

Positivist Mode	Interpretivist Mode
Assumptions	
• Social facts have an objective reality	• Reality is socially constructed
• Variables can be identified and relationships measured	• Variables are complex, interwoven, and difficult to measure
Research Purposes	
• Generalizability	• Contextualization
• Causal explanations	• Understanding
• Prediction	• Interpretation
Research Approach	
• Begins with hypotheses and theory	• May result in hypotheses and theory
• Uses formal instruments	• Researcher as instrument
• Experimental	• Naturalistic
• Deductive	• Inductive
• Component analysis	• Searches for patterns
• Seeks the norm	• Seeks pluralism, complexity
• Reduces data to numerical indices	• Makes minor use of numerical indices
• Uses abstract language in write-up	• Descriptive write-up
Researcher Role	
• Detachment	• Personal involvement
• Objective portrayal	• Empathic understanding

The open, emergent nature of interpretivist approaches means a lack of standardization; there are no clear criteria to package into neat research steps. The openness sets the stage for discovery as well as for ambiguity that, particularly for the novice researcher, engenders a sometimes overwhelming sense of anxiety: "Who else should I be seeing?" "What else should I be asking?" "How can I ever assemble all of the pieces into something meaningful?" The openness of interpretivism also allows the researcher to approach the inherent complexity of social interaction and to honor that complexity, to respect it in its own right. To do justice to complexity, researchers avoid simplifying social phenomena and instead explore the range of behavior. As Eisner (1981, 9) states, "To know a rose by its Latin name and yet to miss its fragrance is to miss much of the rose's meaning." Interpretivism assists you to uncover some of the complexities of meaning.

A Research Home

Different traditions of interpretivist inquiry have developed in different academic disciplines. For example, in the 1920s a group of sociologists from the University of Chicago began doing what they simply called *fieldwork* (Tesch 1990). Influenced by

British social anthropology, sociologists of the "Chicago School" began applying participant-observation techniques to the study of groups within their own culture. This led to series of studies of "urban groups whose ways of life were below or outside the purview of the respectable middle classes" (Vidich and Lyman 1994, 33). Robert Park and Ernest Burgess were two of the influential sociologists guiding the Chicago School movement, which attracted a number of young sociologists between 1920 and 1960, at which time the mode of research became more quantitative.

In the 1960s and 1970s, some other sociologists were attracted to phenomenology. Edmund Husserl (1859–1938) developed the philosophy of phenomenology, contending that "human consciousness actively constitutes the objects of experience" (Holstein and Gubrium 1994, 263). From this philosophy, Alfred Schutz (1899–1959) created social phenomenology as a research mode, arguing that "the social sciences should focus on the ways that . . . the experiential world every person *takes for granted* is produced and experienced *by members*" (Holstein and Gubrium 1994, 263). A phenomenological study focuses on descriptions of how people experience and how they perceive their experience of the phenomena under study. Phenomenology has also been embraced by some psychologists.

For anthropologists, fieldwork has been the rite of passage ever since Bronislaw Malinowski carried out long-term fieldwork (which he called *ethnography*) in New Guinea and the Trobriand Islands between 1914 and 1918. Typically, anthropologists sought to study a group of people who lived in a culture that was remote and quite different from their own. In the early part of the century, an underlying purpose of their work was often that of contributing to a comparative study of evolutionary stages of cultural development that was decidedly Eurocentric. Another tendency was for anthropologists to romanticize life in nonindustrialized areas and to have implicit purposes of wanting to preserve traditional cultures. Although generally descriptive and interpretive, many anthropologists aspired to be as "scientific" as possible by incorporating into their studies various quantitative techniques. In the 1960s, anthropologists increasingly began to reflect seriously on the relationships between themselves and the people they studied as they and others criticized the anthropological discipline for "its historical and ideological role as the hand-maiden of colonialism and neo-colonialism" (Ellen 1984, 3).

Popkewitz places the move from positivism toward interpretive and critical approaches in the larger sociocultural context. Struck by the "contradictions between liberal ideals and institutional processes" in regard to promoting community and personal efficiency, he views changes in the "concepts and methods of study" as "a reaction to the . . . fragmentation in social affairs and the dissolution of moral life" (Popkewitz 1984, 92–93). Preferred research methods reflect personal choices; they are, however, embedded in cultural and historical contexts.

Although some social science researchers (Lincoln and Guba 1985; Schwandt 1989) perceive positivist and interpretivist approaches as incompatible, others (Patton 1990; Reichardt and Cook 1979) believe that the skilled researcher can successfully combine approaches. The argument usually becomes muddled because one party argues from the underlying philosophical assumptions of each paradigm, and the other focuses on the apparent compatibility of the research methods (quantitative and qualitative), enjoying the rewards of both numbers and words. Because the positivist and interpretivist paradigms ask different questions about the nature of the world, they require different procedures to find the type of data needed. This does not mean, however, that the positivist never uses interviews nor that the interpretivist never uses a survey. They may, but such methods are supplementary, not dominant. Different approaches allow you to know and understand different things about the world.

Nonetheless, people tend to adhere to the methodology that is most consonant with their socialized worldview. We are told that the research problem should define whether one chooses a qualitative approach or a quantitative one. This, however, is not how I believe research necessarily is done. Rather, we are attracted to and shape research problems that match our personal view of seeing and understanding the world:

> Our constructions of the world, our values, and our ideas about how to inquire into those constructions, are mutually self-reinforcing. We conduct inquiry via a particular paradigm because it embodies assumptions about the world that we believe and values that we hold, and because we hold those assumptions and values we conduct inquiry according to the precepts of that paradigm. (Schwandt 1989, 399)

As Jill, a student in Vermont, stated, "I felt that I had found a research home when I learned that qualitative research existed." Notwithstanding that you may be taught that there is a preferred way to do research, the particular research mode with which you will find greatest comfort and satisfaction is likely to depend on your personality and background.

The Variability of Qualitative Inquiry

VARIED MODES

Qualitative inquiry is often used as an umbrella term for various orientations to interpretivist research. For example, qualitative researchers might call their work ethnography, case study, phenomenology, educational criticism, hermeneutics, or a number of other terms. Different qualitative research strategies have been grouped and classified in a variety of ways. Wolcott (1992, 23) focuses first on methods and portrays the various approaches as different limbs on a tree. The main limbs of the tree include participant-observation strategies, interview strategies, nonparticipant-observation strategies, and archival strategies. The interview strategies limb, for example, includes minor branches such as oral history, biography, and investigative journalism while participant-observation strategies divide into field study and ethnography branches, each with a number of smaller branches.

Tesch (1990, 72–73) organizes and categorizes types of qualitative research by four areas of research interest: characteristics of language (i.e., discourse analysis, ethnoscience, symbolic interactionism, and others); discovery of regularities (grounded theory, critical research, ethnography, and others); discerning meaning (phenomenology, case study, life history, and hermeneutics); and reflection (educational connoisseurship, reflective phenomenology, and heuristic research). The various orientations are rooted historically in different disciplines and vary in assumptions, focuses, and methods (Jacob 1988). Before claiming that your work is phenomenological, for example, you should explore the literature associated with that orientation, and with other orientations, so that you can broaden your knowledge of ways to approach qualitative research.

This book focuses on ethnographic research techniques. Ethnography comes from the anthropological tradition of illuminating patterns of culture through long-term immersion in the field, collecting data primarily by participant-observation and interviewing. Analysis of this data focuses on description and interpretation of what people say and do. Although definitions overlap, the term *ethnography* is not interchangeable with other forms of qualitative research such as case study, symbolic interactionism, or phenomenology. These and other approaches, however, often use ethnographic techniques as described in this book.

PARTICIPANT-ORIENTED RESEARCH

In recent years, increased sensitivity to issues of power and authority has encouraged a rethinking of research design and implementation. In traditional inquiry, as practiced by both quantitative and qualitative researchers, authority for research decisions resides with the researcher. This position is challenged by critical, feminist, and action researchers who raise questions about how we carry out research. In particular, they cause us to rethink the purpose of research and, thereby, researcher-researched relationships. Accordingly, this book raises some of these challenges to traditional qualitative research.

The following paragraphs demonstrate how specific research frameworks serve as theoretical lenses to shape the kind of research questions asked and the methods used. For comparisons, I focus on traditional ethnography, critical ethnography, and action research. Then I turn to a brief discussion of critical, feminist, and action research, as well as postmodernity, to provide some context for understanding references and comments in the chapters to come.

In 1992–93, I lived for eight months in Costa Rica. For much of that time, I was in a small fishing village working with a local environmental group that was seeking to train young men and women as nature guides and to educate national and international tourists as well as community members about the environment and cultures of the area. The environmental organization was a grassroots group, developed by local people for local environmental efforts. It was headed by an Indigenous man and drew members from all the ethnic and cultural groups in the area—African Caribbean, Indigenous, Hispanic, and European.

Through a mutual contact, I was introduced to the president of the environmental organization to discuss possibilities of my doing research with the group. He suggested that I draft a proposal for the group's board to discuss. The proposal was accepted and I rented a small house in the village. Within this one setting, my research could have taken a variety of forms.

I might have done traditional ethnography. After working with and hanging out with the group for a month or so, I began to see the leaders and activists of the group as "bridges" in a variety of ways. In particular, it seemed that aspects of their lives had required each to learn several different cultural or value systems. In my field log, I was forming a traditional ethnographic research statement: I wanted to understand (1) the motivations and perceived rewards for those who gave of themselves for a greater good; (2) the cultural context that nurtured or provoked such a gathering of varied, talented, committed individuals; and (3) the role of cross-cultural experiences in the philosophical orientations of the leaders/activists.

In a traditional ethnographic study, I would have developed criteria for selection of leaders/activists, set up a series of interviews, and continued "hanging out" with the group, observing actions and interactions. To help in understanding the sociocultural context of the leaders, I may have set up interviews with family members and significant others. Eventually, I would analyze the interview and observation data for patterns and themes and write a descriptive account meant to contribute to the scholarly understanding of activists/leaders. But I did not do a traditional ethnography, as much as those research questions still interest me.

I might have done critical ethnography. Most of the inhabitants of the area were either African Caribbean in heritage or Indigenous. Although patterns of racial and ethnic oppression have taken different forms in Costa Rica than in the United States, both African Caribbean and Indigenous people suffer discrimination. While in the village, I began to hear stories about the ways outsiders (Costa Rican and foreign) were gaining access to land because some local people lacked legal title, in spite of traditional claims to the land.

I could have done research to understand local customs of land tenure and Costa Rican legislation regarding owning land. Then, I might have formed a critical ethnography research statement such as the following: I want to (1) understand ways in which current systems of privilege (class, ethnicity, gender) allow locals to lose claim to their coastal and rain forest land and (2) work with local groups to develop strategies to retain control over their land. Research methods might include creating dialogue groups to discuss experiences with land tenure, the pressures to sell land if title is held, and possible strategies to defend rights and retain land. I would act as a group facilitator and resource person, providing information about legalities where needed. My primary intent would be to help develop strategies and raise awareness of ways to challenge the ongoing loss of land to outsiders. But I did not do critical ethnography either.

Traditional ethnography strives to describe what is, while critical ethnography looks at what "could be" and moves towards action (Thomas 1993). Critical ethnography can be a kind of action research, but not all action research is critical research. Action research has at its essence the intent to change something, to solve some sort of problem, to take action, but the focus is not necessarily emancipatory or political. Through preliminary discussions with the environmental group, action research was the preferred inquiry mode to all participants. If I, with my skills as a researcher, was going to be involved with the group, they wanted me to use my abilities to help their organization in its efforts, not to do research on them for use elsewhere. And I wanted to be of use to the people with whom I was living and from whom I was learning.

My work with the group, however, did not turn out to be typical action research. Instead, I use the words *volunteer researcher* to describe my role. I worked under the group's direction, but retained some control over my participation by nature of the volunteer status. That is, I could choose *not* to participate in some of the information gathering that was desired such as interviewing banana plantation managers about their environmental efforts—a politically controversial topic at the time.

We set up a series of meetings to discuss small-scale research projects that the board desired. I took on several of these projects, often in concert with another member or two. For example, as part of the educational mission of the group, they wanted a booklet created that would describe the area's environmental and cultural diversity and history, with specific information about particular items that visitors often asked about such as indigenous uses of the rainforest. Such projects were an opportune way for me to learn about the area, sponsored by a local group's authority to approach and talk with residents from all ethnic groups about their experiences and knowledge. I met with people, read written information, and analyzed and wrote up the data into an accessible form that, complete with drawings from a local artist, was made available to visitors in both English and Spanish.

In terms of more typical action research, we met formally as a group and informally in conversations to discuss major issues facing the organization. One such issue was how to prioritize group projects and manage time demands since most members were not paid staff. Through facilitating focused discussions and taking notes, I drafted a mission statement and a year-long work plan, delineating tasks, persons responsible, and budget required. All documents went through several iterations with the group as a whole before being accepted as workable.

My role as a volunteer researcher was more amorphous (and less structurally and economically supported) than my action research in Saint Vincent and the Grenadines. As in Saint Vincent, however, I became an integral part of a group and the relational aspects that developed were more authentic and meaningful to me than those I have felt as a researcher studying others. I learned much in this small village and dare to hope that my participation was useful.

Critical Ethnography   The critical ethnography example with the focus on land tenure is a kind of qualitative research that is sometimes categorized variously as *orientational* (Patton 1990), *ideological* (Guba 1990), or *cultural studies* (Gall, Borg, and Gall 1996) research.[2] "Orientational qualitative inquiry begins with an explicit theoretical or ideological perspective that determines what variables and concepts are most important and how the findings will be interpreted" (Patton 1990, 86). Marxist, capitalist, and Freudian theories, for example, have all been used to frame orientational studies. Critical and feminist ethnography are two orientational research perspectives that increasingly influence how we think about doing qualitative research. Both begin with explicit ideological frameworks and both interpret findings based on particular theoretical perspectives.

Critical ethnographers focus on how knowledge is both powerful and political. Focusing on groups marginal to the dominant culture, researchers attempt to understand and describe the experiences, consciousness, and cultural context of people living in asymmetrical power relations (Quantz 1992, 448). They "describe, analyze, and open to scrutiny otherwise hidden agendas, power centers, and assumptions that inhibit, repress, and constrain" (Thomas 1993, 3). Critical ethnographers seek to do more than understand and describe, however; they want to transform unequal power relations. "Conventional ethnographers study culture for the purpose of describing it; critical ethnographers do so to change it" (Thomas 1993, 4). An explicit purpose of this research is change in attitudes, beliefs, and/or social context for research participants and others.

The term *critical* refers to "the detecting and unmasking of beliefs and practices that limit human freedom, justice, and democracy" (R. Usher 1996, 22). It is not just a criticism which is, as Thomas (1993) states, "a complaint we make when our eggs are too cold" (4). Although the doing of critical ethnography does not follow any particular set of methods, a few general aspects of research design are characteristic of critical ethnography.

First, a clear values perspective prevails. Critical ethnographers assert that while values enter into all research, they work to make their values explicit. They see research as a political act because it not only relies on value systems, but challenges value systems (R. Usher 1996).

Secondly, critical ethnographers seek to do more than represent the experiences and perspectives of research participants, a goal of traditional ethnography. Critical ethnographers often question and investigate ways in which "lived experience may be distorted by false consciousness and ideology" (Schwandt 1990, 268). The incorporation of critical reflection as part of the research process is a means toward revealing unexamined assumptions and toward transforming the day-to-day lives of research participants.

Third, critical ethnography can involve study participants as co-researchers of sorts who combine investigation, education, and action (Maguire 1987). Together a group of people investigate social problems of mutual concern, as Maguire (1987) did with battered women in the Southwest, or as Belenky, Bond, and Weinstock (1997) did with economically poor rural mothers in the Northeast. The investigation becomes an educational endeavor through analysis of the problems' structural causes. It then becomes a process of collective action aimed at social change. Ideally, the researcher-researched relationship is marked by negotiation, reciprocity, and willingness on the part of all participants to change and be changed.

For more on critical ethnography, see Carr and Kemmis 1986; Carspecken and Apple 1992; Gitlin 1994; Kinchelow and McLaren 1994; Quantz 1992; Thomas 1993.

Feminist Ethnography   Feminist research is a broad category used to hold multiple perspectives and methods. As with critical ethnography, however, some central beliefs, purposes, and characteristics of research design serve as a thread, running through the fabric of feminist approaches to inquiry. An underlying assumption to feminist work is the belief that women experience oppression and exploitation and that this experience varies, considering the multiple identities of race, class, culture, ethnicity, sexual preference, age, and physical abilities (Maguire 1996).

Like critical ethnographers, feminist ethnographers also focus on issues of justice and power and are committed to uncovering and understanding the forces that cause and sustain oppression (Maguire 1996). They, too, hold as a primary focus of their work the transformation of asymmetrical power relations, particularly as applied to women. Feminist ethnographers describe, contextualize, and raise questions about (problematize) "women's diverse situations" and then "refer the examination of that problematic to theoretical, policy or action frameworks in the interest of realizing social justice for women" (Olesen 1994, 158). This means examining the status of women in a variety of contexts with the goal of challenging an imbalance of power. This does not mean, however, that the focus is exclusively on gender because "gender oppression is not experienced or structured in isolation from other oppressions" (Maguire 1996, 108). Consideration and analysis of race, class, culture, ethnicity, and other identities play a primary role in feminist research as well.

Similar to critical researchers, the work of feminist ethnographers differs from traditional ethnography in several aspects of research design. Feminist researchers ask questions of the role power and relationship play not only at a societal level, but also at the level between researcher and researched. Termed "reflexivity," these questions entail monitoring and reflecting upon the nature of researcher-researched relationships and how those relationships shape the story being told (see Chapter 9 for more discussion on reflexivity). Although all qualitative researchers strive to monitor their subjectivity, feminist ethnographers extend their attention to intersubjectivity, or the interaction between subjectivities of researcher and participants. Intersubjectivity is the awareness that whatever is created through the research is different because two or more people have interacted to build new meaning (subjectivity and intersubjectivity are given greater attention in Chapter 5).

An ongoing conversation among feminist researchers focuses upon what methodological approaches support the purposes of transforming asymmetrical power relations and analyzing power and oppression. For further study of feminist research, you may want to refer to Behar and Gordon 1995; Farganis 1994; Fonow and Cook 1991; Harding 1987; hooks 1984; Lather 1991; Luke and Gore 1992; Maguire 1987, 1996; Mies 1983; Naples 1998; Nielsen 1990; Olesen 1994; Reinharz 1992; P. Usher 1996.

Action Research Action research grew out of the work of Kurt Lewin (1890–1947). His model of action research was grounded in the positivist paradigm with clear separation between the researcher and the researched and with cycles of discovery, intervention, and evaluation (Bryant 1996). It was used particularly in industry research to study ways to make businesses more efficient.

In recent years, action research has experienced popularity again, particularly in education, as a way to improve practice. The cycles of research have evolved to observing, reflecting, and acting (Kemmis and McTaggart 1988; Stringer 1996). Information is first gathered through qualitative and, sometimes, quantitative means. During the reflection phase, the data are interpreted and the multiple viewpoints are communicated and discussed among those with a stake (the stakeholders) in the process. This is followed by the action phase, which involves planning, implementation, and evaluation.

This current form of action research is grounded in the interpretivist paradigm with researcher working with others as agents of change. An assumption of action research is that "those who have previously been designated as 'subjects' should participate directly in research processes and that those processes should be applied in ways that benefit all participants directly" (Stringer 1996, 7). Stringer (1996) elaborates on what he calls community-based action research, which begins with problems as defined by a group, community, or organization, helps people better understand their situation, and then involves them in taking action to resolve their problems. The research process is collaborative and inclusive of all major stakeholders with the researcher acting as a facilitator who keeps the research cycles moving.

Although critical, feminist, and action research promise to contribute much to the researched community as well as to the larger society, the approaches are not problem free. Particularly when the primary researcher is an outsider, there are difficulties associated with defining the research focus, creating action groups where no formal organization exists, and knowing when and how to leave or end the research project. The identified problems and strengths of these modes suggest that much potential lies in the concept of practitioners (e.g., teachers, nurses, social workers) as researchers who investigate, with others, their own "backyard." Practitioners who couple basic research theories and techniques with an action-oriented mode can develop collaborative, reflective data-collecting and analysis teams for their own practices and thereby contribute to the sociopolitical context in which they dwell.

For readings on action research and practitioner research, see Anderson, Herr, and Nihlen 1994; Bartunek and Louis 1996; Bissex and Bullock 1987; Bryant 1996; Cochran-Smith and Lytle 1993; Ebbutt 1985; Goswami and Stillman 1987; Griffiths 1985; Hollingsworth 1997; Hustler, Cassidy, and Cuff 1986; Kelly 1985; Kemmis and McTaggart 1988; McTaggart 1997; Miller 1990; Mohr and Maclean 1987; Noffke and Stevenson 1995; Reason 1988; Stringer 1996; Whyte 1991; and Zuber-Skerritt 1996.

THE POSTMODERN CONTEXT

The term *postmodernity* indicates a break from *modernity,* a historical period of time marked by industrialization in particular. Characteristics of modernity include a belief in formal logic as necessary for reason, the bureaucratization of society, and a belief in science and technology as means to solving problems (Harker 1993). Postmodernists challenge the assumptions upon which modernity rests, seeing them as forces contributing to social homogenization and alienation and to global subjugation (Esteva and Prakash 1998).

Traditional ethnography is affected by postmodern thought in a variety of ways. In particular, some of the basic assumptions of ethnography are debated through questioning the scientific nature of research, the role and authority of the ethnographer, and the way in which reports are written (Fontana 1994). Postmodernism "is not anti-science, but instead emphasizes the need for science to be self-reflexive about its limitations" (R. Usher 1996, 25). It challenges and seeks to remove the dominant position of the ethnographer by making the ethnographer "a visible partner in dialogue, a datum himself or herself" (Fontana 1994, 212). And in reporting fieldwork, postmodern researchers often work to produce a *polyvocal* text, one that has many voices and not only that of the researcher. These are only a few of the ways postmodernity is affecting ethnography. Chapters 5 and 9 address such influence a bit more.

Some feel lost in the shifting sands of postmodern perspectives, their footing undone. Others see new possibilities take form—the need, for example, to explore self as researcher in relationship to research participants; to create interdisciplinary composites; to seriously take on the lenses of other ways of looking at the world, whether these ways be a spirit trance or astrophysics; and to create new forms of representing what is learned, forms that reveal emotions and feeling. Along with the epistemological question of whether we can come to know a phenomenon and what counts as *knowing* rises the ethical question of should (and, if so, how can) researchers work to confront and change oppressive conditions that limit life choices of groups of people and of the ecological planet as a whole. For a deeper understanding of inquiry in the postmodern era, see Denzin 1997; Dickens and Fontana 1994; and Marcus and Fischer 1986.

What Is to Come

Qualitative inquiry is ever changing. "It reminds me of a dot-to-dot exercise that I use with my first graders," said Mary. "One dot of information leads me to another dot, and, in the end, some sort of pattern becomes evident." There are many ways to connect the dots, however. Susan, another student, had a difficult time dealing with the ambiguity that new "dots" presented. After collecting data for a semester, she stated, "I'm ready to throw the whole project out because I've come up with so many new questions. This process has blown me away. I feel like I need to go back and begin all over again." Susan is right. You know best what you should look for, what questions you should ask, and what methods you should use at the end of your study. The process of getting to that end, however, takes you through a terrain that eventually becomes clearer overall, while growing more complex in detail. The combination of your own inquiry, field log, and reading of this text should help you to grasp the phenomenon of your research with the clearer understanding and sense of complexity that are the gifts of qualitative inquiry.

Wolcott (1990) states, "Qualitative approaches beckon because they appear easy or natural. And were it not for the complexity of conceptualizing qualitative studies, conducting the research, analyzing it, and writing it up, perhaps they would be" (11). This chapter has introduced you to some of the philosophical and theoretical contexts of qualitative research. Most of the chapters to come focus on process. They take you through the procedures of research design, data collection, data analysis, and writing, as well as into discussions of rapport, subjectivity, and ethics. Like learning to paint or swim, you will gain skills that can be enhanced only through practice. It is to the complexity of conceptualizing the studies that we now turn.

Exercise

1. Broaden your understanding of the diversity in qualitative inquiry. Choose a qualitative research approach other than ethnography (such as phenomenology, heuristics, ethnomethodology, case study, etc.) and do some reading on that approach. Compare and contrast with ethnography. Share your understandings with the class.

Notes

1. Where I am using positivism, some scholars (Guba and Lincoln 1994) would use the term *postpositivism,* indicating an acceptance that reality is not completely measurable and knowable, but still worth striving to know through primarily quantitative research techniques. Others (Gall, Borg, and Gall 1996) use postpostivism to include research approaches other than those that use quantitative techniques. I am using the term *positivism* throughout this text in an attempt to avoid the confusion generated by the varied use of *postpositivism.*
2. Note that the terms *orientational research, ideological research,* and *cultural studies* are not synonomous, but rather all are categorical terms that include critical and feminist research approaches.

Chapter 2

Prestudy Tasks: Doing What Is Good for You

Researchers make many decisions before they begin collecting data through fieldwork. These decisions generally are embodied in a research proposal prepared for a thesis or dissertation committee or for possible funding agencies. The sections of this chapter raise issues for discussion in the research proposal. You will find also helpful Joseph Maxwell's (1996) book, *Qualitative Research Design: An Interactive Approach,* and Catherine Marshall and Gretchen Rossman's (1995) text, *Designing Qualitative Research.* Both books address in more detail the topics touched upon here.

In proposals, researchers present the possibilities of their study, deliberate on each aspect of the research, anticipate the requirements of their fieldwork, and create guidelines by which to work. Although there is no definitive format for proposal writing, researchers generally consider the following criteria (see Cobb and Hagemaster 1987; Maxwell 1996):

1. purpose and significance of the proposed research,
2. conceptual context, which includes discussion of relevant literature and theory, as well as contribution of pilot studies,
3. research statement and attendant research questions,
4. research methods, which include discussion of sampling design, data collection techniques, data analysis, and write-up,
5. validity issues, which may include the researchers' expertise in doing what they propose, as well as their subjective relationship to the research topic,
6. provision for use of human subjects.

In your proposal, you should address these categories comprehensively, but with the understanding that the resulting document is like a recipe for improvisational cooks. It is a well-thought-out design, but one that may undergo additions, omissions, and new combinations. Your plans will probably change as your fieldwork progresses and the opportunities of the field emerge. If you are inflexible, resolutely tied to your prestudy proposal, then you may forgo the serendipity that the process offers. Yet without a well-thought-out plan, your studies may fall flat, suffer many false starts, and needlessly extend the inquiry. The tentativeness of a proposal may be greatly reduced, however, if written after preliminary pilot fieldwork that sufficiently informs the researcher about the field situation. If the opportunity exists, this is the preferred procedure.

The Research Topic

The first research decision is to determine what you want to study. Unless you are working on a project conceptualized by someone else, you must figure out which issues, uncertainties, dilemmas, or paradoxes intrigue you. Your passion for your chosen topic will be a motivating factor throughout the various research aspects, some of which are intrinsically more interesting than others. You tap into your subjectivity, of which passion is a part, to find topics appropriate to your interests. The topic, however, should not be so personal that it is of little interest to anyone else; nor, as Douglas (1976) warns, should it be in an area where you have major emotional worries. You must be able to distinguish the line between your passion to understand some phenomenon and your overinvolvement in very personal issues that need resolution.

Distinguishing the difference between a topic for research and one for therapy is not always easy. For example, one student, who was also an instructor in a small community college, was about to begin a research class when he received word that his teaching contract was not renewed. Understandably, he was angry and disturbed. Consumed with thoughts on this matter, he decided that for his research project he would interview people at his institution to develop a better understanding of why he was dismissed. The class convinced him not only that such an investigation would be limited in scope, but also that he was unlikely to get honest and complete answers from interviewees. In the end, he explored another interest: attitudes of prison guards toward the private tutoring of inmates, a topic that, as he gathered and analyzed his data, brimmed with fascinating possibilities for continued study.

Asking yourself how your proposed research intersects with your life history and whether you are setting out to prove something that you already believe to be true helps to test your emotional attachment to particular outcomes. Ken, an elementary school principal who had held several different principalships, wanted to investigate the relationship of job stress to administrative turnover. Reflecting on the role of subjectivity in his research, Ken wrote:

> My topic is perfect, I thought. The turnover rate for school administrators is incredible, I know the subject firsthand, I have dozens of contacts in the field, and stress is on everybody's agenda, both public and private sector.
>
> So what's the problem? I care too passionately about the results. I desperately want the study to prove that school boards and superintendents should show some compassion for building administrators. I want taxpayers to recognize the limitations of personnel, resources, and supplies, which make the job of principal so frustrating. I want parents to see that a partnership between school and home is in the best interests of the children. I want to prove that the narrow-minded bigots who persecuted, criticized, harassed, and hounded me were wrong. This is clearly no way to begin an unbiased study.

Interestingly, however, I did not realize the full extent of my personal prejudices until I presented my initial ideas to the qualitative methods class. I was angered and shocked to be accused of having an ax to grind—of having reached my conclusions before I began my research. I was particularly angry because I recognized that they were right.

Ken wanted to justify his own experience. Although he needed to be interested in his research topic, his emotional attachment precluded the open, exploratory learner's attitude that is necessary for good data collection and analysis.

Emotional attachment may manifest itself in other ways. If the very thought of approaching your research participants causes severe anxiety attacks, then you should ask yourself why. Debbie, a special education teacher, new to her school and district, was feeling uncomfortable when designing a project that involved interviewing administrators and supervisors. Finally, she realized that she was threatened by the thought of exposing herself to her bosses in her novice researcher role. She considered alternatives, shifted her focus, and set up a study that required obtaining data from teachers rather than from administrators.

Not everyone works effectively under the same conditions. If you are overly intimidated by the thought of going into the field, then consider reshaping your study in a more inviting way. Some of your intimidation may be the result of feelings or problems that you need to overcome; others may represent feelings and problems beyond your capacity to remedy. The qualitative inquiry process, by nature, is replete with anxiety-producing occasions without the researcher's unwittingly setting up more.

Practical issues such as time and money must also be considered. The conceived study may be appropriate in academic terms but impossible to conduct given practical limitations. Do not begin with a topic so vast in scope that you could never reasonably afford the time or money to complete it.

Although the planned scope for a research topic should be realistic, neither too broad nor too narrow, the researcher cannot always know the ideal scope until data collection is underway. For example, Purvis (1985) originally planned historical research to look at all forms of adult education provisions for working-class women in nineteenth-century England. As she collected and examined documents, however, she realized she had to narrow her study, but how she should focus her research was unclear. Should she investigate forms of adult education provided by the middle class, or types of adult education organized by working-class women themselves? Should she look at all forms of adult education, or concentrate on specific areas? Should she limit her inquiry to education in rural areas or in urban areas, or should she address regional differences? Purvis' range of choices suggests the alternatives available as you consider a research focus; you will find good arguments for supporting many different focuses within the same general area of study. Reading related literature facilitates developing the research focus. It is part of getting started.

Review of Literature

Knowledge of the literature will help you to judge whether your research plans go beyond existing findings and may thereby contribute to your field of study.

Some qualitative researchers argue against reviewing the literature until after data collection has begun, for fear that the researcher will be unduly influenced by the conceptual frameworks, research designs, techniques, and theories of others. Although this is a possibility, I think that literature should be read throughout the research process, including a thorough search before data collection begins.

Reading about the studies of others in a way that is useful to beginning your own work requires a particular frame of mind. First, collect, scan, and read literature to verify that you have chosen a justifiable topic. For example, the many dissertation studies that have investigated why parents send their children to fundamentalist Christian schools have identified and discussed a range of explanations. Another study on this topic, even in a state where no such studies have taken place, could contribute little more of interest. Try to warrant your own project on the basis of what has been done and what has not been done.

Second, use the literature to help find focus for your topic. When you find an article that applies to your area of interest, study the references carefully and seek out the ones that may inform you more. Existing studies show what is known about a general area of inquiry and what is missing. A review of the Christian school literature suggests that very little is known about the lives of adults who as children attended a fundamentalist Christian school. To what extent do they live within the boundaries of the doctrine espoused by their schools? Someone interested in Christian schooling could make a significant contribution by studying this population.

Third, the literature can help to inform your research design and interview questions. Read critically and learn from the successes and failures of other researchers investigating similar phenomena. Did the researcher spend enough time to establish rapport and to probe for more than surface responses? Were the questions asked of a usefully varied group of people? What questions were not asked at all? What situations were (and were not) observed? What directions for future studies did researchers recommend?

Fourth, remember that in qualitative inquiry reviewing the literature is an ongoing process that cannot be completed before data collections and analysis. Your data will suggest the need to review previously unexamined literature of both substantive and theoretical nature. For example, before I began fieldwork in the Caribbean (Glesne 1985), I reviewed rural development literature in addition to agricultural and educational studies and documents pertaining to the Eastern Caribbean. During my time in the field, but particularly after focused time on data analysis, I began to read extensively about dependency theory, which explained economic and power relationships between nation states. Dependency theory became central to my data analysis and discussion, while the rural development literature receded in importance. Regard reviewing literature in interactive terms. You can learn different things from the work of others depending on what you already have learned and what you need to know. You may find yourself both dismayed and pleased to benefit later from material read earlier but overlooked because you lacked the experience to recognize it as beneficial.

Fifth, in conducting your literature search, cast a wide net. Do not confine yourself to your topic, nor to your discipline. If, for instance, your topic involves the use of French in U. S. schools near the border with Quebec, then you will want to collect literature on schooling and bilingualism in general. Delamont (1992) suggests reading for contrast. That is, if you are interested in women in science, then you might also want to read about men in predominantly female professions such as nursing to help generate questions for your study. Sociologists, anthropologists, psychologists, and educators often write on the same topics, but from different perspectives. Try to seek sources from all possible disciplines.

You should not, however, let the widening circles of possibly applicable literature preclude your entry into the field. Remember that data collection and data analysis will also inform your literature search. Ernie was preparing to collect data on professionalization in the field of physical therapy. He reflected on his dance with the literature:

> First of all, I needed to define what professionalization was. Then I felt the need to read enough sociology to understand how people achieved it, which got me into the field of professional socialization. Then if you do achieve it and act it out, you are into the area of professional power and influence. After reading literature about that, I thought I needed to understand professional ethics and how that linked with the idea of the development of community. Finally, I realized that if I didn't go out to the field, I'd spend the rest of my life saying, "Next month, I'll be ready."

Remember that being ready to go to the field is often a state of mind, affected by, but not necessarily related to, having completed the preliminaries.

After you have collected and read a variety of works on your topic, you will need to write the literature review or conceptual context for your proposal. In doing so, organize the review around understandings that come from investigating specific questions of studies and theory that relate to your topic. A literature review is not a summary of various studies, but rather an integration of reviewed sources around particular trends and themes. Quote sparingly—when something is said uniquely and when how it is said contributes to the text. Point out gaps in the literature that relate to your area of interest, thereby using the literature to establish need for more or different kinds of studies. Creswell (1998) suggests creating a diagram as a visual picture of the literature to help organize the review and to figure out how one's own study relates to the larger body of literature.

Some novice qualitative researchers assume that when they have written their literature review for their proposal, they have virtually written a chapter of the dissertation. Literature reviewed as a prestudy task often finds its way into the final write-up, but not usually as a chapter in itself. Wolcott (1990) states that he expects his students to know the literature related to their topics, but he does not want them "to lump (dump?) it all into a chapter that remains unconnected to the rest of the study" (17). He (and I) suggest incorporating the literature as appropriate throughout the telling of the story: "Ordinarily this calls for introducing related research toward the end of a study rather than at the beginning, except for the necessary 'nesting' of the problem in the introduction" (17).

For an informative chapter on reviewing literature, see Delamont's (1992) text, *Fieldwork in Educational Settings: Methods, Pitfalls and Perspectives*.

Theoretical Context

I find it instructive that the word "theory" comes from the same Greek root as the word "theatre." A tragedy or comedy is, after all, no less an inquiry into reality, no less a distillation of perceptions and experiences, than a hypothesis or theory that undertakes to account for the variable incidences of murder or marriage. (Nisbet 1976, 12)

Social scientists define theory in different ways. A prevalent definition comes from Homans, paraphrased by Denzin (1988, 49): "Theory refers to a set of propositions that are interrelated in an ordered fashion such that some may be deducible from others, thus permitting an explanation to be developed for the phenomenon under consideration." The ultimate goal of this form of theorizing is to develop universal laws of human behavior and societal functioning.

Glaser and Strauss (1967) take issue with the conventional deductive approach to research and focus on verification for theory development. In *The Discovery of Grounded Theory*, they propose an inductive strategy whereby the researcher discovers concepts and hypotheses through constant comparative analysis. They advocate theory generation through inquiry, and call the results *grounded theory*. For Glaser and Strauss, the ultimate function of theory is still explanation and prediction. These qualitative researchers and others agree that it is "important to be able to go beyond the local setting of the research and to engage with formal ideas at a more general level" (Coffey and Atkinson 1996, 14).

Interpretivists such as Geertz (1973) and Denzin (1988) offer yet a different understanding of theory based on interpretation, or the act of making sense out of a social interaction. Theory building proceeds by *thick description* (Geertz 1973), defined as "description that goes beyond the mere or bare reporting of an act (thin description), but describes and probes the intentions, motives, meanings, contexts, situations and circumstances of action" (Denzin 1988, 39). The goal of theorizing, then, becomes that of providing understanding of direct lived experience instead of abstract generalizations. These scholars consider that every human situation is novel, emergent, and filled with multiple, often conflicting, meanings and interpretations; they attempt to apprehend the core of these meanings and contradictions (Denzin 1988, 18).

This discussion of theory hints at the difficulty that a novice researcher may experience in deciding the role of theory in a study. In addition, theory is formulated at different levels of abstraction and labeled by different terms.

Empirical generalizations or *substantive theories* are found in both quantitative and qualitative studies. This type of theory is at a low level of abstraction; it consists of outcomes (empirical generalizations) from related studies and mainly functions to raise questions or provide rationale for new studies, and to compare and contrast with study findings. A review of literature related to the study's main concepts provides the base for working with empirical generalizations.

Formal theory (Strauss 1987) is sometimes referred to as *general theory* or as *middle-range propositions* (Turner 1985). "Middle range theories try to explain a whole class of phenomena—say, for example, delinquency, revolutions, ethnic antagonism . . . They are therefore broader in scope than empirical generalizations and causal models" (Turner 1985, 27). Qualitative researchers often make use of these more general theories as a framework for both asking questions of their study and discussing aspects of their findings.

Rebecca Esch (1996), a doctoral student at the University of Vermont, provides an example of using theory in developing the conceptual context for a research proposal. Rebecca was interested in studying adolescent girls' development. After describing the basis for her interest in adolescent girls, she wrote:

> This interest in adolescent girls led me to an exploration of the theories which sought to describe girls' experience of the transition from childhood to adolescence, in addition to theories outlining girls' development, particularly as their development was believed to diverge from traditional theories of adolescent development. My research focused on the ideas of the Stone Center for Developmental Services and Studies at Wellesley College, and the Harvard Project on Women's Psychology and Girls' Development. Both of these groups place the experience of relationship at the center of girls' development. This is in contrast to traditional theories of development which stress individuation and separation.

Rebecca then discussed these theories. After her review of studies and theory regarding adolescent girls' development, she transitioned to literature on friendship, situating the inclusion of this literature in a perceived gap in human development theories:

> My perspective is that although many girls struggle during this period, and perhaps all face the possibility of suffering some ill effects due to cultural, school, and peer pressures, many girls thrive. Thus, one goal of my research is to re-define or re-label the experience of girls' development during this transitional period. Much of this moving away, on my part, from a crisis philosophy, has been generated by my own reflexive search through my adolescent memories, during which I can find little evidence of a similar "crisis." . . . Thus, the question began to form, what of those of us who did not suffer a traumatic transition from childhood to adolescence? What of those of us who did not lose our voice or our sense of self? . . . In thinking about these questions I keep coming back to the idea of growth within relationship and what role my friends have played during the changes and difficulties of my life . . . I began to wonder if perhaps girls' friendship might play an important role during this transitional period.

With this introduction and rationale, Rebecca then explored literature and theory on women's and girls' friendships, and their relationship to the concepts of *developing a sense of self* and *resilience*.

In summary, theory, sometimes referred to as the latest version of what we call truth, is used in a variety of ways in qualitative research. Typically, qualitative research is neither invariably nor explicitly driven by theory, but researchers often use empirical generalizations and formal theory to help form initial questions and working hypotheses during the beginning stages of data collections. As they begin to focus on data analysis, researchers may seek out yet other theories to help them examine their data from different perspectives. Qualitative research may or may not eventuate in statements of theory that are grounded in the data. For more on the role of theory, see Flinders and Mills (Eds.), 1993, *Theory and Concepts in Qualitative Research*.

Research Statement and Questions

A research project is an effort to remedy the ignorance that exists about something. Thinking about what you do not know, as well as what kind of light you hope to shed, is useful for giving direction to your research endeavor. In working out the research statement, begin by jotting down questions about your topic, generated by your reading of the literature and your own experience. When categories for inquiry are exhausted, look at the questions as a whole and figure out the central or overarching question.

The central question becomes the research question or statement (depending upon how it is worded). In one clear sentence, try to describe what it is that you want to understand. Unlike quantitative studies, which identify sets of variables and seek to determine their relationship, qualitative studies are best at contributing to a greater understanding of perceptions, attitudes, and processes. As Creswell (1998) states, "the research question often starts with a *how* or a *what* so that initial forays into the topic describe what is going on" (17). Your statement presents the overall intent of your study and indicates how open or closed it will be. It provides a focus for data collection and analysis. After working on your research statement, look at all the other questions and consider which ones to put on hold for another study and which ones to categorize into subquestions that will assist in investigating your central issue (see Bissex 1987; Maxwell 1996).

Rebecca's and Ashley's work are drawn upon here to provide examples of research statements and questions. Rebecca focused her research with the following statement:

> Through my research I will explore the intersection of girls' friendship and the development of self during the transition from childhood to adolescence.

Rebecca felt compelled to clarify this general statement with several more statements:

> I hope to begin to understand what role friendship plays in girls' developing sense of self. Further, I hope to begin to illuminate whether girls' friendship provides a form of resilience, and/or fosters resistance for girls as they negotiate the transition from childhood to adolescence.

She then created four categories of research questions to help guide her work on girls' friendship and the development of self:

1. How do girls describe the development of their sense of self during this transitional period?
2. What is the experience of friendship for girls during this transitional period?
3. How do girls describe their experiences during this transitional period?
   - What can be understood of a girl's world during this period with respect to family, school, peers/friends, culture, etc.?
   - How does the term "crisis" apply to this period of girls' development? Is there a more positive and proactive way to define, describe, and understand this transitional period?

4. How does an understanding of girls' development and friendships during this transitional period contribute to relational theories of development, and/or other developmental theories?

Ashley was working on a master's thesis in the School of Natural Resources. Her research statement took the following form:

> In this research, I seek to understand how stakeholders involved with the relicensing of hydroelectric projects enter into negotiations and reach consensus concerning resource use and ecosystem protection.

Ashley's research statement is an example of a qualitative study focused upon understanding a process, in this case, the process of negotiating and reaching consensus. She developed four research questions to guide her work:

1. How do stakeholders enter into negotiations and what motivates and constrains them in the negotiation process?
2. What stages are involved in the process of reaching consensus?
3. How do stakeholders perceive the final agreement/outcome?
4. How does legislative context affect the stakeholders (from their perspectives) and the negotiation process?

With research statement and questions developed, both Rebecca and Ashley were ready to consider how they would go about designing their studies to get the data they needed.

Site Selection

With your topic selected and the process of reviewing relevant literature and theories begun, you must decide where to conduct the study, who the study's participants should be, what techniques to use to gather data, and how long to spend in the field. Each decision needs careful prestudy thought, but, as with the research statement, each is subject to change as data collection proceeds and informs you. No guiding list of rules exists for these decisions, yet that does not mean that anything goes. Literature, documents, discussions with potential research participants, guidance of experienced researchers, and your own good judgment all contribute to sound decisions.

In the past, part of the rite of passage for anthropology students was to do research in cultures different from their own. Immersion in a foreign culture was a test, of sorts, of one's ability to learn new modes of behavior and perception. In some ways, however, moving into a new culture is easier than studying your own. When everything is different, you are more open to new understandings. When you are already familiar with a culture or group or school, your angles of vision are narrowed by preformed assumptions about what is going on. Of course, preformed assumptions can accompany you into new settings or cultures as evidenced by Western agricultural researchers who, for many years, ignored the role of women in African agriculture. Assumptions are, however, more easily challenged in new settings.

Currently, many researchers are drawn to studying their own institution or agency, to doing *backyard* research. Doing so is attractive for a number of reasons: They have relatively easy access; the groundwork for rapport is already established; the research would be useful for their professional or personal life; and the amount of time needed for various research steps would be reduced. As a novice researcher, you may be understandably tempted to undertake backyard studies, but you should do so fully aware of the possible problems generated by your involvement in and commitment to your familiar territory. Previous experiences with settings or peoples can set up expectations for certain types of interactions that will constrain effective data collection. When you enter a new culture as a researcher, that is your role, although other roles are often assigned to you by research participants. When studying in your own backyard, you often already have a role—as teacher or principal or case worker or friend. When you add on the researcher role, both you and your others may experience confusion at times over which role you are or should be playing.

Carolyn, for example, was interested in physically disabled children and interviewed special education supervisors about their work. She herself was a mother of a disabled child. She said of her interviewees, "They couldn't disassociate my research role from my role as a parent of a handicapped child." Instead of giving careful answers to her questions, they tended to say, "Well, you know what it's like," or "We've talked about this before."

Gordon was a school principal whose pilot project involved interviewing students in his school:

> Ah! the innocence of the novice researcher! Feeling smug with my own cleverness for choosing a subject both near and dear, I set out to do my research. What could be easier? I was a well-established, well-regarded principal in a small community. Principals are supposed to study student achievement. Thus I had not only the right, but the professional imperative to visit classrooms and interview students if these activities would bring about improvement in the educational program. I knew each subject individually, my teachers respected me (I had hired most of them), and I had control of scheduling. Best of all, I was the main gatekeeper for the school. Thus, through my role as principal, I had the opportunity, the right, and the resources to make short work of interviews and observations. What could go wrong?
>
> Well, several things. First of all, as principal I was on duty anytime I was in the building and crises didn't go away just because I was doing qualitative research. Thus my good intentions to make observations and do interviews were regularly shattered by irate parents, students with personal problems, broken boilers, and wayward buses. Second, as a principal it was my responsibility to protect the education of children wherever possible. How, then, could I justify taking children out of class to interview them about achievement when half of them were reputed to be underachievers? Third, as the primary disciplinarian in the school, I became involved in a long-term disciplinary process with two of my subjects, and I lost valuable data because I was unable to interview them. Finally, as principal, I felt pressure not to upset rapport with teachers, so I found that I tried not to rock the boat any more than I had to. I think I lost valuable data by not interviewing them about their views on the underachievement of students.

What did I learn from all this? First of all, I've found that it's a good idea to go away from home to do your research. Research should be undertaken at least far enough away so that your job role does not interfere with your activities. Second, conduct your research where you are not so emotionally close to your subjects that it distorts your design, preferably someplace where you have not worked and lived for many years.

In addition to the potential access and research design problems that Gordon identified, backyard research can create ethical and political dilemmas. As an established insider, succumbing to the temptation to be a covert observer may lead to guilt or anxiety over that role. Moreover, political consequences are often more challenging in backyard research in that you may have to negotiate with colleagues and superiors not only what data can be collected but also what gets reported. Politically charged situations can leave the researcher feeling vulnerable. Anne, for example, decided to inquire into the use of a particular educational computer program in area schools. What she did not take into consideration at the outset of her research were the people invested in keeping the program in the schools. She states:

> My worst fear of affecting my professional relationships as a result of research came true. Mike explained his opinions of how my biases affected my research, discussed unsubstantiated statements, and pointed out weak writing. He was offended by the analysis. I have now had to edit my analysis to create a less in-depth and more toned down version of the original. My eyes are open to the political ramifications of research. And I have learned to not do research in my own "backyard."

Also, interviews frequently uncover what can be termed *dangerous knowledge* or information that is politically risky to hold, particularly for an insider. Such problems are not limited to backyard research, but they do seem to proliferate there.

Ending the research is also different in backyard versus other settings. Usually, a researcher eventually leaves the researched culture, town, or setting even though connections may remain for life. You don't usually leave your own "backyard," although you may want to do so as a result of some of the "dangerous knowledge" you received in your researcher role.

These warnings against research in your own backyard apply, in general, to traditional ethnographic studies where the researcher is the primary investigator. The situation is different in action research and teacher research. Action researchers work with groups of people to make organizations, projects, curriculum, etc. "better." Teacher researchers often study their own classrooms with the purpose to improve schooling experiences for students. These kinds of backyard research generally remove the confusion over role; either your research role is quite autobiographical in that it is centered upon your own behaviors and thoughts and those of students in your classes or the role is assigned or acknowledged by colleagues as an important role for the organization. This lessens the political challenges because the knowledge gained is either personal knowledge to guide your own teaching or open knowledge from which the group as a whole learns and forms new directions. Finally, in action and teacher research, your being part of the organization is vital because the research is generally a beginning step in a longer, change-oriented process. Indeed, action research is difficult to carry out when you are not part of the organization because the people involved in the research are often those most invested in carrying out the needed changes.

Glen chose, with blessings from his school, to do a formative evaluation of an alternative education program in the high school where he taught science. Reflecting upon his work, he states:

> I cannot imagine a more efficient way to learn qualitative research than being able to do it in a culture and field in which I have some knowledge. This project is more than an individual effort, it is a social journey into my own, and my school's, zone of proximal development. Being able to choose my topic of interest situated in my passion, anchoring it to theory in which I am conversant, not only made it meaningful but made it worthwhile for my institution and community.

Backyard research can be extremely valuable, but it needs to be entered with heightened consciousness of potential difficulties.

If you do not research your own backyard, then how do you go about selecting a site? Often, the selection of research place or places is built into the problem. A colleague, for example, studied what happened when a Japanese firm moved into a predominantly white small American city. His interest grew out of yearlong negotiations that took place in several small Midwestern cities before a Japanese car industry selected one as its base. He then knew where his site would be.

Some research problems do not call for a specific research site; they simply require a setting within some specified geographical boundaries. For example, a study of working single mothers who had been on welfare within the past year does not necessarily involve selecting a single study site, but travel constraints suggest limiting the selection of study participants to nearby locations. Similarly, Rebecca, with her focus on adolescent girls' friendships and development, selected her own community as the site for observations and interviews.

Commonly, however, researchers need to develop a rationale for selecting one or more sites for data collection. Perhaps the phenomenon you wish to investigate exists to some extent everywhere. Do you choose an exemplary site or a typical site? What criteria determine exemplary, typical, or other classifiers? If you select a rural school, must you also look at an urban school? How many sites should you select? To make such decisions, you must look again at your research interests and carefully reflect on what you want to learn. You also may need to try out, or pilot, tentative site selections. The next section, on *Selection of Study Participants,* discusses some sampling strategies that apply to selecting sites as well as study participants.

Selection of Study Participants

Since most research situations are too vast to interview everyone or to observe everything, you will need to devise a selection strategy by which to choose people, events, and times. Random sampling, the strategy often used in quantitative research, is appropriate for selecting a large, statistically representative sample from which generalizations can be drawn. Qualitative researchers neither work (usually) with populations large enough to make random sampling meaningful, nor is their purpose that of producing generalizations. Rather, qualitative researchers tend to select each of their cases *purposefully* (Patton 1990). "The logic and power of purposeful sampling lies in selecting *information-rich* cases for study in depth. Information-rich cases are those from which one can learn a great deal about issues of central importance to the purpose of the research . . ." (Patton 1990, 169).

Patton (1990) identifies and discusses 16 different purposeful sampling strategies. Several of these strategies are presented here (see Exhibit 2.1) as examples of ways in which you might think about what you want to know and, accordingly, the sampling decisions you need to make. Different sampling strategies allow you to learn different things about your topic because each strategy you choose leads you to particular kinds of sites and people. To learn about more sampling strategies, see Patton (1990) and LeCompte and Preissle (1993).

Committee members and funding agencies often expect the research proposal to delineate clearly how many and which persons will be interviewed, as well as how many and which situations will be observed. The researcher is therefore tempted to develop complex selection matrices. Thinking of important stratification criteria is a good place to begin, but do not get overinvested in including all the possible configurations of such variables as ethnicity, gender, socioeconomic class, educational

---

EXHIBIT 2.1
Some Selection Strategies for Research Sites and Participants

Typical case sampling	Illustrates or highlights what is typical, normal. The purpose is to be "illustrative not definitive" (Patton 1990, 173).
Extreme or deviant case sampling	Selects cases from the extremes, cases that are unusual or special in some way, such as high school valedictorians and dropouts; or female scientists who work in Antarctica.
Homogeneous sampling	Selects all similar cases in order to describe some subgroup in depth such as a study of female professors from working-class backgrounds who were the first generation in their families to receive a college education (Clark 1998).
Maximum variation sampling	Selects cases that cut across some range of variation such as students of different ethnic backgrounds enrolled in an environmental studies program. Searches for common patterns across great variation.
Snowball, chain, or network sampling	Obtains knowledge of potential cases from people who know people who meet research interests. Wright and Decker (1997) used this approach to find men and women who were active armed robbers at the time of their research. Snowball sampling is useful for getting started when you have *no other way* to find the participants you want, but it is not always a sufficient strategy in itself for participant selection.
Convenience sampling	Selects cases on the basis of convenience. This strategy has low credibility and is inappropriate for anything other than "practice."

Adapted from Patton 1990, 182–183.

level, and age in your study. Select only those criteria that the literature and your experience suggest are particularly important and remember that the selection strategy is often refined as the researcher collects data.

For example, as Carol began her study of the leisure styles of later-life widows, she assumed that leisure was affected by social class, years of education, employment status, and leisure options locally available. Varying her selection of study participants by these attributes would help her to learn more about her topic. Nonetheless, as Carol began collecting data, she learned of other criteria that appeared to affect leisure styles—such as how recently the women were widowed—and knew she had to include these attributes in her selection strategy.

As she spent time in the field, Carol decided that there was too much variation for her to understand the leisure styles of all later-life widows. She narrowed her focus to one group: high school educated, working, recently widowed urban women. Doing so simplified her selection of participants and allowed her to go deeply into the leisure behavior of a reasonably homogeneous group. What struck Carol as ideal at the planning stage of her project was replaced by something both useful and feasible.

Rebecca also chose a fairly homogeneous sampling strategy since she was choosing depth rather than breadth of understanding. She described her rationale for her selection of adolescent girl participants:

> I am not as concerned about studying a broad spectrum of girls so much as gaining a preliminary understanding of the intersection of girls' friendship and the development of self. . . . Once I have gained an understanding of this issue, I can then move on to exploring how it plays out across a broad spectrum of girls. . . .
>
> By definition, my study requires the engagement of girls who are quite young. To have any breadth of access, I will require the full support and cooperation of their families. Given these considerations, I will choose for my case studies six girls who I either already know, or know of, through my circle of academic relationships and I will ask each girl to invite a best friend to participate with her. . . . Engaging this rather homogeneous circle of girls will allow me to describe their collective understanding of friendship and the development of self with somewhat less confusion from factors such as SES, education [of family], significant family differences, etc. Although drawing on this circle of girls will allow me to gain depth in my understanding and description of girls' friendship, I realize I will lose diversity . . . .

As Rebecca's discussion suggests, in the numbers game, depth is traded for breadth. How many persons must you interview? How much must you observe? How do you know when to stop? There are no magic answers. For in-depth understanding, you should repeatedly spend extended periods with a few respondents and observation sites. For greater breadth, but a more superficial understanding, carry out one-time interviews with more people and fewer observations in more situations. The strategy of participant selection in qualitative inquiry rests on the multiple purposes of illuminating, interpreting, and understanding—and on your own imagination and judgment. Develop an explicit rationale, however, for participant selection based upon theory, personal hunches, and your pilot study.

Selection of Research Techniques

Qualitative researchers depend on a variety of methods for gathering data. The use of multiple data-collection methods contributes to the trustworthiness of the data. This practice of relying on multiple methods is commonly called *triangulation,* a term taken from surveying and navigation. The purpose for methods triangulation is not "the simple combination of different kinds of data, but the attempt to relate them so as to counteract the threats to validity identified in each" (Berg 1995, 5). Although multiple data-collection methods is the most common form of triangulation in qualitative research, triangulation in order to increase confidence in research findings may also involve the incorporation of multiple kinds of data sources (i.e., not just teachers, but students and parents as well), multiple investigators, and multiple theoretical perspectives (see Denzin 1988).

Three data-gathering techniques dominate in qualitative inquiry: participant observation, interviewing, and document collection. Within each technique, a wide variety of practices can be carried out, some more common than others. For example, in participant observation, some researchers use videotaping as a means to replay, slow down, and freeze observed interactions. Many, however, rely on their senses, the results of which are relayed through their pens and stored in their field logs. Some researchers use props such as card sorts or pictures as stimuli for specific information in interviews. Most only ask questions.

These data-gathering techniques are discussed in later chapters; the point here is that, ideally, the qualitative researcher draws on some combination of techniques to collect research data, rather than a single technique. This is not to negate the utility of, say, a study based solely on interviews, but rather to indicate that the more sources tapped for understanding, the richer the data and the more believable the findings.

To figure out what techniques to use, once again contemplate carefully what you want to learn. Different questions have different implications for data collection. In considering options, choose techniques that are likely to (1) elicit data needed to gain understanding of the phenomenon in question, (2) contribute different perspectives on the issue, and (3) make effective use of the time available for data-collection. In your research proposal, discuss each data collection technique that you select as Rebecca did in the following example:

1. **Interviews.** Through the use of interviews . . . I will explore each individual's understanding and experience of friendship. . . . As highlighted in previous sections, my research, by design and by philosophy, requires the involvement of my "others" as co-learners in this study, and the development of a relationship based on trust and rapport . . . I will engage in multiple interviews across which I and my co-learners will collaboratively design, and redesign, the interview structure as we proceed. Given that our relationship will be evolving across these interviews, my hope is that the quality of the information we exchange will also evolve.

2. **Participant Observation and Document Collection.** To create an in-depth case study of each of the girls, I will not only interview them individually, but also spend time with them and their friends at home, at school, and in other settings. I will bring the girls together in groups . . . for conversations about friendship, and, if possible,

employ a videocamera to aid me in analyzing more deeply their interactions and conversations. . . . I will encourage them to keep a journal, draw, paint, take pictures, or engage in any other medium they feel allows them full expression of their ideas. To initiate this exploration, I plan to give each girl . . . a journal upon the embarkation of our journey . . .

3. **Open-ended "Survey."** With the New Moon [magazine] girls I plan to suggest the same sort of creative means of expression as I do with the case study girls. . . . I will ask them to submit a paragraph, essay, picture, photograph, collage, or other creative form which best expresses their feelings about friendship.

Validity Issues

"You must learn to sit with people," he told me. "You must learn to sit and listen. As we say in Songhay: 'One kills something thin only to discover that [inside] it is fat.'" (Stoller 1989, 128)

Chapter 7 discusses some ways to augment the trustworthiness of your research. Trustworthiness or research validity is, however, an issue that should be thought about during research design as well as in the midst of data collection. It is often addressed in one's research proposal. Creswell (1998, 201–203) describes eight verification procedures (summarized here) often used in qualitative research (see also Lincoln and Guba 1985):

1. prolonged engagement and persistent observation—extended time in the field so that you are able to develop trust, learn the culture, and check out your hunches,
2. triangulation—use of multiple data-collection methods, multiple sources, multiple investigators, and/or multiple theoretical perspectives,
3. peer review and debriefing—external reflection and input on your work,
4. negative case analysis—conscious search for negative cases and unconfirming evidence so that you can refine your working hypotheses,
5. clarification of researcher bias—reflection upon your own subjectivity and how you will use and monitor it in your research,
6. member checking—sharing interview transcripts, analytical thoughts, and/or drafts of the final report with research participants to make sure you are representing them and their ideas accurately,
7. rich, thick description—writing that allows the reader to enter the research context,
8. external audit—an outside person examines the research process and product through "auditing" your field notes, research journal, analytic coding scheme, etc.

Attending to all of these means of increasing trustworthiness is not necessary in any one study, but validity issues are important aspects to consider and discuss in your research proposal. Lorraine's work provides an example. She was researching ways in which physical therapists work with elders with dementia.

Subjectivity. I am very invested in the search for a better understanding of how physical therapists work with elders with dementia. My attachment to this field of study may lead me to data that support my own hypothesis. I may hear what I want to hear and see what I want to see. I may easily find ways of discrediting those that disagree. I will address researcher bias by continuously exploring my own subjectivity. By writing both before and after my interviews and observations, I will be able to address pre-conceived opinions and reflect upon my subjectivity.

Negative Cases. My biases may be more apparent to me if I seek out interviews with colleagues that I know to hold differing opinions. These discussions with colleagues will be another method that will allow me to explore my topic, as well as my subjectivity.

Multiple-Session Interviews. Validity of the data may be threatened by the accuracy of participants' testimonies. I need to address the possibility of therapists telling me that they treat patients one way when they actually do not. Truthfulness may be a problem for some therapists since certain opinions or behaviors are not socially accepted . . . Repeat interviews throughout the course of the study will aid in developing rapport and increasing the validity of the interviews. They will also allow the participant time to think more deeply about their own feelings, reactions, and beliefs.

Persistent Observation. It may also be difficult to determine whether therapists are performing in their best behavior rather than their usual behavior, because people act differently when they are being watched. This reactivity phenomenon will be addressed by spending long periods of time in a facility. This will allow therapists to get used to the researcher's presence. By increasing the therapists' comfort with an outsider, they will soon be behaving in their normal fashion.

Multiple Sites. I have chosen to observe and interview in three facilities. Therapists often adopt similar techniques and behaviors of those around them. Looking at three different sites should increase the trustworthiness of common themes.

Many of these procedures for increasing the trustworthiness of your findings receive attention elsewhere in this text. They are introduced here simply to signal another prestudy area for thought. (See Chapter 5 on subjectivity and also Maxwell 1996.)

The Time Frame

You cannot know with certainty how long your research will take. Invariably, you will underestimate the amount of time needed. For example, gaining access to a school may drag on because the school board did not address the researcher's plans on the evening scheduled. Introduction to the school's teachers is delayed because the teacher's meeting was canceled. People reschedule interviews at the last moment, or they don't show up. Unexpected assemblies or field trips change observation schedules.

That things simply take longer than planned is a basic given in qualitative research. Terry Denny advised students at the University of Illinois to figure how much time each step should take and multiply by two and a half. It took even longer than that for Mark, who was studying attitudes of correctional officers toward educational programs for inmates:

> I had expected that contacting the officers and arranging for interviews would have taken a day or two at most. It was over a month between when I scheduled my first interview until I arranged the last one. I had not counted on vacations, weddings, changing shifts, or even officers changing job sites. Not a single interview happened at the time it was originally scheduled. One officer was ordered to work back-to-back shifts because of lack of staff. Twice, officers were ordered to transport offenders to other facilities. One officer was ordered to work an hour longer than her normal shift (due to understaffing) so she could guard the perimeter fence while inmates enjoyed their outside recreation period. No wonder another officer complained in his interview that inmates have more freedom than the officers who guard them.

Despite the delays, do not become discouraged. Rather, remember that unless you are researching your own backyard, you are external if not alien to the lives of research participants. You are not necessarily unwanted, but, because you are not integral to the lives of your others, you are dispensable. You will complete your research tasks, but normally later than you expect.

Institutional structures affect schedule planning. For example, the elementary and high school setting is more structured than the university setting. The scheduling of bells to demarcate set periods assists researchers in planning whom they can interview or when they can observe and for how long. Institutional frameworks also affect the control respondents have over their time. In general, it appears that individuals who hold higher places in the institutional hierarchy have greater autonomy to declare when they are free. Yet they often are busy individuals who reschedule appointments as a matter of course. Those lower in the hierarchy often have little autonomy to set a time to talk. When Lynne interviewed the custodial staff of a university, she had to work through the physical plant manager. He helped develop a schedule, communicate the research intent to the staff, and release individuals for interviews. As a result, Lynne felt caught between management and the workers, grateful to the manager for access and to the workers for their stories, but unsure of how to report the data she received. A way around this situation would be to interview people when they are not at work, although that can create other problems.

In thinking about the time needed for participant observation, find out whether the institution has cycles or seasons of activity, and if it has episodic occasions that affect what goes on. If so, your observations should take account of the different phases of the cycle, as well as the different occasions. This does not mean that observations need to occur every day, but it does mean that time, as well as places and people, must be sampled. Findings from classroom observations made during the first quarter of a school year are likely to differ from those made in the fourth quarter. Classroom observations made only on Mondays may present a very different picture from observations made on other days of the week. Teachers and their students may interact quite differently in September than they do in December, as they may before football games, proms, and all the other big events that temporarily stand a school on end.

Despite the problems that individual researchers face in estimating the time they need to carry out their research, developing a timetable is a good idea. Doing so helps to assess the proposed aspects of the research and to anticipate the requirements of each: arrangements to be made, letters to be written, people to be phoned, and places to be visited. Although somewhat integrated with data collection, analysis and writing should receive at least as much scheduled time as data collection; it is relatively easier to collect data than it is to shape them satisfactorily as words on a page. Finally, the timetable serves as a reality check on the feasibility—given the inevitable constraints of time and finances—of your choice of research topic, methods, sites, and participants.

The timetable is a useful tool, but, like all qualitative research tools, it must remain flexible. In face-to-face interactions, unforeseen circumstances occur that can considerably delay your plans. On one hand, this can be perceived as a source of frustration and anxiety. On the other, the unforeseen is part of the world of exploration, and researchers, if open to what one can learn from occurrences that deviate from their plans, may use it to acquire better data and a better understanding of the people and setting under study.

The Lay Summary

Pre-data-collection tasks are not complete without a developed *lay summary*. Lay summaries are written or verbal presentations of your research that you give to research participants to help explain who you are, what you are doing, and what role you would like them to play in your research. In general, lay summaries address the following points:

1. who you are,
2. what you are doing and why,
3. what you will do with the results,
4. how the study site and participants were selected,
5. any possible benefits as well as risks to the participant,
6. if applicable, the promise of confidentiality and anonymity to participants and site,
7. how often you would like to observe or hope to meet for interviews,
8. how long you expect each session to last,
9. requests to record observations and words (by notes, tape recording, or videotaping).

The lay summary does more than tell what your study is about; it prepares participants to take part most effectively for data collection.

In addition to the lay summary, different interactions with your others may require other discussions as well. The teacher being observed from the back of the room may receive different reassurances than the teacher being interviewed. Observing puts the researcher in a passive role, but the teacher needs to feel reassured about what the researcher is doing "back there," what is being scribbled, and what will happen to the scribblings. Interviewing puts the researcher in the active role of asking questions, which makes confidentiality and anonymity more palpable issues. Also, with its format of questions and answers, interviewing resembles a test and can cause interview anxiety about "right answers." Reassuring participants that they cannot be wrong is necessary. They need to be told that to "do right" they must simply remember and disclose what they can, verbalize their opinions and feelings, and remain comfortable when they do not remember something or have nothing to say to a question.

You should be prepared also for questions that participants might have, such as, "Can I see the data?" or "Will I get a copy of the final report?" Anticipate such questions and be able to give reasonable answers and explanations without promising more than you can deliver.

Following is a copy of Rebecca's lay summary for her adolescent participants.

Rebecca's Lay Summary

You are invited to participate in a research study to learn about girls' friendship and development of their "self" (ideas about who you are and what you are like). This research is being done as part of my program as a doctoral student at the University of Vermont.

I am asking you to participate because I believe that your ideas and feelings about friendship and self would help me to better understand girls' friendship during this time of their growing up. The benefits to you of doing this study is that you might learn some new things about yourself, you might enjoy sharing your ideas and feelings about friendship and self with other girls like you, and you might even make some new friends. In addition, your participation in this study may help me and others better understand how to help girls have good friendships and help them feel good about themselves. There is, however, a risk that sometimes, for some people, talking about relationships and how you see yourself can be upsetting.

I will be the only person (other than your parents) who knows that you are participating in this study. Anytime I use the information you give me, I will always identify you with a fake name (if you would like you can decide what name I use for you). When I interview you I would like your permission to tape-record our interviews, sometimes videotape them, take photographs, and also take notes to remind me about what we talked about. I will be the only one who gets to listen to or see these tapes, videos, and notes, and when I am not using them they will be kept in a locked cabinet that only I have the key to. After I have finished with this study, all of these tapes will be destroyed. I would, however, like to take photographs to include in my presentation of my dissertation. If I use a photograph of you, I will use your fake name to identify the picture, and I will not pair your photograph with what you said about friendship and self. You may choose not to allow me to take photographs of you while you participate in this study. At the end of this consent I will ask you to check off whether you do or do not give me permission to take and use your photograph.

As part of your participation in this study, I will spend time with you and talk with you over the course of a number of weeks. I will first talk with you by yourself for an hour or two and ask you questions about friendship and yourself. During this interview I will also ask you for the name of a friend you would like to have participate in this study with you. After I have arranged for your friend to be part of this study, I will talk with you both together and ask you questions about your friendship and how this friendship makes you feel (about 1–2 hours). Next, I will spend several periods of time with you and your friend so I can see what you and your friend do together and what you talk about (about 3–9 hours altogether depending on what you and your friend feel comfortable with). Then I will have you get together with the other girls like you who are participating in this study and ask you as a group to talk about friendship and self (I think this part will be some sort of pizza party at my house—about 3 hours). This may be the last part of this study, but my plan is to talk with all of you at this point and see if it might be helpful for me to talk to all or some of you some more.

The most important thing for you to remember while you are participating in this study with me is that there are no right or wrong answers to the questions I ask you. All I am looking for is your opinion or ideas or feelings and if I ask you to tell me more, or explain your answer, it is because I want to be really sure I understand what you are telling me. Always remember that in this situation you are the expert, or teacher, and you are explaining to me what friendship and self is like for you and girls like you.

You should also know that you can decide to not participate in this study, or stop doing it at any time after you have started—this is your decision. If you decide to stop doing this study, your decision will not affect any future contact you have with the University of Vermont.

Institutional Review Boards (IRBs) have the responsibility of reviewing all research conducted in an institution receiving funds from the U. S. Department of Health, Education, and Welfare whether or not any of the funds go to a specific study. IRBs are charged with the duty to make sure research participants are aware of both potential risks as well as benefits from taking part in a study. IRB committees look specifically for lay summaries, consent letters, and examples of interview protocols or other research "instruments" in addition to generally assessing the overall design of a study. (The role of IRBs is discussed further in Chapter 6.)

The IRB received Rebecca's research proposal, her lay summary, and consent letter. Because she was going to be doing research with adolescents, her proposal underwent full committee review. They sent her a memo asking for clarifications and lay summary/consent form revisions. In particular, they requested that she provide examples of questions to be asked during the interviews and that she develop a "mechanism for obtaining consent from the parents of the girls recruited through *New Moon*." They also worried about her use of photographs and stated,

There should be two points at which subjects and parents make a decision regarding the photographs: in the initial consent form, they should be asked for consent to take the pictures; and after the text is complete, they should sign a release for the use of the pictures in the document and presentation. Please revise the initial consent form accordingly and develop a second form for the use of the photographs. You also need to make it very clear that the photographs will be part of a permanent, public document.

From the time Rebecca submitted her original protocol to the IRB to the time she received a confirmation letter from the IRB took nearly three months. Because of her work with adolescents, the committee was being particularly careful that the project would not result in any harm to participants. Rebecca eventually got all the pieces in place to everyone's satisfaction, but such are the unforeseen extensions of time that can take place in any research project.

The Pilot Study

A pilot study is useful for testing many aspects of your proposed research. Pilot your observations and interviews in situations and with people as close to the realities of your actual study as possible. Ideally, pilot study participants should be drawn from your target population.

Researchers enter the pilot study with a different frame of mind from the one they have when going into the real study. The idea is not to get data per se, but to learn about your research process, interview questions, observation techniques, and yourself. Clarify your piloting intentions for respondents. For example, "I would like to interview you with these questions and then talk to you afterward about the questions themselves: How clear are they? Are they appropriate? What else should I be asking?" The pilot participants need to know that they are part of a pilot and that, as such, their role is to answer the questions you ask, but with the intent to improve them. Use the pilot study to test the language and substance of your questions, and the overall length of your interview. Use it to determine how your introduction to the study works: Is it too long or not detailed enough? What else do people want to know? Does it inform as broadly as necessary to reassure your others about your proposed project?

Use the pilot study to test your observation techniques: How do those who are observed respond? What would make them feel more comfortable? Can you take field notes as you observe or should you write them up after observation periods? Less obvious than learning about your interview questions and getting a general sense of the nature of your research setting is the need to learn how to be present in that setting. What roles can and should you play in addition to that of researcher? Does the researcher role itself have ramifications that are peculiar to a particular place, ranging from the serious matter of needing clearance from the institution's head for all changes in research routine, to the less serious but still important matter of how to dress. Learning an institution's rules and expectations, its major actors, and its taboos can direct you to personal behavior that will help you to gain access and keep it.

Finally, use the pilot as a chance to inform yourself about the topic itself. How does your research statement hold up? Do new research questions arise? Changes in research focus may indicate poor planning, but they are also likely to indicate new learning. As Carol noted after her pilot project, "qualitative research is like the game of twister. You spin the dial and end up somewhere else." It is important to be open to changes so that the best possible connections between researcher and topic will result.

The pilot study readies you for gathering data. How many people need to be in the pilot? Again, there is no specific answer. The number and variability should be sufficient to allow you to explore likely problems, as well as to give you clues on stratification criteria for selection of participants. With the results of the pilot, you may revise your research statement, research plans, interview questions, and even your way of presenting yourself.

Gaining Access

With all these preliminary tasks taken care of, you are almost ready to begin your research. But first, you must gain access, which sometimes is a simple matter, sometimes not. This section discusses the process of gaining access in general. As with the other aspects of qualitative research, what you do in practice will depend on the context and the researcher-participant relationship.

Access is a process. It refers to your acquisition of consent to go where you want, observe what you want, talk to whomever you want, obtain and read whatever documents you require, and do all of this for whatever period of time you need to satisfy your research purposes. If you receive full and unqualified consent, then you have obtained total access. If your access is qualified somehow, then you must explore the meaning of the qualifications for meeting research expectations: Should you redefine your research? Should you select another site?

If the study involves some sort of organization or agency, then you must first make contact with its *gatekeepers*, the person or persons who must give their consent before you may enter a research setting, and with whom you must negotiate the conditions of access. Since there may be several different gatekeepers, making contact can be complicated, involving different persons at different times. If, for example, you want to study a particular elementary school, do you go first to the principal, the superintendent, or the school board? Starting anywhere but at the top of the hierarchy can be risky because acceptance by those in the lower ranks may be negated by supervisors. Yet gaining acceptance at the top is also risky because others may feel ordered to cooperate or may think that you are somehow politically aligned with one of several factions.

It helps to know an insider who is familiar with the individuals and the politics involved who can advise you in making access decisions. Successfully traversing the often sensitive territory of your research field may require not only your own good sense, but also that of an experienced insider who may work with you as a research collaborator.

If you are interested in individuals unrelated to any organizational structure, then you must make direct contact with these potential participants. Whether approaching gatekeepers or a series of individuals, you want them to say, "Yes, your study sounds interesting. You are welcome." Such a response is more likely if you are introduced by an intermediary whom the gatekeepers or potential participants know and respect. The others then have a way to check you out—to find out informally who you are, what you are like, and whether they would mind having you around. When there is not an intermediary, and even sometimes when there is, gaining access to people within a site is best achieved by first *logging time.* Just being around, participating in activities, and talking informally with people gives them time to get use to you and learn that you are okay. This approach leads to better data than one in which a superior requests a subordinate to cooperate with you. For example, asking the principal to arrange a schedule for interviewing the school's teachers can be an efficient way to obtain teacher cooperation, but not necessarily an effective one.

When meeting the gatekeeper, be prepared to negotiate your access. This involves presenting your lay summary, listening and responding to concerns and demands, and clarifying overarching issues. Make clear that your data—field notes and interview transcripts—belong to you (or to you and the respondent); claim this ownership in the interest of preserving the anonymity and confidentiality that you promise. Second, make clear what you will deliver. This relates to your responsibility to meet respondents' expectations for things such as receiving drafts that they may review and critique, final reports, or consultation about their problems. Third, make clear the emergent possibilities of qualitative research. In other words, make sure the gatekeeper understands that during the course of research, new issues may surface that could require more discussion, initiated by either party. Gaining access is an initial undertaking, but maintaining access is another matter; it may be occasioned by changes that occur in the expectations and needs of both researcher and researched at any time in the course of the research process.

Just as research statements and interview questions may change over the course of fieldwork, so too does trust. Trust needs to be developed before people can be willing to release certain kinds of information. For instance, if you are interested in college students on academic probation, then you should probably wait until after several interviews before requesting access to their academic files. You do not want to put research participants in the uncomfortable position of saying "no" to you; nor do you want to be told no.

Despite utmost care, rejections do occur. It is easy to overreact and become paranoid when faced with negative responses to requests to interview, sit in class, or attend a meeting. Although the negative response may be real, resist concluding that you will not be allowed to do the other things you have requested. The rejection may be unrelated to anything you have done or could have done, but it is, nonetheless, a signal to reflect on what you are doing and perhaps experiment with other approaches.

Sometimes denied access may turn out for the best as it did in Lorna's pilot study of inclusion of special needs children in schools:

> I initially wanted to observe more than two schools. This was probably totally unrealistic, since I very much underestimated the time involved in all aspects of the project. However, I immediately encountered some access problems. I was unable to connect with one building principal to get permission to observe in that school. Multiple phone calls where I did not get further than the secretary left me frustrated. I finally gave up, and focused on the other two classrooms. This is probably the "old blessing in disguise" since I would have felt even more inundated with too much data to deal with.

Researcher Roles

As a researcher, you need to define clearly your research roles. This definition is situationally determined, depending on the context, the identities of your others, and your own personality and values. There are, however, predispositions that all qualitative researchers should carry with them into research situations. First is the researcher's role as researcher. You are a researcher when you are sitting in the back of a classroom taking notes or in the midst of a lengthy interview; you are also a researcher when you talk informally in the grocery store with someone in your study. All of the places in which you present yourself communicate to your others how a researcher acts. As a researcher, ever conscious of your verbal and nonverbal behavior, you are more than usually attuned to your behavior and its impact. This degree of awareness may be uncomfortable to manage, particularly in the early days of your field contacts. Developing a level of self-consciousness that has you habitually attending to your behavior and its consequences, however, is useful. You may want to also seek feedback from trusted persons in the research setting who can see you as you cannot see yourself.

Although often anxiety-producing, the researcher's role can also be ego-gratifying. Students in research classes discuss how they deal with their new credentials as researchers. After being in the field for a while, they find themselves saying to colleagues, "Well, my research shows that . . ." They are asked to give presentations; they begin receiving clips of relevant articles and notices from colleagues and friends; and they begin to gain pleasure from their research role.

The second research role is the researcher as learner. Having this sense of self from the beginning is important. The learner's perspective will lead you to reflect on all aspects of research procedures and findings. It also will set you up for a particular type of interaction with your others. As a researcher, you are a curious student who comes to learn from and with research participants. You do not come as an expert or authority. If you are so perceived, then your respondents will not feel encouraged to be as forthcoming as they can be. As a learner, you are expected to listen; as an expert or authority, you are expected to talk. The differences between these two roles are enormous.

During data collection, expect to feel—at the same time or in close sequence—that you are not learning enough, that you are learning more than you can ever deal with, that you are not learning the right stuff, and that you are learning great stuff but do not know where it will lead or how it will all fit together. Anxieties about your research will change as you engage in each aspect of the process. Anxieties about how everything will fit together signal that you have begun seriously to consider the meaning of the data. As coding and data analysis progress, you will invariably become anxious about how to organize everything into written form.

Accompanying all of the various forms of anxiety is the feeling that your research is running your life. In this research-heightened condition, you will see nonresearch settings as potential research sites. Informal events will trigger thoughts about your research, and those near to you may come to know another person. "I learned about creative chaos," said Andrea, in the midst of her research;

"I was organized in my research, but my house was a total mess. One day I took my son to school without his shoes. My mind was simply on other things."

Neither this chapter nor any other specification of prestudy tasks can exhaust the possibilities of what you personally might anticipate and do before you begin to collect data. You may engage in exhaustive, detailed planning; or you may be comfortable with preparations well short of exhaustiveness. In this, as in so much of research, you need to find your own style, so that you will learn what works for you. Getting ready to conduct your study is not an end in itself. It is a means to the end of data collection. The next two chapters address such activity: participant observation and interviewing.

Exercises

CLASS EXERCISES

1. This exercise goes about research in an unorthodox way—beginning with the research participants in search of a "problem." I suggest this exercise not as a way to *do* research, but as a way to *practice* ethnographic techniques. Consider your classmates the research participants. Now work together to create a research statement to which each student could bring some expertise. Frame your research statement in a clear, focused way. For example, the class may want to describe and analyze how part-time graduate students perceive, manage, and assign priority to their multiple roles. Or, they may decide to explore the role "peer learning" has played in the education of graduate students. Develop what you consider an appropriate qualitative research statement. This statement will serve as the basis for more class exercises in chapters to come.

2. Keeping the research statement (from Exercise 1) as the core, develop three to five research questions that help to focus your topic. List possible aspects of the conceptual context that would guide a literature review if you were to do one.

INDIVIDUAL EXERCISES

1. Diagram your current understanding (working theory) of a research issue of interest to you. What important concepts are part of this research interest and how do they relate? Begin a search of relevant literature.

2. Draft your research statement and research questions.

Chapter 3

Being There: Developing Understanding Through Participant Observation

After a hot, still day, the evening was delightfully cool. Ina, Elija, and Marcus had just entered my house in the Caribbean valley. They had been to a "sing" up on Mango Ridge. A Methodist missionary group from the United States was in the valley for the evening to preach and spread the Word. It was an occasion for a gathering—something out of the ordinary—and many attended. Ina told how a young woman asked him if he had accepted the Lord as his personal savior. Ina had said yes and produced a detailed conversion story when asked for the particulars. All three friends laughed at this and the other invented tales they had told of evil deeds and repentance.

I laughed with them, but felt uneasy. After several months in the Caribbean valley, I suddenly wondered what was real and what was made up in the stories I had been told. Ina, Elija, and Marcus assured me that, although they made up names and made up jobs in their earliest conversations, they no longer did this. After all, I was living in the valley with them; I was "practically Vincentian."

Participant observation provides the opportunity for acquiring the status of "trusted person." Through participant observation—through being a part of a social setting—you learn firsthand how the actions of research participants correspond to their words; see patterns of behavior; experience the unexpected, as well as the expected; and develop a quality of trust with your others that motivates them to tell you what otherwise they might not. Interview questions that develop through participant observation are connected to known behavior, and their answers can therefore be better interpreted. Although participant observation ideally continues throughout the period of data collection, it is particularly important in the beginning stages because of its role in informing you about appropriate areas of investigation and in developing a sound researcher-other relationship. This discussion on participant observation focuses first on the process and then on the researcher. (See also Adler and Adler 1994; Bogdan 1972; Burgess 1984; Jorgensen 1989; McCall and Simmons 1969; Patton 1990; and Wolcott 1981.)

The Participant-Observation Continuum

Participant observation ranges across a continuum from mostly observation to mostly participation. It can be the sole means of data collection or one of several. Although your actual participant-observer role may fall at any point along this continuum, you will most likely find yourself at different points at different times in the data collection process.

Psychologists typically carry out research entirely at the *observer* end of the continuum. This role is more in keeping with the positivist paradigm, wherein the researcher has little to no interaction with those being studied. For example, the researcher may observe children in a university day-care program through a one-way glass. Similarly, the observer may sit on a city park bench, notebook in hand, observing town square activities. At the complete observer end of the continuum, your others often do not know that they are being observed.

Observer as participant is the next point on the continuum. The researcher remains primarily an observer but has some interaction with study participants. When another graduate student and I assisted Alan Peshkin in a study of a fundamentalist Christian school (Peshkin 1986), we interacted with students and teachers, but for a semester we were primarily observers, taking notes from the back of a classroom. We did not teach; give advice; or assist teachers, students, or administrators.

In contrast, I was more of a *participant as observer* during my work in Saint Vincent (Glesne 1985). I was interested in nonformal education and interacted extensively with others throughout my year's residency in their village. I assisted in agricultural work, socialized, and became an intermediary, if not an advocate, in interactions with agricultural agencies. A paradox develops as you become more of a participant and less of an observer. The more you function as a member of the everyday world of the researched, the more you risk losing the eye of the uninvolved outsider; yet, the more you participate, the greater your opportunity to learn.

The *full participant* is simultaneously a functioning member of the community undergoing investigation and an investigator. In order to learn about the politics and workings of a social welfare agency, for example, a researcher may seek employment with such an agency. Doing so is not as easy as first perceived because the researcher must manage two, sometimes conflicting, roles. Jan Yoors, in his book *The Gypsies,* describes the dilemma of becoming a full participant: "I was torn between two worlds and unable to choose between them despite the Romany saying that *Yekka buliasa nashti beshes pe done grastende* (with one behind you cannot sit on two horses)" (Yoors 1967, 47).

Where on this continuum *should* you place yourself? Your answer depends on the question you are investigating, the context of your study, and your theoretical perspective—to restate some of the contingencies underlying this much-used response. What applies to so much of the conduct of qualitative inquiry applies here: What is best done is less a case of what is established as right than of what your judgment tells you is fitting. If you are interested, as Woolfson (1988) is, in the nonverbal interaction between medical doctors and their patients during the initial, symptom-description phase, then you need to observe as unobtrusively as possible. Woolfson operated a video camera from outside the room where doctor and patient sat.

The context of the study can also affect your position on the participant-observer continuum. Because neither I nor Peshkin is fundamentalist Christian, we could never, without more deception than we could justify, be full participants in the study of the Christian day school. In his study of ethnicity in a California high school, Peshkin (1991) found himself moving from his usual "observer as participant" role to more of a "participant as observer" because he was easily and readily incorporated into the lives of the people there. Your place on the continuum also depends on your theoretical perspective. If you are doing action research, you are more likely to be a full participant than if you are doing traditional ethnography.

Participant-Observation Goals

Some people and some places are much studied. People can become jaundiced by the presence of outsiders who stay too short a time to get the picture that local folks have of themselves. Robert Caro, author of a book on Lyndon Johnson, describes his entry into the thinly populated county where Johnson grew up. At first the local people did not trust him. Too many reporters and journalists had already come for a day or a month and had invariably misrepresented the place and its people. Caro (1988) says,

> The people felt—and they were right—that they were being used, and that the things that were being written didn't accurately reflect and convey the country they loved. When I moved there, as soon as I said "I love it here and I'm going to live here and I'm going to stay here as long as it takes to truly understand it," their attitude really changed. (227)

In contrast to the general journalistic tendency to swoop in and swoop out, the ethnographic researcher means to stay long enough to get full description and a deep understanding.

The main outcome of participant observation is to understand the research setting, its participants, and their behavior. Achieving this outcome requires time and a learner's stance. Hymes (1982) states:

> Much of what we seek to find out in ethnography is knowledge that others already have. Our ability to learn ethnographically is an extension of what every human being must do, that is, learn the meanings, norms, patterns of a way of life. (29)

"Rather than studying people," agrees Spradley, "ethnography means learning from people" (Spradley 1979, 3).

As a learner, you are not in the research setting to preach or evaluate, nor to compete for prestige or status. Your focus is on your research participants, and you work to stay out of the limelight. To maintain this stance, be flexible and open to changing your point of view. Mary Catherine Bateson (1984) describes the importance of this attitude in the lives of her parents (Gregory Bateson and Margaret Mead) and in anthropological fieldwork in general:

> In anthropological fieldwork, even when you take with you certain questions you want answered or certain expectations about how a society functions, you must be willing to turn your attention from one focus to another, depending on what you are offered by events, looking for clues to patterns and not knowing what will prove to be important or how your own attention and responsiveness have been shaped. (164)

Through participant observation, you also seek to make the strange familiar and the familiar strange (Erickson 1973). The strange becomes familiar in the process of understanding it. To make the familiar strange is often more difficult because you must continually question your own assumptions and perceptions, asking yourself: Why is it this way and not different? Overcome your disposition to settle into a way of seeing and understanding that gives you the comfort of closure at the price of shutting down thought.

In the end, your new understandings—achieved through your learner's stance, your flexibility, and your emphasis on making the strange familiar and the familiar strange—provide new vantage points, new ways of thinking about some aspect of social interaction.

The Participant-Observation Process

In everyday life you observe people, interactions, and events. Participant observation in a research setting, however, differs in that the researcher carefully observes, systematically experiences, and consciously records in detail the many aspects of a situation. Moreover, a participant observer must constantly analyze his or her observations for meaning (What is going on here?) and for evidence of personal bias (Am I seeing what I hoped to see and nothing else? Am I being judgmental and evaluative?). Finally, a participant observer does all of this because it is instrumental to the research goals, which is to say that the observer is present somewhere for particular reasons. In your ordinary, everyday life, you may be a good observer of the interaction around you, but you do not consciously record and analyze what you hear and see in the context of particular goals that direct your behavior.

EARLY DAYS OF FIELDWORK

The first days in the field are the most anxiety-producing, as you question whether people will accept you and whether what you are doing is "right." The early days are also exciting and full of new learnings, but the many unknowns can create stressful situations.

Do not feel the need to "get in" with everyone, everywhere. Look for easy openings, that is, with friendly, welcoming people. Spend time with them, but never to the neglect of others at the site. Spend enough time with them, however, for them to get to know what you are doing, how you will be present, and what it is like to have you present—so that they can reassure others about you.

Figure out where the safe places are in the setting—safe because they are not controlled by any one person. In a school, this might be the cafeteria, the teachers' lounge, hallways, and the grounds outside the school. Spend time in these places, getting to know people and letting them get to know you, so that they will feel comfortable with you and will be more apt to respond positively when you ask to observe in "their" space.

Look for entry into closed places that in some ways are controlled by a person or group, possibly by arranging for introductions through mutual friends. Do not seek administrative-ordered permission to enter closed places in institutions, such as schools; if formal permission is given, do not take it as a proper invitation. Instead, arrange for the administration to announce your presence; then, address all of the teachers with your lay summary, clarifying that you want to come to their classes but that you will not do so unless they agree. Before-school in-service sessions are a fine time to introduce yourself and your project.

If the teachers do not routinely introduce you to the students during your classroom visits, ask if you can do so the first time you come to a class. This allows you to reassure the teacher and the students that you are there to observe, not to judge or evaluate. You can also more easily interact with students because they know who you are and why you are there.

When visiting classrooms, arrive at the beginning of a period and leave when the period is over. Be unobtrusive; do not call attention to yourself. Take notes only when doing so is understood and accepted by the teacher. Do not leave without a word of thanks to the teacher. If you are lucky, you will be invited back "anytime."

Finally, guard against bringing preconceived opinions to your participant observation. This is particularly easy to do if you are or have been a teacher, nurse, or social worker yourself and then become a participant observer in a similar site. Even though you were once "there," you cannot safely assume that you know what the people are like in your research site. All schools, hospitals, and social work agencies are not the same. For example, Sandy taught in a school where teachers were very critical of professors from a nearby university. Therefore, when she began participant observation in a school in another university town as part of her dissertation research, she was hesitant to identify herself with the university—when in fact the school chosen for her study had a good working relationship with the university. Do not assume that you know nothing about schools, hospitals, or village life, but do assume that you have to learn about the particular site and its people.

OBSERVATIONS

When you begin your role as a participant observer, try to observe everything that is happening: make notes and jot down thoughts without narrow, specific regard for your research problem. Study the *setting* and describe it in words and in sketches, using all your senses. How does the setting sound and smell? In what ways does a setting change from place to place throughout your research site? For instance, if you are doing research in a K–12 school, then in what ways is the first grade setting similar to and different from a twelfth grade classroom? Work on making the familiar strange. For example, if you notice that classroom doors tend to be left open (or closed), then ask yourself what this signifies.

Take note of the *participants* in the setting. Who are they in terms of age, gender, social class, ethnicity? How are they dressed? What do they do and say? Who interacts with whom? Make note of the conversations you hear.

Take note of *events*, differentiating between special events and daily events; then look for *acts* within those events. In the fundamentalist Christian school, for example, the first event of every day was a teachers' meeting. What kind of greetings do teachers offer during teachers' meetings, and to whom do they offer them? What do they informally talk about with one another? What kinds of questions do they ask of the principal? In other words, what "acts" make up the "event" of a teachers' meeting?

Another category for observation is people's *gestures*. How do students show enthusiasm and boredom? How does the teacher? What gestures help the principal to deliver his or her points? Observe which gestures jump out at you, which you take for granted, and which you might be misinterpreting. If a child lies with her head on the desk while the teacher is talking, is she sleepy, bored, or concentrating?

Cross-cultural research brings with it the recognition of either new gestures or new meanings to familiar gestures. A whispered "pssst" in the Caribbean can be a friendly "hello." Sucking air in through one's teeth with an upward motion of the head, however, is not the desired reaction to one of your serious comments—it signifies disregard, disagreement, or disdain. But you need not go to another country to find differences in how gestures are used. Native American children may opt for collaborative work assignments and avoid ones that draw attention to individual success (Sindell 1987). African American children may seek eye contact with the teacher but at a different rate than white children do (McDermott 1987). Just as teachers, to be effective, need to be aware of cultural differences in gestures, so too do researchers.

As a participant observer, then, consciously observe the research setting; its participants; and the events, acts, and gestures that occur within them. In the process, note what you see, hear, feel, and think. Begin to look for patterns and to abstract similarities and differences across individuals and events. For example, Ginny chose to practice her observation skills in the lounge of a squash facility during a men's round-robin tournament. After a period of jotting notes, she began to see a pattern:

> The winners of matches seem to stand or walk around after the match is complete. The losers always sit immediately. Blue headband wins. Red sits. Blue goes off to find a towel and water. Blondy, who had mentioned a head problem earlier, wins a match with Glasses. Glasses sits down. Blondy walks around and asks the director who is winning.

Ginny continued with more examples and concluded with questions about the behavior of male winners and losers during sports competition. She was able to move from the individuals in her observation, to their behavior, to thoughts about the more general behavior of men in sports events.

Wolcott (1981) suggests four strategies to guide observations:

1. observations by a broad sweep,
2. observations of nothing in particular,
3. observations that search for paradoxes,
4. observations that search for problems facing the group.

In the broad sweep observations, you try to observe and record everything. Since doing so is impossible, you begin to be selective about what to observe and record and then need to reflect upon your choices. When you search for nothing in particular, you begin to note what stands out, what appears as unusual. And when you search for paradoxes and for problems, you begin to look more deeply into the interactions before you. Such strategies help you to make the familiar strange and to ground you in the research context. (See also Bogdan and Biklen 1992 for an excellent discussion of field observations.)

FIELD NOTES

Notebook Form   The field notebook or field log is the primary recording tool of the qualitative researcher. It becomes filled with descriptions of people, places, events, activities, and conversations; and it becomes a place for ideas, reflections, hunches, and notes about patterns that seem to be emerging. It also becomes a place for exploring the researcher's own biases.

The actual form of the field notebook varies with the preferences of the individual researcher. Some arrange everything chronologically in spiral-bound notebooks; others keep loose-leaf notebooks so that different kinds of notes can be easily separated; yet others take notes on pads of paper, later transferring them to computer files. Peshkin (personal communication) used to complete data gathering with a large box full of spiral-bound notebooks, until his school and ethnicity research in Riverview, California, when he replaced his notebooks with 5 × 8 cards. He limited one point to a card and gave each card a date and a topic label, such as "Filipino," or a general label for later categorizing. Since during data analysis he always organized his field notes onto 5 × 8 cards, he reasoned that he might as well start out with them that way. Not only did this save him the laborious process of cutting up photocopied field logs and attaching them to cards, but it also motivated him to develop preliminary categories or codes early on.

Writing directly on cards may be a good method for those who can work from their handwritten notes. Those who prefer to transcribe everything into their computer are increasingly served by computer programs that assist in the coding and sorting of data (more on this in Chapter 7).

What form you choose for keeping notes is not important. That you keep a field notebook, however, is vital. (See Sanjek's 1990 edited volume *Fieldnotes.*)

Making Notes   Lofland (1971) distinguishes among mental, jotted, and full field notes. Mental notes are made of discussions or observations when pulling out one's notebook would not be prudent. In the fundamentalist Christian school, since Peshkin, the other research assistant, and I did not take notes during chapel, we made mental notes and wrote them up later. Jotted notes may be done in private or in public. They are the few words jotted down to help remember a thought or a description that will be completed later on. The full field notes are the running notes written preferably throughout the day, but sometimes, depending on the circumstances, after the observational period.

If possible, carry a notebook with you at all times and make it known that, as a researcher, you will write in your notebook. Your role will become that of inscriber, and soon it will be expected that if anything at all is going on, you will write it down. Of course, not all situations lend themselves to full note-taking. Agar (1973) could not take his notebook with him when doing research on drug addiction in New York City. Even in safe places, some researchers suggest that you should ease into writing. While doing research in a school, you may say that you plan to take notes, but this does not necessarily mean that you should or will do so at the outset of your fieldwork. You may want to spend from a few days to a few weeks just hanging out, getting to know the people and the place before you judge that it is acceptable to begin note-taking and determine just when and where it is acceptable to do so.

All notes should be expanded later, preferably the same evening. Some studies indicate that you can sleep on a day's events and retain your recall abilities, so that you could write up field notes the morning after participant observation. Ability to remember the details needed for field notes declines rapidly after that period of time, however.

Allot ample time for working on field notes. If you are making only mental or jotted notes, some researchers suggest that you give as much time to writing up your notes as you did to being in the field. If you are taking full field notes, then allow several hours to read through your notes to clarify and expand on them and to add your reflective thoughts and ideas. If this all seems rather much, be assured that your ability to write quickly and to observe and remember what you saw and heard does improve with practice. You will be pleased with the trouble you take to prepare clear, ample notes when later you sit down to analyze and write. One caveat: Your comfort zone may be breached by the demands of note-keeping. Find a balance between preparing notes that support your research needs and preparing them to an extent that makes research an aversive act.

Descriptive Notes   Your field notes should be both descriptive and analytic. In recording details, strive for accuracy, but avoid being judgmental. Make sure that your notes will enable you, a year later, to visualize the moment, the person, the setting, the day. Summarizing observations into succinct abstract statements will not do the job. For example, after observing a class, you might be tempted to write, "The class was disorderly and noisy." This statement does not present a clear picture of the classroom, and it is judgmental because it relies on the researcher's conceptions of "disorder" and "noise." The following statements are more concrete in their descriptiveness:

> The fifth grade class contained fifteen girls and twelve boys. When I entered, they were clustered loosely into six groups. One group of four girls was trying to see who could

blow the biggest bubble with their gum. A group of five boys was imitating a Kung Fu movie they had seen on tv the evening before . . . .

When you observe and describe the interactions taking place, you invariably look for patterns in what at first you might perceive as chaos and disorder. Check your field notes for vague adjectives such as *many* or *some* and replace them with more descriptive words. Look for and replace with descriptions words that convey an evaluative impression, that obscure rather than clarify, such as *wonderful, mundane, interesting, doing nothing, nice,* or *good*.

Make note of the dialogue that occurs. In particular, focus on words frequently used in or unique to the setting. Such terms help in wording interview questions and often become *native* or participant-generated analytic categories in the final write-up. Be alert for familiar words that assume very different meanings from your usual understanding. I spent a month in Saint Vincent before I understood that Vincentians did not use the word *country* to describe any nonurban area. Instead, they used "up country" to refer to the windward or eastern side of the island. A young man who lived in the capital city, Kingstown, but went "down leeward" (to the western side of the island) every weekend to help his grandmother on her land could honestly answer that he could not remember when he was last "in the country."

Drawing sketches also helps you to visualize a setting. Focus on where people and inanimate objects are located in space. Are there patterns? Do they change over time?

Your eyes, ears, and hands join forces to capture the details of a setting in your field notes, particularly early on in your fieldwork, when you are trying to capture an overall picture of the setting and its people. Through note-taking, you reflect on the appropriateness of your problem statement and become increasingly focused. Then, what you record and what you omit will begin to depend on your ever-refined, ever-clarified purpose. If you decide to emphasize, for instance, the interactions of international children in a university day-care center, then you do not need to describe in detail the teacher's curriculum. If, however, you are looking at the role religion plays in Christian schools, then you do note where in the curriculum religion does and does not play a part.

The following is an example of descriptive notes from my field log of the Saint Vincent setting in which I lived:

The valley stretches from the sea four-and-a-half miles inland until lost in the interior's 3,000-foot peaks. At 6:00 A.M. on a November Sunday morning, the bay is already a scene of relaxed activity. As a light rain develops, old men move into the fishermen's bamboo shelter. One curses another about his chickens. At the mouth of the river, men, women, and children gather to catch tree-tree (fish no longer than one's fingernail) by weighting burlap sacks on the river bottom with stone and then covering the sacks with "bush" (branches of trees and shrubs). The small fish seek the shelter of the leaves but are caught when the fabric is suddenly lifted from the water. On down the black sand beach, young women and children sit where the water meets the shore. Young men swim to a fishing boat anchored farther out, climb aboard, and talk as the boat gently rocks with the rising and falling sea. A rainbow stretches from beyond a "board house"

(house made of wood) on a point of land bathed in yellow light to the middle of the sea. In the other direction lies the valley, green and pastoral, with rugged hills covered in clouds.

A lane lined by sprouting fence posts leads into the valley. Cattle, horses, and sheep intermingle on the lush, river-mouth land. Thorny, palmlike trees stand out on the nearby cliffs. They soon give way to coconut palm, mangoes, breadfruit, and citrus trees. A mile into the valley, where most of the villages are, one forgets the immensity and varied moods of the nearby sea and is only aware of the enfolding mountains, often misty with rain. Villages sprinkle the two miles of arterial road which, after the last village, winds on up into the mountains a short distance before becoming a track for walking and climbing to land terraced and planted primarily in eddoes or bananas. The fields continue as the land slopes steeply, but then give way to natural vegetation.

These descriptive notes were intended to portray the context in which more focused observations and conversations took place. They set the scene for discussion of the life of young people within that valley. They do not analyze or try to explain what was going on; they only describe.

In addition to setting the scene, good descriptive notes capture specific interactions among research participants. For example, Yvette was studying how adult learners perceive, create meaning, and support one another in long-term or intensive learning groups. Through multiple observations of core courses, she focused on the interactions of adult learners in two different cohorts:

3/3/97, 4:00 PM, Doctoral Cohort Observations

Students are arriving, they are sharing ideas about their projects with peers in the same project group. Most are sitting in the same seats as last week. *Will students sit in the same seats throughout the semester?*

Prof (professor) tapes the multicolored handprinted (newsprint paper) agenda onto the classroom's right cinder block wall.

K (s—student) passes out a photocopied bibliography from the 1997 NAWE Conference as a resource for books on the writing process.

C (s) shares information about a local conference students could attend.

K (s) passes a flier around the student circle (more of a square made up of long black lunch tables placed end to end, surrounded by molded black plastic chairs, the table square fills the room) on Women's History Month. All look at it with varying degrees of interest and then pass it on to the next student.

C (s) Asks the group to tell her which group she is now in from last month.

D (s) Asks group about information she never received because she wasn't at the fall retreat. She is told to call the program administrative assistant. She doesn't understand why she didn't get the information.

L (s) Shares the title of a book on the future millennium. The group listens but is slowly breaking into whispered conversations.

Whole group begins to engage in (full volume) side conversations with people with whom they are sitting.

Several handouts are passed around the circle for everyone. Some are for upcoming student presentations.

Photocopied material appears to be an artifact of the group, a resource for their learning process, work process, class act—activity. Higher education culture—and the meaning of photocopied materials? Everyone knows the passing routine.

Although Yvette's observation notes are primarily descriptive, she did not hesitate to insert a thought or question as it occurred to her. Some of her questions became part of formal interviews; others, she inquired into more informally. Yet other questions helped to guide her subsequent observations. Her noting "the passing routine" is an example of "making the familiar strange," as she observed what went on around her.

Analytic Notes   Mary Catherine Bateson (1984) says of her mother, Margaret Mead,

> Margaret always emphasized the importance of recording first impressions and saving those first few pages of notes instead of discarding them in the scorn of later sophistication, for the informed eye has its own blindness as it begins to take for granted things that were initially bizarre. When something occurs to you, *write it down*, she said. (165)

This is good advice to follow.

Analytic notes—those recordings of things that occur to you—are sometimes called *observer comments,* but they should be more than comments. After each day of participant observation, the qualitative researcher takes time for reflective and analytic noting. This is the time to write down feelings, work out problems, jot down ideas and impressions, clarify earlier interpretations, speculate about what is going on, and make flexible short- and long-term plans for the days to come. Of course, reflective and analytic thoughts may come to you during participant observation and at other times as well. It is important to make note of these thoughts too—to write *memos* to yourself (Glaser and Strauss 1967) as Yvette did in the example above. Otherwise, the thoughts are apt to slip away. Mark these memos in some way to identify them easily as your own thoughts and wonderings. Analytic noting is a type of data analysis conducted throughout the research process; its contributions range from problem identification, to question development, to understanding the patterns and themes in your work.

As an example, I draw again from Yvette's field notes, this time from her reflective analytic notes after an observation session:

3/25/97, Field Reflections

There is a marked difference between the participation and interaction patterns of the whole group and small groups. In large group the dialogue is constructed by often the same people who offer statements that often act to support the group's dialogue in the same way each time. There are those who speak openly and more often than others (Martin, Alexis and Dee). Some (Travis and Mel) speak at the end of dialogue segments to confirm or wisely summarize (rarely taking chances). Becky contributes statements that ask for clarification of tasks and ideas, Suzanne's statements seem riskier in that she experiments with articulating what she is learning to the group for verification. Beth questions authority.

There are those who rarely speak, they watch and respond when it is safe, after others have structured the dialogue direction. In addition to the large group dialogue, there are often whispered dialogues taking place simultaneously (Katrina and Beth). What are the whispered dialogues about? Will I see changes in the dialogue patterns as time passes and topics change? When and why?

So what is happening?

1. Are adults negotiating the public/private duality of speaking and acting in the larger group where instructors are present? Is there a feeling of fear and uneasiness with the readings and project task that reduces iteration? No one wishes to appear unprepared, unintelligent. No risk taking?
2. Women are quiet except for a few who are used to public speaking. Some males dominate and have to comment on what just about everyone says. Some males are quiet.
3. Lack of time, and over-ambitious project is taking away the time for corridor talk. The report is that students are becoming bitchy with each other. Could it be stress, pressure to perform, no time to thoughtfully communicate, reflect, engage in praxis . . .

Yvette's analytic notes moved beyond her initial descriptions of details in cohort members' interactions to reflecting on the patterns within those interactions and to raising questions about their meaning.

Noting Advice   The following six guidelines are, in a sense, tricks of the participant observer's trade gained through experience. They are lore about the process of *noting* as a participant observer, some of it inapplicable if you use a word processor.

1. When taking notes by hand in a notebook, write only on one side of the paper. This reduces confusion if notes are later photocopied and cut into chunks for data analysis.
2. Leave ample margins on either side of your notes for coding and for afterthoughts.
3. Create your own form of shorthand to assist you in note-taking. For instance, in the Christian school study *Christian* soon became Xn, *student* S, *knowledge* K, *teacher* T, and *school* sch. I also used the same shortened forms for similar prepositions and other commonly used words, relying on the

context to differentiate them. Thus, *became* and *because* were both noted as b/c, *with* as w/, and *without* as w/o. If you know shorthand, then you may see this made-up shorthand as inefficient; if not, then my advice is to develop your own system.

4. When taking jotted notes, do not discuss your observations with someone else before writing up full field notes. Such talk not only dissipates the need to get your observations and thoughts down on paper, but also can modify your original perceptions. This does not mean that you should not compare your interpretations with others, but first record your own observations and reflections.

5. Even if you have been taking full, running notes throughout the day, your work is not done when the school bell rings or the sun sets. Read through the day's notes. Fill in remembered descriptions, clarify and expand briefly noted events or actions, and then reflect on the day and write your thoughts.

6. Invariably, unplanned occasions provide data relevant to your research question. Include these casual encounters in your field notes. Qualitative research is not delimited by time or space, even though when focusing on an institution such as a school, data collection generally occurs within set hours in a set location. This does not preclude collecting data in other places at other times.

Do not worry if at first you feel either overwhelmed with all the activity in your site and unable to focus, or disappointed in that nothing special is happening. Lorna felt both when she set out to observe a special needs child who had been mainstreamed into a regular classroom:

> My first observation left me feeling quite overwhelmed. I immediately was swept into a land of little, cute beings, who seemed to be swarming all over the place, chaotic, yet with some vague sense of order. Noisy, chattering, munching at snacks, getting up, sitting down, yawning, whining, working, listening, leaving, moving. At first, I couldn't even find the identified special needs child. With all that activity, I discovered how difficult it was to take notes. What should be written down? How do I stay focused? How do I deal with the little boy who asks me to help him with his spelling? And though I was specifically looking for interactions with the special needs child, at first, I found nothing out of the ordinary interactions, or almost none. At first glance, except for the "shadow," the aide, I couldn't see any impact of his being in the room. Dismayed, I decided, prematurely, that this data analysis will be boring, if not simple. I was wrong, of course.

Lorna had to stick with her observations over time before she began to see "the extent of and interaction of compassion, affection, and challenge involved in including these children in regular classes."

Finally, be reassured that variety in observations does not mean that someone got it wrong. Journalist Joan Didion (1988) describes how both she and her husband wrote very different books about El Salvador despite being together all of the time that they were there. Differentiating between "institutional" and "cultural" studies of pupils, Ball states, "The landscape looks different depending on the particular hill you happen to choose to stand on" (Ball 1985, 28). Subjective dispositions direct people to a variety of different things. This variety reveals the multiple realities of any social phenomenon, which together provide a fuller picture of the people, the times, and the place. Mary Catherine Bateson (1984) observes,

> You record carefully what your attention has allowed you to see, knowing that you will not see everything and that others will see differently, but recording whatever you can so it will be part of the cumulative picture. (164)

Other Fieldwork Allies: Collaborators, Photographs, and Documents

COLLABORATORS

Anthropological and sociological ethnographers often develop a close working relationship with a member of the researched group. This person is sometimes referred to as an *informant*, but also as a research *collaborator*. The collaborator plays a variety of roles, limited only by researcher imagination and the collaborator's willingness and capability, such as making introductions, alerting the researcher to unexplored data sources, and helping to develop theories grounded in the data. Although it has not traditionally been the case, the collaborator is sometimes a true partner in all or most aspects of the research process.

In Peshkin's study of a school and a rural community (Peshkin 1978), a teacher volunteered himself as collaborator, asking, "Do you want to know what really is going on here?" And in the Christian school study (Peshkin 1986), one student slowly emerged to play this role over the course of many interview sessions. By all indicators, the student was a faithful Christian, but he had reserved some type of autonomy that was expressed in his particularly forthcoming conduct.

Collaborators are indispensable partners in the conduct of qualitative inquiry. There will be much that you could not know without the interpretive knowledge, sensitivity, and insights of insiders, from the development and wording of interview questions to understanding hierarchies of power and authority. Remember, however, that the perspective of your collaborator may not represent that of all research participants. As Freilich (1977) and Moreno (1995) have warned, those who first befriend the outsider are often marginal, themselves, in some way. In fact, you may seek out more than one collaborator, and you may have recourse to different collaborators at different times in your research process.

Seek out and be ready to nurture the relationship with those willing and able to serve in the collaborator role. In this, as in your other research relationships, you must be attuned to the responsibilities of reciprocity, and to the need not to offend or exploit as you develop what ideally is a mutually rewarding association. (For extended accounts of "informants" in the lives of famous anthropologists, see Casagrande 1960.)

VIDEO AND PHOTOGRAPHS

Photography and videotaping techniques can enhance observation, and they can be employed in a variety of ways. Grimshaw (in Bottorff 1995) describes the primary advantages of videotaping as *density* and *permanence*. The density of data collected with videotape is greater than that of human observation or audio recording, and the nature of the record is permanent, in that it is possible to return to the observation repeatedly.

For microanalysis, or focusing on one aspect of everyday interaction, videotaping is invaluable. For example, Pat wanted to understand how low-income mothers help their children to learn. She had access to videotapes of such mothers and their children in laboratory-play situations, and she observed the tapes over and over. Then she interviewed the mothers, using her observations as a guide for question development. Through her observations and interviews, Pat developed a detailed coding manual that incorporated both behavioral and cognitive information for analyzing the videotapes. Bottorff (1994) warns, however, that the limitations of this type of data collection include the lack of contextual data beyond the recording, and the missed opportunity to be an active participant, able to test emerging theories as they develop. By relying too heavily on this type of data collection, you can lose the value of the *participant* in participant observation.

In *Visual Anthropology,* Collier and Collier (1986) discuss photography in fieldwork from its use in building rapport, conducting cultural inventories, and probing while interviewing to analytical procedures. They see photography as "an abstracting process of observation but very different from the fieldworker's inscribed notebook" in that photography gathers *specific* information "with qualifying and contextual relationships that are usually missing from codified written notes" (10). This was certainly true for Munoz (1995), who studied work, love, and identity in youths living in Puerto Rico. She reflected upon how photography contributed to her work:

> Photographs still what is moving so I can see it without blur: time, place, a glance, posture, details (What does her face express? What do his eyes say? What color is the dress she's wearing? The shirt he's wearing? What kind of material? Does she have earrings on? Do they have wedding rings? What is their hair like? What are their hands like?) All these combine to give a portrait, in black and white of a person caught at a particular moment in time . . . Photographs provide another approach to knowledge that literally brings me face to face with my questions and their answers. (60–61)

The qualitative researcher remains open to creative ways to enhance data collection as special educator Bruce demonstrated with his use of photography. Bruce was interested in familial perceptions of their children with disabilities. He gave a roll of film to each family and asked them to take pictures of the child and family members in everyday activities. A member of his research support group suggested that he give the families another roll of film and ask each member to take five pictures that for him or her symbolize the child but without the child in the picture. He could then interview each family member about his or her pictures and perhaps uncover items that he would not see or otherwise ask about.

Photographs also provide useful data for the historical background of your study. Peshkin (1978) asked residents of his rural school-community study to show him their family albums, which contained pictures dating back as far as seventy years. Such pictures not only captured the past in a special way, but they also served, as in Bruce's research, as the basis for interviewing. The utility of photographs and videotaping is limited only by your imagination (see Becker 1986a; Bogdan and Biklen 1982; Collier and Collier 1986; English 1988; Fetterman 1989; and Hagedorn 1994).

DOCUMENTS

Archaeologists reconstruct life in past times by examining the documents left behind. These documents, usually called artifacts, provide archaeologists with the basis for hypotheses about how people fed, clothed, and housed themselves; with whom they communicated; and how they thought about gods and an afterlife. Archaeologists cannot observe and participate in the everyday life of their others; they cannot interview men and women and children. Yet, from the records people leave behind, archaeologists can recreate their probable lives.

You have it easier than the archaeologist because you can both observe people in their normal interactions and ask them about the meanings of their actions. This is not to suggest, however, that you should ignore documents as a source of data. Documents corroborate your observations and interviews and thus make your findings more trustworthy. Beyond corroboration, they may raise questions about your hunches and thereby shape new directions for observations and interviews. They also provide you with historical, demographic, and sometimes personal information that is unavailable from other sources.

As a society that venerates the written word, we have many types of written documents. Diaries, letters, memoranda, graffiti, notes, memorials on tombstones, scrapbooks, membership lists, newsletters, newspapers, and computer-accessed bulletin boards are all potentially useful documents. A comparison of graffiti on the bathroom doors in the fundamentalist Christian school (only two statements observed all year, both witty but tame) with that found in the community's public school (many and of various natures) reinforced the image of the Christian school students that our observations and interviews had provided us.

Students in the Christian school, as with students everywhere, passed notes to one another during classes, then crumpled them and left them behind. These notes became artifacts in our research—consistent with our other findings. Compare, for example, the substance of the message from a Christian school student (in the first letter below) with that from a public high school student (in the second letter below):

Joe

I'm not the kind of girl who lets a guy boss me around. I don't like any guy doing that to any girl. . . .

If you save me a seat at lunch, I'll sit with you. . . .

I'm not going to meet you anywhere on my bike 'cause Mom will somehow find out and I'd be in big trouble.

Plus, I'd feel very bad 'cause I'd have to lie about where I was going and what I was doing. . . . Talk to you later.

Rachel

(Peshkin 1986, 155)

Fran,

I'm gonna kick this girl Nicky's ass in 3rd period. She has a smart ass mouth! I'm 'bout to hit her in it.

Are you going to the class meeting today? I might. I'm going to the junior prom, my mom's going to get a dress for pregs but in style.

Bell just rang finish later.

Lisa

(Peshkin, unpublished letter 1986 fieldwork)

To understand a phenomenon, you need to know its history. Reviewing a town's newspapers and institutional newsletters is one way to get started. A town's library archives are a good place to begin, but you will most likely get access to even more useful historical documents by letting it be known that you are interested in old letters, scrapbooks, and minutes of meetings. Such matters often work in a network fashion; once you find someone delighted by your historical interests, that source will usually lead you to someone else.

You can ask research participants to produce documents for you: to keep diaries, journals, or other kinds of records. If working in a school, you may be able to collaborate with teachers so that assignments simultaneously meet the needs of students, teachers, and researcher. For instance, if you are interested in children's self-concepts, then you may be able to persuade English teachers to ask their students to write self-portraits and then let you read them.

Notwithstanding your comfort with the written word, do not forget other forms of potentially useful documents, such as films, drawings, paintings, and music. While in Saint Vincent, I asked the children who found my home an entertaining hangout to draw themselves as they imagined they would be when grown. From these drawings I pulled out themes for comparison with the themes that emerged from interviewing young adults. I also analyzed the reggae and calypso music played in Saint Vincent (particularly that composed by Vincentians for Carnival) for its agricultural and educational messages; my findings were consistent with hunches gleaned from participant observation and interviews.

Graffiti, notes, and songs are all *measures of accretion,* or things people have created. You can be on the outlook for *measures of erosion* as well, things people have worn away such as the paths across the grass on college campuses or the shine on handrails in front of popular museum exhibits. And as Stoller (1989) urges, think about using all your senses, not only sight.

Documents and other unobtrusive measures provide both historical and contextual dimensions to your observations and interviews. They enrich what you see and hear by supporting, expanding, and challenging your portrayals and perceptions. Your understanding of the phenomenon in question grows as you make use of the documents and artifacts that are a part of people's lives. (See also Berg 1995 and Merriam 1988.)

The Participant Observer's Role

The participant observer's role entails a way of being present in everyday settings that enhances your awareness and curiosity about the interactions taking place around you. You become immersed in the setting, its people, and the research questions. One way to test if you are being there appropriately is whether or not you are seeing things you have never noticed before. After Andrea began her study of a community, she wrote the following in her field log:

> I went to a local restaurant for breakfast, caught myself watching the gathering of men at the breakfast bar, and found myself wondering for the first time: Who are those men? Why do they come here? How come I never noticed them before? Should I find out who they are—perhaps they represent some potential research rock yet unturned? I enjoy this newly honed sense of seeing.

After a period of time in the field, another test is whether you find within yourself a growing determination to understand the issues at hand from the participant's perspective. This indicates that you have been able to suspend your personal judgment and concerns. In the words of Sigmund Freud: "I [Freud] learnt to restrain speculative tendencies and to follow the unforgettable advice of my master Charcot: to look at the same things again and again until they themselves begin to speak" (Malcolm 1987, 95).

Another gift of immersion is that everything you read and hear can be connected, or at least considered for connection, to your phenomenon. (For more on connectedness, see Gould 1990, 3–6.) Ideas are generated and notes pile up. It is a time of transformation, when a research persona emerges with a life of its own. This persona is the one that fits your research field. It is not that you become some unrecognizable other person, but that, as you respond to the needs of being present somewhere in the role of researcher, you learn that you cannot just be the person you are in other settings playing more familiar roles. You are more and less yourself, moved to unexpected behavior in order to facilitate research opportunities and constrained from ordinary behavior that would interfere with your progress.

ANXIETY: A RESEARCH COMPANION

Immersion in and connection to others' lives do not occur without tensions and problems. After finding a place to live in the Vincentian village, I wrote the following in my field log:

> I am moved into the house—complete with bats that fly out of the sink drain, a cockroach apartment complex in the kitchen cabinets, a strange smell of something dead under the kitchen floor, bat races in the ceiling every morning at four A.M., no refrigeration so that even bread does not last the night without molding, and a toilet which leaks.

> Moving in is easy, though, compared with moving out into the community to begin observation and informal interviews. I finally forced myself outside around nine A.M., although I was ready to go at 7:30—I just couldn't make my feet walk out the door. I felt out of place, näive, unsure . . . .

Although my work took place in another culture with its attendant novelty and strangeness, immersion into an unfamiliar setting within your own country can be as anxiety-producing. Expect to feel like a somewhat awkward newcomer, as people rightfully wonder who you are, why you have come, what you will do, and what sort of nuisance you might prove to be.

New participant observers often feel timid, sensing that as invaders of someone else's territory, they are unwanted and unnecessary. It is true that, unless engaged in collaborative research, you are neither invited nor necessary. If, however, you retain that timidity, then you will limit your success because you will be too restrained about where you go, who you see, what you ask, or how much time you take. With a little effort and time, plus some skill, this awkwardness passes, your presence becomes "natural," and you begin to feel at ease. You need not become an essential presence to feel at ease and be welcomed; you just have to behave well, fit in with the local behavioral norms, and be agreeable, interested, polite, and respectful. In fact, you may find yourself behaving "better," that is, more properly than you otherwise do in your nonresearch life.

Feeling at ease does not, however, happen all at once with all participants in all sites, and it may never happen with some people in some places. Occasionally, overcoming timidity and fitting in may mean finding a role in the setting where you contribute in some way, although such roles are not always necessary, not always possible, and not always useful. What you do and how it is received depends on your skills, research needs, research participants, and setting.

Once accepted into the research setting, your companion anxiety latches onto new worries: Are you talking to the right people, observing the right events, and asking the right research questions? Soon after beginning his ethnicity study in Riverview, California, Peshkin (1991) noted the following in his field log:

> Titles keep popping into mind. This process begins earlier in each study. It is more than just a game. I really don't know what I can, should, or want to do. What stories does the place support? Today I got the first of my sinking feelings that I'm lost. The place is too big for me, and I won't be able to handle it. (personal communication)

He was able to "handle" it, and he did learn at least some of Riverview's stories. Anxiety of varying degrees is our constant companion: we need to acknowledge its presence, take account of its messages, and then continue our work.

In addition to courting anxiety, researchers face mental and physical fatigue from overdoing, especially from "overbeing," which is a sense of always being on stage and therefore on best behavior. Fatigue generally finds researchers after they have been in the field for an extended time; burnout becomes a possibility. When feeling overwhelmed with fatigue, it is clearly time to consider interspersing work with breaks of various sorts taken both inside and outside the field.

PARTICIPATING

As discussed earlier, how much of a participant you can or should be in a study varies. Horowitz (1986) takes issue with the implication that the researcher is essentially free to choose the degree and form of participation:

> I will argue that fieldwork roles are not matters dictated solely, or even largely, by the stance of the fieldworker, but are instead better viewed as interactional matters based on processes of continuing negotiation between the researcher and the researched. Together, the qualities and attributes of the fieldworker interact with those of the setting and its members to shape, if not create, an emergent role for the researcher. (410)

Research others often assign the researcher a role in keeping with their own conceptual frameworks. Horowitz was identified as a "lady" (which meant she was sexually unavailable) and as a "reporter" by the young male gang members she studied. The roles allowed her access to considerable information, but kept her from some areas of discussion and participant observation. In Saint Vincent, I became the "agriculture lady" who relayed messages to both governmental and nongovernmental agricultural organizations with which I had contact. Peshkin found himself functioning in a "teacher" role several times in his ethnicity study. The following is an example from his field log:

> The class was devoted to students writing paragraphs to go with their thesis paragraph, already submitted. The thesis paragraph contained a quote from Huck Finn, a statement given to them about Twain, and their opening statements. The students worked on their own or came to Jane [their teacher] for a reaction to their paragraphs. Then they started coming to me and kept coming for about half the period. They seemed to have decided that I was functioning as if I were a teacher.

He worried about this role:

> I've never been co-opted to a teacher's role before. I like doing it, but I do have misgivings. Kids may forget that I'm the book-writing guy to whom they can say anything with impunity, if what they think of when they see me is that I'm some sort of teacher, not quite like their regular one, but a teacherlike person, nonetheless.

Balance the costs and benefits of your participation. What you do in an effort to reciprocate may conflict with your role as researcher. If, for example, a teacher asks you what you see from the back of her classroom, and you respond with advice or reinforcement, then you assume a judgmental expert role and risk losing your credibility as a nonjudgmental researcher. If you are enlisted as a free substitute teacher and do well with a class, then you make teachers aware of your teaching assets and, possibly, their teaching liabilities. If a class needs a driver for a field trip and you volunteer, then you may be overdoing the good-person role because of the resultant time drain on your work. Being the field trip driver, however, may provide an opportunity to observe students and teachers in a different context from the usual one. Do participate, but in a way that does not get you inextricably incorporated in a setting's ongoing affairs unless you are choosing to do more action-oriented research. If you become incorporated, then you might have to take a position that alienates you, that makes you reactive, that makes you take sides.

REMAINING MARGINAL

In traditional ethnography, researchers are sometimes called "marginal natives" (Freilich 1977) because, although they grow close to their others, they generally remain sojourners who are physically and psychologically at the margin of life in the research setting. In physical terms, the researcher attends events but stays on the fringes, at the back of classrooms and meetings.

Although researchers and participants interact freely, the interaction usually is within a frame of guarded intimacy. The researcher does not take charge or play the role of change agent or judge, but stays also at the psychological margins of interactions. Remaining marginal "allows one to continue to spend time with groups when they are no longer friendly" (Horowitz 1986, 426) with each other. The point of the margin is that it offers the vantage of seeing without being the focus of attention, of being present without being fully participant, so that you are free to be fully attuned to what occurs before you, which, after all, is the point of being there.

Realize, however, that in some situations you may alienate your research participants by choosing to remain marginal. They may see you as aloof and even as exploitative. In *Death Without Weeping: The Violence of Everyday Life in Brazil,* Nancy Scheper-Hughes (1992) describes how, as a Peace Corps volunteer, she had spent time in an economically poor community in Brazil. She was active immunizing babies, administering penicillin injections, and working as a community organizer to create a community center and cooperative day nursery. Fifteen years later, she returned to the same community as an anthropologist to study "mother love and child death." Old neighbors and friends welcomed her back, but grew weary and disillusioned with her proclaimed role. They wanted her to help them as she had before:

> But each time the women approached me with their requests, I backed away saying, "this work is cut out for you. My work is different now. I cannot be an anthropologist and a *companheira* [comrade, friend 'in the struggle'] at the same time." I shared my new reservations about the propriety of an outsider taking an active role in the life of a Brazilian community. But my argument fell on deaf ears. (Scheper-Hughes 1992, 17)

Scheper-Hughes continued to conduct interviews and to remain somewhat marginal to the community until confronted by the women:

> Why had I refused to work with them when they had been so willing to work with me? Didn't I care about them personally anymore, their lives, their suffering, their struggle? Why was I so passive, so indifferent, so resigned . . . the women gave me an ultimatum: the next time I came back to The Alto I would have to "be" with them—"accompany them" was the expression they used—in their *luta,* and not just "sit idly by" taking fieldnotes. "What is this anthropology anyway to us?" they taunted. (18)

Scheper-Hughes returned five years later and assumed the combined role of anthropologist-*companheira*. Although she found this role difficult to balance and "rarely free of conflict" (18), it also served to enrich her understandings of the community as she demonstrates in her moving ethnography.

As participation increases, marginality decreases, and you begin to experience what others see, think, and feel. This can be absolutely worthwhile for yourself and research participants; no amount of advantageous marginality can replace the sense of things that participation offers. The most fruitful strategy is a judicious combination of participation and observation, as dictated by what you hope to understand, your theoretical stance, and your research others.

GAINING AND LOSING SELF

"In short, she could not unself herself and become other people" (Pritchett 1987, 134). This criticism was said of writer Rebecca West and her failure to become an actress when she was young. In a sense, qualitative researchers are like actors; they must be able to "unself" themselves as they enter the lives of other people. They do not "become" other people, but they do manage the impressions that they give.

Participant observation places researchers in the lives of others in a self-consciously instrumental way. Participant observers are not merely visiting with the hope to see the sights, have a good time, and, in passing, learn a little about how the natives live. Researchers have ends-in-view, purposes—however incipient—that underlie their presence in particular settings and direct their behavior while there. The inescapable truth is that researchers are not merely present as they would be in other ordinary circumstances of their lives. Given purposes to pursue, they shape their behavior to be efficacious in light of these purposes, managing selves that are instrumental to gaining access and maintaining access throughout the period of study in a way that optimizes data collection.

You have control over your words and actions, but less control over other aspects of yourself—sex, age, religion, and ethnicity. But even with seemingly unchangeable characteristics such as gender or ethnicity, you do have some choice in how you present yourself. For example, Daniels (1967) elaborates on her "learned responses" to behave "appropriately" when working as a woman sociologist among Army officers:

> Certain behavior was considered inappropriate or even insulting from women: a firm handclasp, a direct eye-to-eye confrontation, a brisk, businesslike air, an assured manner of joking or kidding with equals were all antagonizing. Most galling of all was my naïve assumption that, of *course,* I was equal. It was important to wait until equality was *given* me. When I learned to smile sweetly, keep my eyes cast down, ask helplessly for favors, and exhibit explicitly feminine mannerisms, my ability to work harmoniously and efficiently increased. (275)

Most research situations do not call for such extreme impression management. In Saint Vincent, I always wore a skirt because shorts and slacks were not considered appropriate dress. In the Christian school, Peshkin shaved his beard, and we both carefully removed any minced oaths from our speech, such as "gosh," "darn," or "gee." Researchers often have to work for their acceptance, and this frequently entails a nonaggressive style or, as Lofland puts it, becoming "a socially acceptable incompetent" (Lofland 1971, 101). The extent to which you should modify behavior for research purposes is difficult to define: Where are the boundaries of integrity? When does adaptation go too far? In everyday life, you present yourself differently in different situations. Research is one more occasion for fashioning a presence, albeit more self-consciously than is ordinarily the case. At some point, however, does this impression management become a lie and transgress the boundaries of ethical warrant?

A number of people have collected research data through covert participant observation and, in so doing, monitored carefully their presented self. Dalton (1959) worked covertly as a firm manager to investigate management; Homan (Homan and Bulmer 1982) studied a Pentecostal sect as if he were a novitiate; Sullivan (Sullivan, Queen, and Patrick 1958) lost weight, altered age, and adopted a "new personality" in order to study Air Force recruits; and Humphreys (1970) studied homosexuals by taking on the role of "watch queen" in public restrooms. Researchers who study the powerful, the illegal, and the marginal often have used covert means of gathering data.

Although some (Douglas 1976) would argue that ordinary social life is characterized by deceit and impression management, others say that no research should consciously deceive. Covert research is fraught with questions and problems, discussed to some extent in the ethics chapter (Chapter 6). On one hand, some argue that the rights of subjects override the rights of science and that covert observation is harmful to subjects, researcher, and the discipline. On the other hand, some believe that a measure of deception is acceptable in some areas when the benefits of knowledge outweigh the harm, and when the harm has been minimized by following conventions of confidentiality and anonymity.

BEING EFFECTIVE

Learning to be an effective participant observer takes some doing. Begin by asking what there is about your identity or persona—such as gender, age, ethnicity, or country of origin—that might affect your access and data collection. Are there ways in which you can monitor yourself to gain more information? Second, before entering a setting as a participant observer, investigate the scene or use collaborators to discover normal attire and acceptable behaviors. You will make mistakes in your research interactions, but being prepared lessens the probability of major mistakes. Third, as you begin your role as a participant observer, be on the lookout for ways to adjust or accommodate yourself so that you "fit in" in a manner instrumental to gathering data. For example, this may mean brushing up on the latest music when working with teens, or keeping up with football scores when working in a male-dominated education department in the Midwest. Fourth, as participant observation continues, be aware of the different groups in the setting and carefully consider whether or not to become aligned with any one group. Unless your focus narrows so that you are concerned with only one group, such as the athlete student group, then it is probably best to remain un-aligned. Finally, a natural disposition is to share what you learn with others whom you know would be interested. Don't. Learning to be judiciously silent is critical, so that everyone who talks to you knows that he or she can safely tell you anything.

BITTERSWEET TIMES: DISENGAGING

Leaving the field may be a bittersweet time. You are glad to be done and have your life return to normal; you can finally get to the neglected tasks in other aspects of your life; and you can once again spend time with family and friends. Still, you are sad because something you have invested in highly is over. You may be leaving good relationships and good times. Even if you never personally accepted your others' ideology, most likely you came to empathize and enjoy interacting with them. It may be that you will never return to the setting under the same circumstances.

You may feel dislocated when you return full time to pre-fieldwork life. After all, you have adjusted to living properly in someone else's life. You may also feel different about yourself; long-time immersion in someone else's life enhances your general self-awareness and tells you about yourself as a fieldworker. You feel relief at not always having to be watchful, yet you find yourself reevaluating your "normal" life through comparisons with the lifestyle of your research participants. You miss people, places, and ways of doing things. Of course, leaving a Caribbean village is different from leaving a secondary school in the city in which you normally live, but departure from both places tends to be bittersweet.

Exercises

1. Take a notebook with you to a public setting where social interaction takes place (restaurant, public library, public park, shopping mall, airport, etc.). Observe as though you are a stranger in a new country, trying to make sense of the action around you. Be as descriptive as possible. Observe for an hour, then write up your notes into a descriptive vignette, looking for patterns in events and actions.

2. Go to your research setting with your field notebook. Concentrate on observing the context only. Describe how things look, smell, sound, feel. Write up your observations into a vignette with the intention of having readers feel as though they are in the school, nursing home, physical therapy clinic, or whatever may be your research setting.

3. Brainstorm ways to gather data on your topic other than through participant observation or interviewing (taking photographs; collecting diaries, letters, minutes of meetings, old high school annuals, scrapbooks kept by research participants; drawing or asking participants to draw; etc.). Discuss ideas with classmates and then pilot with a research participant. Reflect upon what you learn and what new questions arise.

Chapter 4

Making Words Fly: Developing Understanding Through Interviewing

Think of interviewing as the process of getting words to fly. To be sure, they do not fly with the regularity and predictability of balls emerging from batting-practice machines that baseball teams use. Interviewing is a human interaction with all of its attendant uncertainties. As an interviewer, you are not a research machine, but you do "pitch" questions at your respondents with the intent of making words fly. Unlike a human baseball pitcher whose joy derives from throwing balls that batters never touch, you toss questions that you want your respondents to "hit" and hit well in every corner of your data park, if not clear out of it—a swatted home run of words. As a researcher, you want your "pitches"—your questions—to stimulate verbal flights from the important respondents who know what you do not. From these flights come the information that you transmute into data—the stuff of dissertations, articles, and books.

Getting words to fly is the subject of this chapter. It is a simple matter to express: Develop a clearly defined topic; design interview questions that fit the topic; ask the questions with consummate skill; and have ample time to "pitch" the questions to forthcoming and knowledgeable respondents. As with pitching balls, however, the process of creating good interviews takes practice.

Interviewing: An Interaction

What type of interaction is the interview? An interview is between at least two persons, but other possibilities include one or more interviewers and one or more interviewees. Interviewing more than one person at a time sometimes proves very useful: children often need company to be emboldened to talk and some topics are better discussed by a small group of people (often referred to as a *focus group*) (for discussion of group interviews, see Berg 1995; McMillan 1989; Morgan 1988; Van Galen, Noblit, and Hare 1988–1989).

Researchers ask questions in the context of purposes generally known fully only to themselves. Respondents, the possessors of information, answer questions in the context of dispositions (motives, values, concerns, needs) that researchers need to unravel in order to make sense out of the words that their questions generate. The questions, typically created by the researchers, may be fully established before interviewing begins and remain unchanged throughout the interview. Questions may emerge in the course of interviewing and may be added to or replace the preestablished ones; this process of question formation is the more likely and the more ideal one in qualitative inquiry.

The questions you bring to your interview are not set within a binding contract; they are your best effort before you have had the chance to use them with a number of respondents. However much you have done to validate the utility of your questions, you should think of them tentatively, so that you are disposed to modify or abandon them, replace them with others, or add new ones to your list or *interview schedule*. The more fundamentally you change your interview schedule, however, the more frequently you may have to return to people whom you thought you had finished interviewing in order to ask them questions that emerged in interviews with others. In general, it is not advisable to say final good-byes to respondents; leave the door open to return.

Interviews can figure in a research project in different ways. In the positivist tradition, they can be the basis for later data collection, as in the form of a questionnaire. Not knowing enough about the phenomenon of interest, researchers interview a sample of respondents in the hope of transforming what they have learned into the necessary items and scales. Schuman (1970), also in a positivist vein, advocates the interview as a validity check of the responses given to questionnaire items. For example, what do respondents mean when they select "strongly agree" or "strongly disagree" as their response to some item? Probing in depth with a small sample of respondents who account for what they meant when they disagreed or agreed can indicate whether different respondents perceived the question in reasonably similar terms, as well as what underpins their reactions to it. In the interpretive tradition, the interview can be the sole basis of a study, or it can be used in conjunction with data from participant observations and documents.

Given the face-to-face nature of ethnographic research, you may ask questions on the many occasions when something is happening that you wonder about. You inquire right then and there without formally arranging a time to ask your questions. *Structured interviewing*, in contrast, is a more formal, orderly process that you direct to a range of intentions. You may want to learn about that which you cannot see or can no longer see. Jan Myrdal (1965), in *Report from a Chinese Village*, reconstructs—through oral history interviews with many people—the transition in rural China between the passing of Chiang Kai-Shek's regime and the ascendancy of Mao Zedong. *Oral history interviews* focus on historical events, skills, ways of life, or cultural patterns that may be changing (Rubin and Rubin 1995). Mary F. Smith

(1954), in *Baba of Karo,* re-creates—through life history interviews with one person—the life of a Nigerian woman of the Hausa tribe. *Life history interviews* focus more on the life experiences of one or several individuals. Both oral history and life history interviews are examples of focusing on concepts of culture. "In cultural interviewing, researchers learn the rules, norms, values, and understandings that are passed from one generation of group members to the next" (Rubin and Rubin 1995, 168). The kinds of questions in cultural interviews "get people talking about their lives, experiences, or understandings" (178). Observations puts you on the trail of understandings that you infer from what you see, but you cannot, except through interviewing, get the actor's explanations.

You might also interview in search of opinions, perceptions, and attitudes toward some topic, for example, asking teachers their opinion about the substance of the state-mandated changes in the middle school science curriculum. How do they perceive the impact of the changes on their work as teachers? What is their attitude about this impact? Concerned about the utility of the state's curricular mandate, you might conduct interviews to obtain data that will be instrumental for understanding teacher conceptions of science and the obstacles to implementing proposals for reform. This would be a form of *topical interviewing* that focuses more on a program, issue, or process than on people's lives.

The opportunity to learn about what you cannot see and to explore alternative explanations of what you do see is the special strength of interviewing in qualitative inquiry. To this opportunity, add the serendipitous learnings that emerge from the unexpected turns in discourse that your questions evoke. In the process of listening to your respondents, you learn what questions to ask. For more sources on interviewing, see Bernard 1988; Brady 1976; Burgess 1984; Enright and Tammivaara 1984; Fetterman 1989; Fontana and Frey 1994; Gorden [1969] 1975; Hyman [1954] 1975; Kvale 1996; Patton 1990; Rubin and Rubin 1995; Seidman 1991; and Wildavsky 1989.

Developing Questions

QUESTION CONTENT

What is the origin of the interview question? In qualitative research, the experience of learning as participant observer often precedes interviewing and is the basis for forming questions. The things you see and hear about the people and circumstances of interest to you therefore become the nuggets around which you construct your questions. Of course, participant observation does not and cannot always precede question making. What then? Turn to your topic and ask, in effect: If this is what I intend to understand, what questions must I direct to which respondents?

Novice researchers sometimes confuse their research questions with their interview questions, thinking that they can modify their research questions to produce their interview schedule. "Your research questions formulate what you want to understand; your *interview* questions are what you ask people in order to gain that understanding" (Maxwell 1996, 74). Although there should be a relationship between research and interview questions, interview questions tend to be more contextual and specific than research questions. And their development "requires creativity and insight, rather than a mechanical translation of the research questions into an interview guide" (74).

Among the more important sources of questions is the theory, implicit or explicit, underlying some behavior. Daren, for example, planned to investigate what he called "the returning dropout," young people who dropped out of high school but later returned to study in an adult education program. Daren's questions originated from his knowledge of the literature and from his reasoning. Over time, they were modified by pilot testing and through consultation with other researchers and informants. They reflected theoretical considerations. He asked, for example:

1. for what reasons returnees left school in the first place (suggests a connection between leaving and returning to school),
2. how parents reacted to their decision to drop out (suggests the likelihood of a parental role in leaving and returning),
3. whether they have friends who also dropped out (suggests that peer influence could motivate leaving and returning),
4. how they learned about the adult education program (suggests the possible influence of the source of knowledge about the program),
5. in what ways treatment of students and contents of instruction were different in the adult program than in their high school program (suggests the appeal of some particular features of the adult program compared with the high school program).

These discrete questions do not amount to a theory; they do, however, point toward an understanding of the complex phenomenon of returning to school, which is a precursor to theory. In short, with the answers Daren received from each of his returning dropouts, he advanced his ability to explain why dropouts return to school.

By whatever means obtained, the questions you ask must fit your topic: the answers they elicit must illuminate the phenomenon of inquiry. And the questions you ask must be anchored in the cultural reality of your respondents: the questions must be drawn from the respondents' lives. Thus, when Sarah interviewed student teachers about their classroom practices, she knew what to ask because she had both sat in their prepractice teaching methods class and later watched them perform in their own classrooms. But she also could have known what to ask by having taught a teaching methods class and supervised student teachers. In both cases, she could enhance the experiential foundation from which she generated questions by use of knowledgeable informants, such as former student teachers and supervisors of student teachers, as well as by reading the relevant literature.

THE MECHANICS OF QUESTION DEVELOPMENT

Todd, interviewing parents about their perceptions of portfolio use as a means of assessing their child's performance in school, stated, "I found I spent 45 seconds explaining each question, so I had to work to simplify them." Researchers often begin with questions that make perfect sense to them, but are less clear to their research participants. Michael Patton (1990), in his chapter on interviewing in the text *Qualitative Evaluation and Research Methods,* has some of the best advice around concerning the development of good interview questions. He talks about kinds of questions, urging the researcher to ask questions from a variety of angles.

Kinds of questions that Patton (1990) describes include experience/behavior questions, opinion/values questions, feeling questions, knowledge questions, sensory questions, and background/demographics questions. Experience/behavior questions are generally the easiest ones for a respondent to answer and are good places to begin to get the interviewee talking comfortably. Knowledge questions, in contrast, can give the impression of being tested. Respondents can readily feel embarrassed or at least uneasy when they have to say "I don't know" to a question that you assumed they would know. If a knowledge question is information that can be obtained from documents or from one person in the know, such as the department chair, get the information there and drop the question from your interview list for all respondents.

Patton (1990) also reminds us that we can ask our questions of the present, past, and future. Questions that ask for hypothetical musings about the future, however, tend to provide data that is neither "thick" in description, nor very useful during data analysis. The question, "How would you like the university to be in ten years' time?" generates little other than a wish list. Exceptions exist, of course, but the past and present tend to be richer ground for stories, descriptions, and interviewer probes.

"The way a question is worded is one of the most important elements determining how the interviewee will respond" (Patton 1990, 295). Not only must you think about different kinds of interview questions, but also you need to work carefully with shaping the question as Todd discovered in his portfolio interviews with parents. Look through your questions and rework any that are dichotomous yes/no questions ("Do you participate in volunteer activities?") because such questions guide your respondent to give short answers. Rethink multiple questions ("Tell me about the last time you volunteered, how long you worked at the activity, and how you felt about doing so") because your respondent will most likely talk more fully about one of your several questions and forget the others. "Why" questions ("Why do you do volunteer work?") can also be problematic because each respondent might answer from a different perspective, even though he or she could speak to several (Patton 1990). As researcher, you would want to investigate the primary categories or perspectives with all respondents. For example, one interviewee might answer why she does volunteer work with a discussion of childhood experiences. Another might talk about his need to give something back to the community. Yet another might report how volunteer work puts her in contact with people she would not be with otherwise. As a result of your "why" question, you will generate a list of reasons for participation in volunteer activities, but your understanding of volunteer work might grow even deeper if you asked each respondent about the role of family socialization, moral beliefs, and perceived rewards in his or her participation in volunteer work.

One kind of question to think about using is the *presupposition question,* a question in which "the interviewer presupposes that the respondent has something to say" (Patton 1990, 303). Novice interviewers often perceive the need to begin with a short-answer question such as, "Are you satisfied with your volunteer work?" followed by the more open-ended questions: "In what ways are you satisfied?" and "In what ways are you not satisfied?" You can often presuppose that satisfaction (or some other attribute) is a part of the work and begin with a statement such as "I'm going to ask you now about your satisfaction and dissatisfaction with your volunteer work. Let's begin with the ways in which it is satisfying for you."

Presupposition questions are useful. Leading questions are not. It is sometimes easy to confuse the two. *Leading questions* "give the interviewee hints about what would be a desirable or appropriate kind of answer" (Patton 1990, 318). In leading questions, the interviewer makes obvious the direction in which he or she would like the answer to go. Imagine if you began a question with the following, "It often seems that much of our population is focused on themselves, never thinking about environmental problems, homelessness, or poverty except as they, individually or possibly as a family, are affected. What does volunteer work mean to you?" If the questions were asked in this way, could a respondent easily tell you that he spent spring break with Habitat for Humanity because his girlfriend has signed up to go? A presupposition question might, in contrast, presuppose that there are ways in which volunteer work is and is not meaningful (satisfactory, useful, etc.) to the respondent, but it does not lead the interviewee to answer in any specific way.

Some examples of questions are drawn from the study that Peshkin (1991) conducted in the pseudonymous Riverview High School in California. He planned to explore how, if at all, ethnicity figured in the life of a high school. The questions are not intended as model questions, but as types of questions that can be raised for qualitative inquiry. They also demonstrate the importance of planning a series of interviews over time so that rapport can be established and time can be sufficient for learning from your respondents.

Some questions were addressed to each group interviewed—counselors, teachers, students, and parents; others were designed for a particular group only. One set of questions for counselors was planned to encompass three or more interview sessions. The introductory interview covered background data and explored the process of becoming a counselor; it was intended as a time to become acquainted, build rapport, and ease the counselor into the role of interviewee. In the next session, planned as an after-school meeting, the counselors were told, "I'd like to get a general picture of what you do in the course of a day, not necessarily the very special things, just the routine type of things. Take today, for instance. What did you do?" Included with this introduction were these notes to the interviewer: "Make a list of these things. Get elaboration of anything not perfectly clear. Categorize discrete activities." Spradley (1979) refers to this type of question as a *grand tour* question, a request for the respondent to verbally take the interviewer through a place, a time period, a sequence of events or activities, or some group of people or objects.

Peshkin's idea was to complete this picture as a setup for the third session, which opened with a review of the types of activities the counselor reported. Then, the counselor was told, "Okay, now I'd like to take these activities one at a time and learn something about their operation. Were the student a Filipino [the type of student was, alternately, a Filipino, Hispanic, African American, or Italian], what would your thinking be about how the matter is best handled?" The goal was to learn if and how counselors differentiated their professional behavior on the basis of a student's ethnicity. Peshkin assumed that it would take at least two sessions to establish rapport and set up the necessary structure of concrete objects (the list of a counselor's ordinary activities) in order to elicit effectively a report of behavioral distinctions on the basis of ethnicity. A common mistake in interviewing is to ask questions about a topic before promoting a level of trust that allows respondents to be open and expansive.

Another mistake is to ask questions about something that is too vague to elicit the most comprehensive response. The record of the counselor's day is the concrete object toward which further questions were directed. Other such objects can be obtained by asking the respondent to recapture something by imagining it. For example, if you want to understand how nurses with varying years of experience construe the initial entry period into their profession, you could say, much as might a hypnotist: "I'd like to have you go back to a time in your professional life that you've probably not thought about for years. Remember when you finished your schooling? You found a position and where ready to begin your first day on the job," and so on. The idea is to provide mood and props for interviewees to recall something likely to be long unthought-about. For your purposes, you want them to recapture time, place, feeling, and meaning of a past event. The straightforward "Let's talk about the early days of you work as a nurse" just might fail to get the words to fly.

Another type of concrete object would be a quotation that you select from another source that contains ideas on which you wish your respondents to comment. The value of the quotation is that it allows you to attribute to someone else ideas that are usefully provocative but that you would prefer not be put in your own voice. Peshkin and I did this in the Christian school study. We used a quotation from Jerome Bruner's (1960) *Process of Education* that contrasted education that inculcated in students a way of viewing the world with education that helped students to find their own way of viewing the world.

Advice questions ask the interviewee to imagine a conversation with a hypothetical person: "What advice would you give to a niece considering nursing as a career?" This is an indirect form of asking, "What do you think about . . ." or "What do you do in the case of . . . ?" The advice-question format elicits possibly more idealized responses, but perhaps more complete answers than one might get otherwise. In asking questions, you have a choice of voices, and thus of degrees of directness and generality. You can ask "do you," "do teachers like you," "do teachers in your school," or "do teachers in general." The scope of the voice increases with each example as, accordingly, the degree of personal disclosure decreases. Whenever you judge your questions to be too personal to be asked directly, you can use another voice, and assume that the longer the respondent talks, the more likely he or she is speaking in a personal voice.

In the ethnicity study, Peshkin sought out the *native language* of his participants—what terms students used to refer to ethnicity. In one of the early interview sessions, students were told the following: "From the looks of the kids here I see that there are lots of different races and nationalities and ethnic groups. Before we go on to some other questions, I'd like to be sure what word or words you use to describe the different groups of kids. Is it races? Or nationalities? Or ethnic groups? Or what?" Then, in order to be able to make accurate reference to each student during later questions, Peshkin followed the above with, "Do you consider yourself to be part of one or more of these groups?"

Interviewing that is preceded by or accompanied with participant observation creates chances to derive some questions from sheer fortuity. One day in class Peshkin heard a student tell a story to other students that ended with, "It's stupid to trip off of people's color." That statement became the first line in a question that began with, "I heard a student say . . ." and continued with: "what do you think that means? In what ways do people trip off of color in Riverview? How about in Riverview High School?"

That some questions are designated as warm-up questions suggests that others are best asked at the end. When you are reasonably comfortable with the form and substance of your questions, begin to give attention to their order. Which belong at the beginning because they are easy to answer and answering them will reassure respondents that your questions are manageable? Which belong at the beginning because they are foundational to what you will ask later, or because they will give you the time needed to promote rapport? Which questions should be asked in special sequence? Which should be kept as far apart as possible because you want to minimize how the answer to one question might affect the answer to another? Which should be asked at the end because they are of a summary or culminating nature? Of course, we all know what happens to the best-laid plans of researchers. Your logical order may be sundered by the psychological order that emerges from your respondents' answers. Not needing to keep things straight, as you see it, they may talk in streams of language that connect to various of your questions, but in no way resemble your planned order. You then learn new ways that your questions connect.

REVISING AND PILOTING

View the preinterview process of question construction as a continuing interaction between your topic and questions and collaborators whom you enlist to play several facilitative roles in this process.

First, think of the prepilot testing period as a three-way interaction among the researcher, the tentatively formed topic, and interview questions—tentative because in so thinking you are optimally open to what is known to be most realistic: that interview questions will change. Write questions, check them against your topic, possibly revise your research statement, and reconsider the questions.

Then, think of prepilot testing as a four-way interaction when the collaborators enter the picture. These collaborators or facilitators are your agreeable peers, who will read drafts of your questions in light of what you communicate as the point of your study. They bring their logic, uninvested in your study, to the assessment of your questions, and give you the basis for returning to your work table to create still one more draft. Such facilitators tell you about grammar, clarity, and question–topic fit. In addition, some facilitators may be informed by experience with the people and phenomena of your research topic and thus can ascertain if your questions are anchored in the respondents' cultural reality. No doubt, the most effective collaborators are the persons for whom your questions are meant. Your greatest challenge is to create questions that your respondents find valuable to consider, and questions whose answers provide you with pictures of the unseen, expand your understanding, offer insight, and upset any well-entrenched ignorance.

Finally, pilot your questions. Ideally, your pilot respondents are drawn from the actual group that you mean to study. Urge your pilot respondents to be in a critical frame of mind so that they do not just answer your questions but, more important, that they reflect critically on the usability of your questions. Since formal pilot studies are not always feasible, you might design a period of piloting that encompasses the early days of interviews with your actual respondents, rather than a set-aside period with specially designated pilot respondents. Such a period, if conducted in the right frame of mind—the deep commitment to revise—should suffice for pilot-testing purposes. Sean, in reflecting on developing interview questions about the experiences of first-generation college students, observed

> It was the actual pilot interview phase which most clearly informed my interview questions. Which questions resonated with my interviewee, and which ones fell to the ground (both figuratively during the interview and literally during the coding of the interview)? It is also the point at which the experience of the first generation student leaves the crisp pages of research documents and becomes a responsive, interactive experience . . . one which says, "Huh?" at the end of a poorly worded question, or continues at length in response to a good one.

Be prepared to let some questions fall to the ground.

The following example (Exhibit 4.1) is taken from work Kristina did on her questions for interviews with African women about their perceptions of their legal rights as women. Presented here are only a few of her questions from each of her subsequent drafts so you can get an idea of how her questions evolved through her dedication to making them good questions and through feedback from her professor, peers, and eventually several pilot interviews.

The process of drafting and redrafting interview questions required time, thought, and effort on Kristina's part. Her research benefited, however, with her later questions eliciting interesting and engaging information. The data you get are only as good as the questions you ask.

Setting Up to Interview

Where will you conduct your interviews? Convenient, available, appropriate locations need to be found. Select quiet, physically comfortable, and private locations when you can; they are generally most appropriate. When respondent convenience is the overriding consideration, agree, knowing that their willingness to cooperate with you may be contingent on how unbothersome it is to see you. Defer to your respondents' needs because their willingness is primary, limited only by your capacity to conduct an interview in the place that they suggest. If, for example, a location's lack of privacy dampens if not defeats open discussion, or if its noise level precludes

(*Continued on p. 78.*)

EXHIBIT 4.1
Example of Developing Interview Questions

Drafts of Kristina's Questions	Brief Comments on Each Draft

Draft 1, October 2

Draft 1

1. How would you describe the position of women in your country, both economically and socially?

Notice how broad and general the first question is. Because it is such a large question, it would be difficult to know where to start in answering it.

2. I want to talk to you about any experiences you or your mother, or other women that you know have had, about owning property. How did you or the women you know gain property?

Again, where does one start and with whom–you, your mother, or other women? And what is meant by "gain"; what is meant by "property"?

3. How did you come to understand what rights a married woman has compared to her husband?

Question 3 is less broad than the others, but it still feels vague. How would you answer it?

Draft 2, October 9

Draft 2

In many countries around the world, women have inferior social and economic positions compared to men. This inferior position sometimes makes it difficult for women to exercise their rights in issues of marriage and property. I want you to describe first the rights women in your country face when it comes to marriage issues, and then we'll come back to the rights of women relating to property.

These preliminary words, an attempt to be more conversational in her approach, clearly state Kristina's position and could silence or lead women to answer in certain ways.

1. What kinds of rights do women have in your country around the issue of marriage?

Question 1 remains quite broad and vague and asked at a general level rather than engaging the women in discussing their own experiences.

Now I want to talk to you about issues relating to marriage. I'm going to divide this issue into two topics. First I want to talk about what rights a woman has when she is married, the kinds of things she can and cannot do, and rules or laws which may apply to a married woman. Then I want to talk about the same issues only concerning divorce.

Kristina's preliminary to the next questions is a worthwhile attempt to be more conversational and to alert the women to what kinds of questions are to come, but the words "I want to talk to you about . . ." or "I want to talk about . . ." do not work to bring the interviewee into the interview. It is also difficult to follow all the information presented.

2. What kinds of rules or laws apply to married women?

Question 2, like 1, is too broad, vague, and general.

3. What experiences have you had which helped you to understand what rules or laws apply to married women?

Question 3 finally gets at the woman's experience. Look at how this question seems more engaging than Question 3 of Draft 1.

Drafts of Kristina's Questions	Brief Comments on Each Draft
Draft 3, November 11	**Draft 3**
1. If you had to generalize and describe how women in your country live, what would you say?	Nice beginning, but again very broad and difficult to answer.
Now I want to talk to you about issues relating to marriage. I'm interested in the sorts of rights a married woman has, the kinds of things she can and cannot do, what kinds of rules or laws apply to married women. These rights don't necessarily have to be actual laws but can be what is expected of a married woman.	Kristina might say "Now I would like to hear about . . ." which situates her as the learner in the interview process. What she goes on to say is useful and clarifying information for the interviewee.
2. What kinds of laws or rules apply to a married woman?	Question 2 continues to be asked at a general level, but the introduction makes it easier to think about an answer. Being a "knowledge" question, it could be regarded as an uncomfortable kind of test question by interviewees.
3. What do you think about these kinds of rules or rights?	Question 3 is a nice follow-up, and, I suspect, where the interviewee information will become more interesting.
Draft 4, November 18	**Draft 4**
I want to talk to you about your understanding of how women perceive marriage, divorce, and property rights in your country. I'm mostly interested in your perceptions of these issues, regardless of your knowledge about specific laws which apply to women. I'm going to break this interview into three sections beginning with marriage, then we'll talk about divorce, and finally we'll talk about women's property and inheritance rights.	Nice, clear introduction that sets out the scope of the interview and specifies that Kristina wants to understand the women's perceptions, not their knowledge of their country's laws.
1. I'd like you to tell me about the laws or customs concerning women and marriage in your country. How would you describe them? (probe for role of women, role of men, how roles have changed)	Question 1 is at a general level, but clear and direct with good prompts for areas in which to probe.
2. How were you raised to think about marriage? (probe for role of mother, father, friends, school, government programs)	Question 2 gets at the interviewee's socialization. It would prompt reflective, and, most likely, engaging answers.
3. What would you teach your children about women and marriage? (probe for differences between teaching sons and daughters)	Question 3 is an excellent question to get at the interviewee's values and opinions.

hearing, then the available site is not workable. If meeting where radios or televisions blare—the normal background sound in many homes—your gentle request will generally suffice to get the sets turned off. An office set aside for the researcher on a regular basis is ideal for interviews with students conducted at school. Otherwise, you may have to use your creativity and move around, depending on the time of day—the lunchroom, auditorium, backstage, campus picnic table, and gymnasium are possible places. Teachers, counselors, and administrators are easier to meet because they have classrooms and offices.

When will you meet? "Convenient, available, and appropriate" apply also to the time of the interview. By appropriate, I mean a time when both researcher and respondent feel like talking. Again, however, you take what you can get and defer to the preferences of the respondent. School-based interviews usually follow a teacher's free-period schedule and a student's study-hall period. Barring these class-time opportunities, before and after school and lunchtimes are other possibilities. Consider evening meetings if they are a teacher's preference. To meet counselors and administrators requires fitting into their schedules when free of appointments.

How long will your interview last? An hour of steady talk is generally an appropriate length before diminishing returns set in for both parties. There are exceptions, for example, when less time is available to the respondent. Take what you can get, while trying to promote regularity—of location, time, and length of interview—so that you can say to your respondent at the interview's end, "Same time and place next week?"

How often will you meet? This is variable, although most studies require multi-session interviews to obtain trustworthy results. Just how many will depend on the length of the interview schedule and interview sessions, the interest and verbal fluency of the respondent, and the probing skills of the researcher. You might say to your respondents, "I would like to meet with you at least two times, and maybe more, certainly no more than is comfortable for you. And you may—without any explanation—stop any particular session or all further sessions." Then, it is your challenge to make the interview experience so rewarding that having more than two sessions, if needed, is unproblematic to the respondents.

How will you note your studies? Whether by hand, audiotape, or videotape is a matter of your needs and the respondents' consent. It is not quite a toss-up as to whether you note by hand or tape recorder. With handwritten notes (or notes typed into your laptop computer), you are closer to being done writing when your interview is done; this is their distinct advantage. Also noting by hand is less obtrusive and less intimidating to some persons. But be aware of the message your respondent may deduce whenever you stop taking notes: the risky, "I no longer am noteworthy." You will also feel less in control of the interview when, as you handwrite notes, your attention is focused on the struggle to keep up with the respondent's talk (even knowing that this generally cannot be done), and you can only intermittently maintain eye contact and attend to all of the verbal and nonverbal cues that have bearing on your procedure. Interviewees may generally be patient and slow down, even wait for you to catch up if you explain your desire to capture their words as fully as possible. The tape recorder, however, provides a nearly complete record of what has been said and permits easy attention to the course of the interview.

Most persons will agree to the use of a tape recorder, and for most research purposes an audio record is fully sufficient. Depending on the sensitivity of your topic and the unease of your respondents, you may want to wait until the end of the first session before you ask for permission to tape record. Tape-recording requires an electrical outlet; using batteries is acceptable but somewhat risky. Give due attention to the quality of your cassettes, tape recorder, and microphone. Choose to activate the recorders yourself. Voice-activated machines omit telling silences and often the first words after a silence. Tape recorders that make a sound when the end of the tape has been reached save you from continuous peeking at the tape to check its proximity to the end, and from calling attention to your taping. Most recorders have built-in microphones, which are less effective than an external microphone; best of all are lapel microphones that can be attached to both researcher and respondent, particularly if there is sound around your interview site or you are interviewing persons who are soft-voiced.

If you are conducting a lot of interviews, you may want to obtain a transcribing machine with headphones and a foot pedal for reversing and advancing the tape, so that your hands are free to transcribe (see Fetterman 1989). Lorna reflected upon her transcription process without a transcribing machine:

> The worse problem was in transcribing the interviews verbatim. My initial attempts at home left me somewhat crazed; it took me about one hour to transcribe about ten minutes of conversation. In desperation, I hired someone to do this. However, the expensive transcriptions contained numerous "???," where the words were obscured. . . . I then had to go over the entire tapes to fill in missing parts of the interaction.

Whatever means can be afforded to minimize the agony of transcribing tapes—estimate five-plus hours per 90-minute tape done by an experienced transcriber—should be seized. The good times of data collection can quickly pall if the transcribing doldrums set in. To avoid them don't assume that you must have a verbatim transcript. Reflect carefully on your needs. Replay your tapes on the way home from interviews. Browse through tapes and judge how much you need transcribed. Merriam (1988) suggests an *interview log* as an alternative to full transcription. The researcher sets the tape counter on zero, puts in the tape, and begins to listen, jotting down verbatim phrases or sentences that appear important as well as the number on the tape counter. In a column to the right of the recorded words, the researcher makes more analytical comments about the script such as "importance of people and financing in establishment of programs" (Merriam 1988, 85). The interview log is coded along with other data and the researcher can easily return to a desired portion of an interview later on.

Regardless of the means you select to record your interview, keep an account for every interviewee that includes the following: old questions requiring elaboration; questions already covered; where to begin next time; special circumstances that you feel affected the quality of the interview; reminders about anything that might prepare you for subsequent interviews; and identification data that at a glance give characteristics (such as age, gender, ethnicity, socioeconomic status, experience, or occupation) that have bearing on your respondent selection. These identification data allow you to monitor the respondents you have seen, so you can be mindful of whom else to see. Review your notes, listen to the tapes, and transcribe as soon after the interview as possible. In these ways, you also gain some idea of how you are doing as an interviewer, what you need to improve, what you have learned, and what points you need to explore further. If you wait until you have completed all of your interviews before hearing your tapes (or reviewing your notes), then you have waited too long to learn what they can teach you.

The Nature of Interviewing

Conducting interviews is well within the capacity of most researchers, although it is clearly true that some people take to it naturally, and readily get better and more proficient. Others take longer to become adequate interviewers, particularly in learning how to probe and how to wait with silence.

Interviewing is not quite the same process for all its practitioners, any more than teaching, nursing, counseling, or drawing is. Its variability derives from who is conducting the interview with whom, on what topic, and at what time and place. Interviewing, in short, brings together different persons and personalities. As you move from respondent to respondent, the nature of the interaction will change, as will, depending on the topic discussed, the location of the interview, and the temper of the times. If you are a European American researcher interviewing a Mexican American official of the Mexican American Political League on the subject of farm workers, in the League's business office, during the heated times of a strike, you will conduct an interview that is imaginably different from one you would conduct if you are a Mexican American researcher, interviewing the same officer, on the same subject, in your office, at a time when labor peace prevails.

But even if all variables were the same and just the researcher changed, the interview process could be expected to be observably different—albeit possibly equally good, for there is no one person who is exactly the right interviewer, any more than there is a "right" practitioner in the case of teachers, nurses, or social workers. Each researcher has personal strengths and weaknesses that form the basis of his or her interview style. Just as in nonresearch life, some persons engender nearly instant trust; they can safely ask direct, probing questions on hot topics early in an interview relationship. Some can make blunders and get excused over and over because they are eminently forgivable. Some create such an atmosphere of good cheer and nurturance that respondents line up to be interviewed by them. Learn who you are, how you operate, and make the best of it. Do not expect the same reception from all respondents. They will take to you as variably as people do in general. This means that some will give you wonderful interviews, and others may not be helpful at all. Of course, your unsuccessful interview encounters should not occur always with the same type of person. It would never do to have your unsuccessful respondent group be confined, for example, to middle-aged males who always vote Republican.

Interviewing is a complex act. In the early days of interviewing it might be easier to conclude, "This is not for me" than to exult, "I have found my niche!" Because there are so many acts to orchestrate, effective interviewing should be viewed the way that good teaching is: you should look for improvement over time, for continuing growth, rather than for mastery or perfection.

A number of things occur simultaneously in interviewing. Of course, first and foremost is your listening. Interviewers are listeners incarnate; your machines can record, but only you can listen. At no time do you stop listening, because without the data your listening furnishes, you cannot make any of the decisions inherent in interviewing: Are you listening with your research purposes and eventual write-up fully in mind, so that you are attuned to whether your questions are delivering on your intentions for them? If they are not, is the problem in the question, in the respondent, or in the way you are listening? Has your question been answered and is it time to move on? If so, move on to what question? Should you probe now or later? What form should your probe take? Do you need to probe further the results produced by your probe? Have your questions been eliciting shorter and shorter if not monosyllabic returns, suggesting irritation with the topic or tiredness? The spontaneity and unpredictability of the interview exchange precludes planning most probes ahead of time; you must, accordingly, think and talk on your feet, one of those many interview-related skills that practice improves.

You listen and you look, aware that feedback can be both nonverbal and verbal. You observe the respondent's body language to determine what effects your questions, probes, and comments are having, in order to decide whether you will adjust your conduct accordingly. Do you see indicators of discomfort, and is the source of that discomfort in the physical conditions of your interview site or in the topic to which you are stimulating a response? Do you see signs of boredom, annoyance, bewilderment? What might be their source and their remedy, and is it within your means to find a remedy? Dick wrote in his log of causes that were beyond his control:

> I arrive at school on a day when classes have been called off because of a power outage at 7:30 a.m. on a cold winter day. The principal is afraid because it came back on some time afterward, but not before she had made the decision to call off school. Parents will be angry because they had to make alternative arrangements for child care when the child could have been in school.

Dick needed to decide whether to proceed as planned with his interview.

Although listening and looking are critical, you forgo their gains unless you remember. You want to remember your questions so you won't constantly look down at your list, and so you won't be taken off guard when your questions are being taken out of order. You want to remember what has been said—by you and your respondent—in this session and in previous ones. You want to recall what you have heard, so that you can pick up on past points in order to make connections, see gaps and inconsistencies, avoid asking some questions, or rephrase other questions when you know that your first attempt at questioning fell short of your expectations and needs. You must of course remember to bear in mind your research purpose so that what you are listening to is being assessed in respect to your research needs. Flying words and worthy words are a necessary condition for judging your interviews to be successful.

You must also remember your responsibility for the quality of the respondent's experience. Are you attending to aspects of the interview that make it not just agreeable but pleasurable for the respondent? Just as your pleasure may be confined to the verbal goods you receive, your respondents' pleasure derives from the satisfaction of talking to you. How satisfied respondents are can affect their willingness to continue to talk to you, the effort they put into their talk, and what they may tell other interview candidates about being your interviewee.

Related to monitoring the quality of the respondent's experience is remembering to control your negative emotions. Although expressing such emotions may be permissible in ordinary conversations, the interview is not an ordinary conversation; hence, unless involved in some feminist and critical research projects that focus on learning through dialogue, you do not have the license to manifest your anger and irritation at any "disagreeable" views you may hear. When Bonnie learned from interviewing nurses that they often are seriously uninformed about the care and treatment of older, confused patients, she could not vent her feelings to the nurses and still maintain her role as a researcher. The venting may be acceptable and consistent with her role as a caring nurse, but not with her role as a researcher. Keeping roles separate is hard but essential if you mean to collect data from people whose experiences and perspectives differ from yours. Moreover, you may be disappointed with the quality of your respondent's answer; nonetheless, you mask any feelings that express this disappointment and look for positive means to improve the quality of your respondent's answer.

Finally, remember to keep track of time, so that time remains for you to make some usefully culminating statements, such as, "Here's the ground we covered today. I was pleased to learn about such and such. Would it be okay for next time if we went back to this and that point before we turn to the subject of the declining market for fresh ostrich eggs?" In this way, you review and pave the way for your next interview session. You keep track of time so you can keep your promise to talk only for an hour and avoid overstaying your welcome. Take the time to negotiate and verify details of your next meeting, and be punctual for each appointment.

To listen, look, and remember in the comprehensive terms suggested here requires developing your concentration. This means shutting off the myriad other aspects of your life so that you can fully attend to the needs of your interview. Achieving the appropriate level of concentration can be physically and emotionally draining, particularly in your early days as an interviewer. Accordingly, a depletion of your personal resources is yet one more aspect of those things that occur simultaneously while interviewing. It is not excessively far-fetched to say that if you are not tired at the end of an interview session, then you might wonder about the quality of the session.

Interviewer Attributes

The attributes described below do not ensure high-quality interviews; they are simply useful attributes to consider as you embark on research involving interviews. To what extent you must master these attributes, which ones have primacy, or which others may be substituted depends on you and the interview situation. Each attribute completes the sentence "The good interviewer is . . ."

ANTICIPATORY

As a good interviewer, you look ahead and ask, "What does the situation call for?" Some of the specifics about what to anticipate already have been mentioned. Your lay summary is an example, in which you consider both what you must say in order to present yourself and your project cogently, and how what you say may vary from situation (the superintendent of schools) to situation (the parents of students). What materials and equipment do you need to assemble for your interview session? Who should you see next, in light of what you have been learning and not learning, and what arrangements need to be made to set up the next interviews? Anticipation feeds off the results of taking stock, an activity that might well be included at the end of the day in the daily task of log writing. Reflecting on each day is preparatory to anticipating what is next, both broadly in terms of your inquiry, and narrowly in terms of your next day's activities.

ALERT TO ESTABLISH RAPPORT

Rapport is tantamount to trust, and trust is the foundation for facilitating full and detailed answers to your questions. Many of the attributes below contribute to rapport, though they may be intended to accomplish something else, as well.

You promote rapport by the interest you show in what your respondents say. By your verbal and nonverbal behavior you demonstrate that you appreciate what you are hearing. Almost everyone gets satisfaction from being able to evoke interest in the listener. Furthermore, although your expression of interest promotes rapport, it also communicates just what it is that interests you. Your interest shapes the respondent's behavior by selectively reinforcing the respondent's discussion of some topics. You shape behavior, even when not intending to, by the form and content of your questions, by the nature of your reactions to the answers you get, and by the rapport that you develop. Rapport is more fully discussed in Chapter 5.

NAIVE

Naive characterizes the researcher's special learner role. It entails a frame of mind by which you set aside your assumptions (pretensions, in some cases) that you know what your respondents mean when they tell you something, rather than seek explanations about what they mean. Often, the hazard is that your research is on a topic about which you may know a great deal through study and personal experience. What you know is the basis for the assumptions that preclude you from seeking explanations and that shut down your depth-probe inclinations. If you second-guess your respondents, then you forego the chance to say, "Tell me more." The difficulty of being naive is that assumptions generally are useful for simplifying relations with others. In your research capacity, you need not be relentless in asking "What do you mean?" in the many guises you can give it, but you must be alert to the value of being naive.

Claudia faced the hazard of not being usefully naive in her study of families at risk of losing their children. She is an "expert" on the subject; she trains people to work with such families. Her expertise may obviate her asking some questions, and, as well, her respondents from discussing matters they assume she already knows. Claudia must convince her respondents by all she says and does, both before and during her interviews, that she is a learner, not an expert. Not being naive interfered with Ned's asking his extension agent respondents to explain what they meant when they spoke of "small land holders." He failed to ask because he had once been an extension agent, used the term himself, and thereby assumed he knew to what amount of land the term applied. But because the meaning of what respondents said would change depending on the amount of land involved, the referent of the expression had important consequences.

Pat reflected upon her role as interviewer and learner:

> I found that I enjoyed the interviewing process, but I had to be careful not to make it into a performance where I was the "star interviewer." Instead, I had to be aware that I was just the "seeker of knowledge." This became an important distinction for me when I first started because I had been concerned with how I would do as the interviewer—I had to shift my attention from me to the topic at hand and when I did this successfully, I found the interview to be enjoyable and meaningful.

Casting yourself as learner correspondingly casts the respondent as teacher. For many, this is a flattering role that enhances the respondent's satisfaction with being interviewed. And when you are a learner, you get taught.

ANALYTIC

Analysis does not refer to a stage in the research process. Rather, it is a continuing process that should begin just as soon as your research begins. It follows, then, that interviewing is not simply devoted to data acquisition. It is also a time to consider relationships, salience, meanings, and explanations—analytic acts that not only lead to new questions, but also prepare you for the more concentrated period of analysis that follows the completion of data collection.

Gloria interviewed women who had left and then returned to the university. All had children. One woman told her that being away from home so much required that her husband change his participation in family life. Hearing this should have set bells ringing in Gloria's mind, but bells did not ring. She was not listening analytically at the time. The respondent's husband had to redefine his roles as spouse and father. Gloria needed to focus on the husband's behavior: include questions about it, probe it, and consider its meaning for other respondents. By not listening analytically, she could not make further use of what she was hearing.

As much as you might try to give your interviews the character of a good conversation, remember that research talk differs from other talk because it is driven by research purposes. The distinguishing mark of a good interview is not good conversation but good data. When your data collection is complete and you enter a period of extended data analysis, you will find the analysis easier if all along you have been listening analytically and converting the results of ongoing analysis into further questions and notes that highlight thoughts and ideas.

NONDIRECTIVE AND THERAPEUTIC

As researcher you are an interested, emotional person who, most likely, has an opinion on the topic into which you are inquiring. But as researcher, you want to learn the respondents' beliefs, experiences, and views rather than to persuade them of your perspective. This need to learn from the other guides the researcher's behavior into a nondirective and somewhat therapeutic role.

As researcher you apprehend what your respondents mean and feel, and you rightly communicate that to them. What you, as researcher, do not ordinarily communicate is that you also share (or do not share) these meanings and feelings. For to do so would enable your respondents to shape their comments in reaction to you. You want your respondents to be as protective of spotted owls or as supportive of loggers' rights as they really are.

To be nondirective is not to be robotlike or impassive, behaviors which would indicate that you were unaware of the sentiments that your respondent expressed. Similarly to counselors, interviewers can make comments that reveal that they have both heard and empathized with what their interviewees have said. Comments such as "that must have hurt" or "that must have made you feel good" (and their numerous variations) are nonformulaic combinations of thoughts to express. The idea is to make clear that you did hear what your respondents said, and that you do grasp their feelings.

Your need is to manifest your understanding without saying "I'm with you, on your side," and, of course, without saying, "I'm not with you." It is the clarification of where your side is, where your preferences, values, and antagonisms are, that will make you reactive. The danger of reactivity extends beyond its possible distortion of the respondents' comments to the more general hazard of being refused access to a whole set of potential interviewees who feel you have taken sides. In research studies that involve sides, you must be able to learn about everyone's pains and pleasures without looking as if you have been recruited to anyone's cause. Some respondents may insist on knowing where you stand as a condition for continuing to talk with you. In this case, my perspective is that ethically you need to reveal your position and accept the possible consequences.

What specifically is therapeutic about the interview process is the unburdening effect of the respondents' saying safely whatever it is they feel. This effect is enhanced by the Rogerian "Mm hmms," "How did you feel about that?" "Would you tell me more about that?" Much of what you do and say is feedback, which again has the effect of indicating to your respondent that you grasp what he or she is saying and feeling, as well as what you found informative (which is a crucial part of helping respondents play their unaccustomed role of talker for research purposes).

The therapeutic dimension of good interviewing is part of what you can return to your respondents. It will not be uncommon for you to receive words of gratitude from respondents who are pleased with the opportunity for the profound, pro-longed expression of personal views that your multisession interviews afford. Knowing that it is a way of reciprocating, make the most of your interview's therapeutic aspect.

AWARE OF STATUS DIFFERENCES

Particularly through the work of feminist and critical researchers, the hierarchical nature of even the interview process is undergoing challenge. Fontana and Frey (1994) state,

> . . . the emphasis is shifting to allow the development of a closer relation between inter-viewer and respondent, attempting to minimize status differences and doing away with the traditional hierarchical situation in interviewing. Interviewers can show their hu-man side and answer questions and express feelings. (370)

Yet, how to minimize status differences is difficult when research roles are different from everyday interactions. In discussing interviews to gather information on the lives of women, Davies (1996) notes how, even though we may work to structure an interview so that "it is the woman's own logic and ideas that steer the conversation" (584), the interview is still different from a conversation: "it is not a discussion where mutual information is shared, but one where the interviewee's experience is placed at the centre" (584).

How much you work to make the relationship less hierarchical depends on the research purpose, topic, and desires of research participants. Orientational re-search and action research are more likely to involve research participants as co-re-searchers of sorts. The dialogical process is inherently valuable to the process of learning more about each other and each other's perspectives as part of the re-search. In traditional ethnographic research, some topics more easily lend them-selves (and call for) a more dialogical sharing than others. For example, in the Christian School study, expression of our beliefs and opinions would have denied us access to the school. In Busier's (1997) case studies of women in recovery from anorexia, the sharing of her own experience with anorexia allowed her access to women who would not have talked about their own experiences with someone who had not "been there."

Qualitative researchers are neither always emotionally removed and solely con-trolling of the research process, nor always openly sharing of their own opinions and seeking collaboration. Be mindful, however, of status differences inherent in any research interaction and work to minimize them where possible. Consider ways in which you can include research participants in the research process. You might begin with various forms of member-checking. For example, Young began to share her record of her interviews with Tardif in regular "have-I-understood-you" sessions (Young and Tardif 1988). Also consider ways in which you can give back both dur-ing and after data collection. Finally, if you remain uncomfortable with the decid-edly hierarchical nature of traditional inquiry, choose topics that allow or require more sharing of self, work only on projects requested by research participants, or explore further the possibilities of feminist, critical, and action research.

PATIENTLY PROBING

For qualitative inquiry, the interview is rightly conceived as an occasion for depth probes—for getting to the bottom of things. By so doing you do justice to the complexity of your topic. Qualitative researchers operate from the assumption that they cannot exhaust what there is to know about their topic. They may stop their investigation because they have run out of time or satisfied their particular research conceptualization. While the research remains in process, interviewing is a "what-else" and "tell-me-more" endeavor. The next question on your interview schedule should get its turn only when you have stopped learning from the previous one and its spin-offs. This is where patience comes in.

You need to concentrate on being patient in order to give due, unrushed attention and deliberation to the responses you elicit from each question you ask. Rush and the world rushes with you: If you communicate your satisfaction with your respondents' short-shrift replies, then you teach them how minimal your expectations are. Say, "Tell me more," and your interviewees will learn how to respond accordingly. You will find that the better you probe, the longer your interview time becomes. Short and few interview sessions are generally the mark of inexperienced or poor interviewers. With experience, the number of sessions increases.

Your probes are requests for more: more explanation, clarification, description, and evaluation, depending on your assessment of what best follows what your respondent has said. Probes may take numerous forms; they range from silence, to sounds, to a single word, to complete sentences. Learn which forms work best for you. Silence is easy to use, if you can tolerate it. Too little silence, and you may fail to have made clear that you were inviting more respondent talk; too much silence, and you may make your respondent squirm. The magical right amount of silence indicates, "Go on. Take some more time to think about your reasons for entering a graduate program. I'm not in a hurry."

Silence literally leaves more time for thought. Its use saves you from the common practice of offering your respondents a multiple-choice menu from which to select an answer to your question. Silence is better than a menu of choices, as is rephrasing the question if it elicits no answer, or saying, "We can come back to that later if nothing comes to mind." Used judiciously, silence is a useful and easy probe—as is the bunched utterance, "uh huh, uh huh," sometimes combined with a nodding head.

Longer, more directive probes take various forms. A couple of examples of the many possibilities are, "I'm not sure I got that straight. Would you please run that by me again" and (accompanied by a summary of what you thought you hear), "Did I understand you correctly?" Both types invite a rethinking by the respondent, and with rethinking may come elaboration. The summary alternative can also be used to preface, "Is there anything more you'd like to add to this?" Probes also can be simple questions: "How did that happen?" "What made you feel that way?" And more complex conditional questions: "If you had returned to graduate school fifteen years ago, how might your life look different now?"

The following example (Exhibit 4.2) is a portion of Terry's interview with David, a child in her elementary classroom. Terry was interested in learning styles and in how children described their own learning processes. She talked to her class about theories of learning before interviewing some of the children. In this example, Terry used probes to open up and more fully understand David's perspective on his learning. The left column presents a portion of the interview while the right column contains comments on the probes.

As Terry demonstrates, it is clearly not the form of your probe that is most critical. It is your intent to probe, supported by your patience to linger and inquire rather than get on with completing the interview. The more nervous you are, the less patient you will be to probe and the less you will find occasion to do so. Missed opportunities for probing, however, plague us all. You will read your interview transcripts and find many occasions to groan over opportunities forgone. You were too tired, too satiated with ideas, or just didn't grasp what was being said. Given the intent to probe, the requisite habit and skill will develop—although you will always probe less than you could (as you learn in the ex post facto replaying of your tape or reading of your transcript).

There are other qualities that could be used to describe a good interviewer. Among them is the quality of being nonthreatening. Tardif comments on its corollary—the sense of safety she felt in talking to Young, a sense that Young could convey by being outside Tardif's personal and professional world:

> I found it easier to discuss my thoughts and feelings regarding some of my professional decisions with Beth [Young] than I did with many of my colleagues. There was a freedom of expression afforded me in these sessions that was not present in my everyday contacts. Beth was not a threat to me in any professional sense—she did not have a stake in any of the issues that had been discussed. (Young and Tardif 1988, 8)

Young's advantage as a nonthreatening outsider is a part of the case against doing research in your own workplace or with people with whom you already have a relationship.

Of course, a good interviewer never does anything to make respondents look or feel ignorant. Equally obvious, you should be calm and reassuring. Your nervousness can exacerbate the respondent's own nervousness. Be attuned to the respondent's anxiety at the prospect of being interviewed. When trying to make interview arrangements, you will discover that respondents often try to excuse themselves on the grounds that they have not had enough schooling or they don't know enough. Even otherwise sophisticated respondents will be diffident about their performance, saying, "I don't know if that's what you're looking for or not."

Respondents may perceive your questions as testing, in the way they thought of questions as students at school. You may inadvertently present your questions and respond to answers in tones that suggest you are testing. Accordingly, you need to reassure, not only when you present yourself at the outset of interview arrangements, but also in the course of the interviews when respondents understandably want to know if they are being helpful to you. You need to reassure that it is perfectly permissible to say, "I don't know," "I have no idea," or "I never even thought about that before."

—————————————————————— **EXHIBIT 4.2** ——————————————————————

Examples of Using Probes in an Interview

Interview Transcript	Comments
T: I'd like you to go back to when you were in kindergarten, a time you probably haven't thought about too much.	Good preliminary introduction to a question that eases the interviewee back to a past time.
D: Oh yeah, I can sort of remember some parts of it.	
T: Can you remember some thing that you learned back then?	Yes/No question. "Tell me about . . ." might have worked better.
D: Here's something that I can remember. I learned that when you are studying castles—I learned that they have arrow holes in the walls.	**D** gives a short answer about one item.
T: How did you learn that?	**T** opens up the interview with this probe.
D: The teacher said it. We were having a rug discussion, I think. The teacher was telling us some facts about castles. And I also remember how to divide stuff up equally. That's why I'm okay at dividing. . . . And I learned a trick in spelling "said." The teacher said, "it's sa-id in-stead of sed." I remember every single morn-ing or almost every single we would play bingo on the rug until we could memorize our letters. I remember the first day I ever read a book. It's *Alligator in the Elevator*. It was my first book. I remember that after that I read all the books they had in the kindergarten. And then just kept on reading higher and higher levels. And by first grade I was reading adult books. I read the first book in the Tarzan series.	**D** can suddenly remember lots of things. He is not, however, really answering the "how" question except for learning specific things from his teacher.
T: Do you remember when you first learned to read?	Although a yes/no question, **T** is picking up on reading as an area to probe for the "how."
D: This is what I always do. I can remember I did this when I learned to walk. I don't really do it, I just kind of stand back and practice ways of doing it for a while. I'm usually late at doing things. For instance, I was never really a toddler. . . . The first day I took a step, I just walked around. I never fell either, unless I tripped or slipped. In reading, I kind of looked at signs and I read little things at first and then I just tried reading a book after a while and I could read it.	And **D** addresses the "how."

Finally, the good interviewer is "warm" and "caring." When you are warm and caring you promote rapport, you make yourself appealing to talk to, and, not least, you communicate to your respondents, "I see you as a human being with interests, experience, and needs beyond those I tap for my own purposes." It should be more than just tolerable to be with you in your role as researcher. In an effective interview, both researcher and respondent feel good, rewarded, and satisfied by the process and the outcomes.

Some Typical Problems

Fortunately, it is only once that you can do something for the first time (or do we believe that because it is consoling?). Helen reflected in somber tones about the beginning of her interviews:

> Things don't always work the way you plan. It took me a month to get access. Then when I got there I learned the interview guides had not been passed out. I had asked the principal to identify teachers who knew a lot, and found he had simply told various people that they would meet with me. About a third of the way through the first interview I realized that the pause button was still on my tape recorder.

Everything that can possibly go wrong did not go wrong for Helen. None of her respondents, for example, had brought with them to the interview young children who could not sit quietly for an hour—so that the parent's attention was consistently drawn away from the interviewer's questions. Making the best of bad times may be all that you can manage as you try to salvage something from an interview, at least chalking it up as an occasion to get to know your respondent.

Remembering to check your tape recorder comes easier after your initiation. Beyond problems most commonly associated with the novice's early days are others that can occur to anyone at any time. For example, your respondents do not answer the question you ask. What is going on? The reason may simply be that the respondent has innocently (without a hidden agenda) taken a fancy to discussing something else. If you can listen as gracefully to their off-target (in your terms) as you do to their on-target talk, then the time that you lose may be more than offset by the enhanced quality of your respondent's answers. With the serendipity that abounds in qualitative research, the perceived off-target talk may even lead you into a relevant and related territory of which you were not even aware, opening up a whole new path for understanding. Or it may simply be that your question was not clear or the respondent was too nervous to concentrate. Look for suitable other words in which to recast your question. If restating does not help, go on to other questions rather than risk the respondent's developing feelings of inadequacy.

The reason for not answering a particular question, or for respondents' turning the focus of talk to topics of their own, may be more complex. Jennifer had a respondent who brought the talk around to safety in the nursery school, when Jennifer had the virtues of outdoor play on her mind. In time, Jennifer realized that her respondent gave very little time in her program to outdoor play and was saving herself from embarrassment in an interview that was directed exclusively toward outdoor play. In still more time, Jennifer realized that she needed to preface her interviews with the clearest possible statement that her inquiry on outdoor play was free of advocacy, so that respondents could continue to feel good about themselves—whether they did or did not include play in their nursery school program.

Such prefacing is critical to effective interviewing, because respondents logically conclude that if you ask a lot about something, you must think it is important. This may be true, but it does not necessarily make you an advocate. To the extent that you appear as an advocate, your respondents may become defensive or tell you what they think you want to hear. Try explaining to them that you believe there are both successful and unsuccessful teachers who emphasize outdoor play; that you are not making judgments about success; that you want only to understand the place of outdoor play, or lack of it, in their nursery school curriculum. If it is there, what are the reasons? If it is not, then, again, for what reasons?

When respondents show a pattern of turning away from your questions, they may be saying obliquely what they won't say directly: "I don't want to continue this interview." Other forms of resistance to being interviewed are missed appointments and monosyllabic replies. The resistance may be apparent or real. Apparent resistance may result from respondents' being preoccupied with personal matters that preclude concentrating on your matters. If they want to talk about their personal problems, your listening may clear the deck for them to return to your questions. Cutting short your current session or postponing further sessions for a few weeks may suffice to return to normalcy. Do not prematurely conclude that respondent resistance is tantamount to their wish to terminate all further interviews. It may be that your questions are treading on matters too sensitive for them to discuss with you. Be gently direct. If you observe resistance, ask about it: "It seems to me that you have not been comfortable . . . Are there areas you'd rather not talk about?" You might even ask, "Do you think we ought to stop the interviews?" If you do not hear yes, then you can continue interviewing and judge the quality of what you're hearing. If it is poor, shorten your list of questions and end the sessions as soon as you can manage to do so.

Far removed from the problem of resistance is the problem of the nonstop talker. Respondent fluency is wonderful if it is on your research topic, but if not, then you need to learn to redirect the flow of talk. Making a wordless sound or a physical sign, such as a slightly upraised hand, may stop the stream of words so you can apologize for your interruption and pick up on something the respondent has said that you can probe. Or summarize what the respondent has said and then bridge to where next you wish to go. The idea is to avoid making an abrupt shift to a topic distant from where the respondent's talk had been.

In interviews, as in ordinary conversations, people make contradictory statements. Consider the possibilities that contradictions connote: the evolution of the respondent's thinking about the topic; the respondent's confusion about the topic; the respondent's being comfortably of two minds about the topic. Is the topic generating the contradictions worthy of clarification? If so, then you need to probe further into the respondent's most recent statement, right then and there.

In addition, you can raise the topic again at your next session, inviting more thought to it. If it is not too obvious, you can take the two contradictory statements and put them in the mouths of two hypothetical persons: "I've heard some people say . . . I've heard other people say . . . What's your thinking about these two positions?" When the respondent has replied, you can continue: "Is it possible that both are right?" The point is, when you ask questions, especially about complex matters, you cannot reasonably expect complete, carefully considered responses to be ready at hand. If you allow respondents time to think, then you will get more trustworthy data.

Though not a problem in the same sense as those above, you may find it problematic to decide whether or not the interviews—a particular session or the entire series with one person—went well. In one sense, "going well" means getting answers that fit the questions you ask and that you can visualize as part of your forthcoming text; careful listening will indicate whether this criterion is met. In another, more serious sense, going well means getting trustworthy data. Trustworthiness, certainly a relative consideration, is likely to increase with time and the establishment of a trusting relationship with your respondent. Clearly, the more one deems a person trustworthy, the more he or she will speak fully and frankly to that person. What a respondent says may be reinforced or undermined by what you learn from other interviewees, as well as from other data sources such as documents and participant observation. Thus, judging how the interviews are going may be tentative at first—you feel good about the interview because the flow of talk was easy, smooth, uninhibited, and on target—and confirmed or challenged later as you acquire data from other sources.

Concluding Considerations

When you consider the time, effort, cooperation, and flying words that respondents give you, you need to be able to communicate at the end your gratitude. Leave time after your interviews for the expression of your gratitude and for other informal talk. In fact, during such informal time (with tape recorder off) you may occasionally learn more of value than when you were plugged in.

Your gratitude to interviewees for their investment in your research project is readily within your power to provide. Another type of return is not necessarily within your grasp, though it is a common by-product of the interview process. A Vincentian young man told me in the course of an interview, "I tell you things I've never told myself." Given the amount of time qualitative researchers spend with their respondents, the research experience can affect respondents' thoughts and behavior. Questions raise consciousness. Respondents learn about themselves, you, and research.

Researchers get more than data from their interviews. They speak of the exhilaration of conducting interviews as did Glen, who interviewed people involved in an alternative educational program: "Every interview provided another angle, and more capacity than the last. I began to realize that the interviewing was becoming slightly addictive, like endorphins after a good run." And researchers tell of the rewards of meeting new people and of coming to understand some they thought they might not want to meet. Andrea commented,

> One of the most enjoyable surprises was finding common ground with those respondents I was least inclined to interview. I would be struck, upon leaving, at how pleasant a time we had together. . . . I wrote in my journal: "Up close, these people don't seem so extreme to me as they appeared before I met them."

The type of interviewing emphasized in this chapter is *structured*—you have specified questions you know you want to ask; *open*—you are prepared to develop new questions to follow unexpected leads that arise in the course of your interviewing; and *depth-probing*—you pursue all points of interest with variant expressions that mean "tell me more" and "explain." The intent of such interviewing is to capture the unseen that was, is, will be, or should be; how respondents think or feel about something; and how they explain or account for something. Such a broad-scale approach is directed to understanding phenomena in their fullest possible complexity. The elaborated responses you hear provide the affective and cognitive underpinnings of your respondents' perceptions.

Interviewing is an occasion for close researcher-other interaction. Qualitative research provides many opportunities to engage feelings because it is a distance-reducing experience. The feelings in question are those that are involved in the researchers' relationships with others—the matter of rapport—and those that are involved in the researchers' reactions to what they are learning in the world of their others—the matter of subjectivity (the issues in Chapter 5).

Exercises

CLASS EXERCISES

1. The following activity is adapted from Berg (1995, 63). Turn to a classmate and decide who will be the speaker and who, the listener. The instructor assigns a topic that students know about, but are not particularly invested in, such as their opinions on the tenure and promotion process for university professors. The speaker talks for 30 seconds on the topic and then the listener repeats what he or she has heard, using the speaker's words ("I" statements). Then students change roles and repeat the exercise. The instructor then assigns a more personal topic such as "first conscious awareness of racism" and increases time allotment to a minute. Students follow the same procedure as above. At the end of the exercise, discuss nonverbal aspects of the two scenarios: What were differences in body language? in the level of sound? in the tone of what was being said? Which kind of topic would make for a better interview? What kinds of things should the interviewer observe, in addition to listening to the words being spoken?

2. Return to your class's *Practice* research statement developed at the end of Chapter 2. As a class, create five interview questions that would help one

understand the chosen topic. Pilot the questions by interviewing each other. Each student should have time to be both interviewer and interviewee. As interviewers, students take full, running notes of the interview. As interviewees, students reflect on the questions and make suggestions to reword, extend, or delete. After the interviews, reflect as a group both on the questions and the interviewing process. As homework, type up your interview transcript, filling in details where remembered. Hold on to these transcripts for a later exercise.

INDIVIDUAL EXERCISE

1. Create five to ten open-ended interview questions for your own research project. Pilot the questions with a classmate, asking her or him to pretend that she or he is one of your participants. Work together to reshape the questions. Then pilot the questions with someone who has had experiences similar to your research population or ask the questions of a research participant who is willing to collaborate with you on developing your questions. Reshape the questions again after reflecting upon what worked, what did not, and what new questions arose.

Chapter 5

The Personal Dimension: Rapport and Subjectivity

When I stayed away too long, they scolded and snubbed me. When I was not completely fair (and sometimes even when I was) in the distribution of attention, I paid dearly for it. (Myerhoff 1979, 27)

In qualitative inquiry, the nature of relationships depends on at least two factors: the quality of your interactions to support your research—or rapport—and the quality of your self-awareness of the potential effects of self on your research—or subjectivity.

The term *rapport* describes the character of effective field relationships. Just what that character is, however, is vague and sometimes confusing. The first half of this chapter attends to rapport, but it does not delineate steps for achieving rapport; there is no such list, although there are some apparent antecedents of rapport.[1] Rather, the discussion explicates some of the issues that complicate establishing and maintaining rapport.[2] The second half of the chapter focuses on how awareness of *subjectivity* contributes not only to more trustworthy research, but also to greater understanding of yourself and your psychological investment in your research.

Definitions of Rapport

The dictionary defines rapport as the "relation characterized by harmony, conformity, accord, or affinity," and notes that it refers to the "confidence of a subject in the operator as in hypnotism, psychotherapy, or mental testing with willingness to cooperate" (*Webster's* 1986). Rapport is an attribute that is instrumental to a variety of professional relationships, from used-car salesperson to marriage counselor. Its function, however, varies with each relationship. For example, counselors establish rapport so that clients can feel sufficiently comfortable to disclose information;

their intent is to attain ends shaped by the clients' needs, as they and the clients ascertain them.

Researchers, to the contrary, traditionally establish rapport to attain ends shaped primarily by their own needs. In qualitative research, rapport is a distance-reducing, anxiety-quieting, trust-building mechanism that primarily serves the interest of the researcher. Spradley gently acknowledges rapport's acquisitive functions: "Rapport encourages informants to talk about their culture" (Spradley 1979, 78). Freilich is more pointed: "The researcher . . . 'engineers' people and situations to get the type of data required by the study" (Freilich 1977, 257). Rapport is a necessary but not sufficient condition for obtaining good data; researchers partake in the opportunities it enables by virtue of other skills.

Rapport is sometimes used interchangeably with *friendship* in the fieldwork literature. Although the line between the two is often hard to distinguish, they are not the same thing. A friend is "one that seeks the society or welfare of another whom he holds in affection, respect, or esteem or whose companionship and personality are pleasurable" (*Webster's* 1986). Friendship means mutual liking and affection and implies a sense of intimacy and mutual bonding. You trust your friends; even more, you like them and will do things for them that you would not do for others. A relationship characterized by rapport is marked by confidence and trust, but not necessarily by liking; friendship invariably is. "One can learn a great deal from people one dislikes or from people who dislike one" (Wax 1971, 373). You do not need to like or be liked by your others, although your work will be even more rewarding if mutual liking occurs. In research relationships, your ordinary need to be liked is overshadowed by the necessity of being accepted and trusted.

Authority over the relationship also distinguishes rapport from friendship. Friends are (or should be) equal actors in establishing and maintaining their relationship. The rapport relationship is more asymmetrical, usually with the researcher desiring and working to achieve rapport. Control, however, is never totally in the hands of the researcher. Rapport is a process of interactions with the researched (Mitchell 1993). It is something that is continually being negotiated between researcher and researched and can, at any time, be rejected by research participants. (The distinction between rapport and friendship is addressed in more detail later in this chapter).

Factors Bearing on Rapport

The literature and lore of fieldwork often portray consummate researchers as sensitive, patient, nonjudgmental, friendly, and inoffensive. They have a sense of humor and a high tolerance for ambiguity; and they learn the other's language, wear appropriate dress, and maintain confidentiality. These factors affecting rapport are personal characteristics that, to some degree, the researcher can manage.

You manage your appearance and behavior in rapport-building efforts in order to acquire continual access to information. Measor (1985) discussed the role of appearance and shared interests in her data collection in a British school. She found that how she looked mattered to both students and teachers and that this in itself caused a problem because each group had a different notion of appropriateness. As a result, Measor sought a compromise that showed she was fashion conscious, but not too much so. About her overall presentation of self, Measor observed, "In a research relationship, one presents a particular front or a particular self. My own view is that it is important to come over as very sweet and trustworthy, but ultimately rather bland" (Measor 1985, 62).

In order to maintain access, you need to act continually in culturally appropriate ways. This may mean "getting mad" or "causing a disturbance," as Pettigrew (1981) discovered while working among Sikhs in the Punjab. When someone made a derogatory remark, she could not ignore it with a tolerant, indifferent attitude. In keeping with cultural rules, she had to display her opposition in order to maintain respect and rapport. Conversely, when Pettigrew witnessed the blatant sexist treatment of women, she could not object, or she would not have been allowed to stay.

Your appearance, speech, and behavior must be acceptable to your research participants. This may be hard to manage at first because you are habituated to acting in certain ways that reflect your personal sense of propriety, dignity, and integrity—and to taking offense when your strongly held values have been assailed. It is important to learn, however, that your strongly held values often are not appropriate guides for conducting your research. For example, teachers in the Christian day school that Peshkin (1986) and I studied were actively involved in rallies protesting the Equal Rights Amendment. As researchers concerned with rapport, we not only had to keep our thoughts on this topic to ourselves, but we also were restricted from partaking in any pro-ERA rallies that might be televised throughout the state. We could not be seen endorsing what was antithetical to core fundamental Christian belief. Thus, rapport can place limitations on the researcher's ordinary interactions and expressions.

Although the accommodations you make to be inoffensive in your research role do not ensure rapport, they do enhance the prospects of its establishment. Whitehead and Conaway's (1986) edited book *Self, Sex, and Gender in Cross-Cultural Fieldwork* contains many examples of ways in which researchers managed their behavior and appearance to build and maintain rapport. For Regina and Leon Oboler (1986), working with the Nandi in Kenya, developing rapport meant that they could not openly display affection for each other, a condition they met:

> It pleased us when people would comment to us, with approval, that we acted just like Nandis because this implied that they viewed us as unlike the Europeans they had previously encountered. (43)

You consciously monitor your behavior so that people who are unaccustomed to the presence of researchers in their lives will be at ease in your presence. Your challenge is to fit in.

You do not, however, have to always agree with your research participants in order to fit in. Sometimes when researchers question participants' viewpoints, they receive information they would not obtain otherwise and are even more accepted into a group as a result of open dialogue. "Fieldworkers worry," state Kleinman and Copp (1993), "that participants will interpret disagreement as unfair criticism or rejection, and thus it will drive a wedge between them. But . . . saying what one thinks can be an *engaging* experience and thus constitute closeness rather than distance" (40). When to disagree and when to keep opinions to yourself is one of those issues that depend upon other factors such as your mode of inquiry, the nature of your topic, and the kind of relationships you have developed with your others.

As mentioned in Chapter 3, gender, age, and ethnicity—attributes over which the researcher has a lesser degree of control—can also make a difference in access to data. For example, Banks, a black anthropologist, may have had an advantage in developing rapport among Malaysians who were resentful of the British (Lawless, Sutlive, and Samora 1983). Characteristics such as color, age, gender, and nationality are not amenable to manipulation, but you do have other attributes that are and which you can emphasize in the effort to overcome disadvantages that might result from ascribed attributes.

Perhaps to some extent it is possible to counteract potential impacts of ascribed characteristics. By acting in ways that others did not expect women to act, Hunt (1984) modified the effect of gender in her study of city police. In addition, European and European American women doing cross-cultural research often comment upon ways in which they are allowed more androgynous behavior (or "honorary maleness") than local women in their research sites. As Warren (1988) states, "Both whiteness and foreignness permit woman fieldworkers more cross-gender behavior than that allowed to native women" (21).

Appearing as if one is something that one is not can also extend some degree of control over personal attributes. For example, Robbins (Robbins, Anthony, and Curtis 1973) appeared to be a member of a proselytizing group known as "Jesus Freaks," even though he was not. The use of an as-if posture rests on the researcher's sense of what is ethical, not on the demands of rapport. Clearly, in research, as in other matters, what works is not necessarily good.

The ideal of rapport is developing sufficient trust for the conduct of a study. Sufficiency is largely contextual, depending on your goals; the personality, age, gender, and ethnicity of all participants; and the setting and time of the study (Glazer 1972; Gonzalez 1986; Spradley 1979). In the end, you will know when you have rapport, because you will see it in the willingness of others to allow access to those parts of their lives of interest to you.

Developing and Maintaining Rapport

When asked, "How do you know when you have rapport," students in my qualitative research course replied:

- The way the interview goes shows rapport. When the interviewee keeps looking at her watch, you know you have not achieved good rapport.
- Rapport comes when the interviewee gets something out of the interview. One person told me, "No one has asked me this before." In good interview situations, people get to think about things that they have not put together before. They learn about themselves in the process. Another person told me, "I think I got more out of this than you did." You feel good then.

The first student describes how being attuned to the nonverbal language of your others can inform you about your research relationship, although people do check the time for reasons other than boredom. The second student introduces the concept of reciprocity into the relationship. Rapport is more easily achieved if both parties get something out of the interaction. Often research participants will find being part of a study flattering; they will welcome the attention and enjoy the opportunity to reflect on matters of importance to them.

This willingness can be found where least expected. Andrea received a letter from one of her interviewees after their first meeting. The interviewee expressed sincere desire to get together again, sent information relevant to their discussion, apologized for being too enthusiastic, and complimented Andrea on the approach she was taking to investigating change in a small rural community. The interviewee was a developer with whom Andrea has postponed talking because she feared her ability to keep an open, interested, learner perspective. Ironically, she found herself fascinated both by what he had to say and by his clear, logical, sensitive way of expressing his point of view. Rapport, obviously, had been achieved.

Generally, people will talk more willingly about personal or sensitive issues once they know you. In most cases, this means being perceived as someone who is willing to invest the time truly to understand them. Sometimes it simply means giving the person time to learn that you are an all-right sort of person. Dick tells of doing an interview with a teacher aspiring to be a principal. Dick had a single, one-and-one-half hour interview scheduled and felt dismayed going into it. "These people," he said beforehand, "will never tell a stranger all this information." But the interviewee was someone who talked easily, and Dick responded appropriately with "umms" and "uh huhs." After 45 minutes, during which Dick thought he was getting good information, the interviewee asked, "Now that I know you, can we go back to one of the earlier questions?" Dick was delighted that he had been able to develop rapport sufficient for the interviewee to reveal deeper layers of information comfortably. He also learned that many layers of data existed and that, even though his single-session interviews might give him enough data for his purposes, he was getting "thinner" data than he could through multiple interviews.

Although contact over a long period of time does not assure the development of rapport, time may prove to be a determining condition once you have attended to other matters. If you are around long enough, you can verify that the self you have been projecting is an enduring self: You have said that you will maintain anonymity of respondents and you always do, and you have said that you have not come to find fault and you never do. Time allows you to substantiate that you will keep the promises you made when you were negotiating access and that you will remain the person you have been showing yourself to be.

Juefei Wang (1995), an educational researcher from China who has been living in Vermont, reflected on the role of time in the development of rapport in U.S. and China. He indicates that rapport building may look very different in diverse cultures. After a short introduction to a study, most Vermont respondents were willing to talk openly with Wang. Most Vermonters were also willing to participate in his research, but some would simply decline with a "No thank you, I'm not

interested," or refuse to answer certain questions saying, "I don't know." He con-
trasts the U. S. response to that in China:

> Among the people I have interviewed in China, probably over a hundred altogether, I
> have never had the case of fast-paced trust building. Even with young, open people, it
> takes me longer to build the trust. I have to find a way to make the interviewees believe
> that I am one of them. They talk about their families; I ask questions about their par-
> ents, wives, husbands, and children, and tell them about mine. They complain about
> their low pay; I tell them my pay is not high either. This is the process to build trust. It
> takes much longer, yet it can be long-lasting.
>
> In China, I have never had any refusal for cooperation. The frank American way of
> saying "I don't know" would not be acceptable by most Chinese. . . . They would always
> try to save face for me by not refusing me, yet they can always find a way not to give me
> anything valuable or anything at all. (2)

Wang describes how it took him over a week in China to get personal information
from a school principal that, in the United States, he would have received in less
time. He states:

> Modesty is still a virtue of the nation. This fact makes it very difficult when a researcher
> tries to find out about the interviewee's roles in an organization. The interviewee talks
> about other's contributions without talking about him or herself. (3)

Part of your role as researcher is to learn the culturally appropriate ways to develop
rapport. When you do not obtain the kind of information you seek, it may be because you have not made the necessary cultural bridges in your own expectations
and behavior.

Developing and maintaining rapport with children and adolescents also adds
extra dimensions to the research process. The role (supervisor, leader, observer,
friend) the researcher takes in relationship to children affects not only the kind of
information gathered but also the nature of rapport needed. Fine and Sandstrom
(1988) distinguish researcher relationships with children on the dimensions of (1)
extent of positive contact between child and adult and (2) extent to which the
adult has direct authority over the child (14). In particular, they explore what it
means for an adult to be a "friend" with a child.

Rebecca, in her dissertation research with adolescent girls and the role of
friendship in their lives, finds herself in a "friendly" role with the girls. The contact
with them is highly positive. She arrives at their homes with art supplies, drives
them to ice cream shops, and engages them in talk that has led to their requests for
personal advice from Rebecca. Although responsible for the girls when with them,
she does not have authority over them. Her evolving connection to the girls, however, has led her to realize that she will not simply say "good-bye" when her data
collection is through. Rebecca plans to maintain contact with each girl as long as
the girl desires.

Whether with adults or children, rapport, like access, is something to be continually negotiated. Negotiating rapport means conscious attunement to the emerging needs of a relationship. An interviewee may become distrustful and uneasy after several sessions of interviewing. Pick up on these reactions and find ways to be more reassuring and to build trust (this may mean revealing more of yourself or your research thoughts). Alternately, you may find that you have to withdraw from certain research relationships. Many fieldworkers advise awareness and avoidance of a society's "marginals"—frequently the very ones who, because of their fringe status, are most open to rapport and friendship with researchers. According to Mitchell (1993, 15–16), the "naïve-sympathetic novice" researcher going into new territory is sometimes perceived as prey, available for exploitation, by marginal others. In addition, it does not reassure your research participants if you are identified with someone whom they see as undesirable.

Developing and maintaining rapport obviously involves more than consideration of one individual at a time; it calls for awareness of social interactions among participants. Researchers enter into social systems in ways that demonstrate that participants are valued, that is, that the worth of their time and attention and association is appreciated. Thus, if you are not equitable in the time you allot to participants, you may risk bruising feelings or eroding relationships, as Myerhoff (1979) observed in the opening quotation to this chapter.

You may need to remain uninvolved in the politics of your site, but this does not free you from needing to understand the political landscape and the pitfalls into which you might tumble. Maintaining rapport is associated with becoming informed about your setting's social and political structure so that you can shape your conduct with the sure-footedness that such knowledge affords. It is no small matter to be aware of the formal and informal loci of power, of the issues that irritate, and of the history that continues to shape current behavior. All of this is part of rapport—both developing it and keeping it—for it is the knowledge that helps you fit in.

SAFETY VALVES

"Once we feel connected to the people we study, we think we must consistently feel good about them" (Kleinman and Copp 1993, 28). Always feeling good about your participants, however, may not be the case. Given the stress of fieldwork, maintaining rapport sometimes requires safety valves. Immersed in a life that is not your normal one, which, accordingly, abnormally constrains you, you periodically need to get away to be with people from your own subculture and talk to those who have similar beliefs and ideas. You may need to blow off steam or simply disappear for a few days so that you do not destroy the rapport that has been developed.

Fieldwork accounts do not always address this need, but field notes or journals do. Malinowski's (1967) diary while among the Trobriand Islanders is a well-known example. It became the place for him to vent his feelings and make statements that would not have endeared him to his host community. You won't earn a merit badge if you persist in unbroken duty to the obligations of your study. Immersion is valued, but it can be overdone. Sustaining the needed degree of rapport depends on your capacity to continue making careful, considered judgments. Taking breaks promotes your ability to mindfully make the multitude of daily decisions needed in your work. Gaining distance by whatever means—trips, reading, strongly worded personal journals—is advised.

Rapport and Friendship

When a distinction between rapport and friendship is made in qualitative litera-ture, the overwhelming tendency in the past was to warn against forming friend-ships because of the hazards of sample bias and loss of objectivity. These hazards were linked to overidentification, also called *over-rapport* and *going native* (Gold 1969; Miller 1952; Shaffir, Stebbins, and Turowetz 1980; Van Maanen 1983).

Qualitative researchers have written about how friendship biases data selection and decreases objectivity primarily in three different ways (Gans 1982; Hammersley and Atkinson 1983; Pelto and Pelto 1978; Zigarmi and Zigarmi 1978). In the first situation, data bias can result from a somewhat unconscious subjective selection process. Researchers are tempted to talk primarily with people they like or find po-litically sympathetic. If they follow such impulses, Gans suggests that "the pleasure of participant observation [would] increase significantly, but the sampling of peo-ple and situations . . . may become badly distorted' (Gans 1982, 52). Or it may be that researchers talk to a variety of people, but overidentify with one group. They then hear what this group has to tell them, but less fully what other groups tell them. Therefore, they may censor their own questioning process to avoid alienat-ing those with whom they are overidentifying. They also may be tempted to give such friends confidential information that would help them.

In the second situation, researchers are consciously aware of their best data sources, but they are denied access to some of them because of their friendship with others. "Every firm social relationship with a particular individual or group carries with it the possibility of closed doors and social rebuffs from competing seg-ments of the community" (Pelto and Pelto 1978, 184). In the Caribbean, I at-tempted to maintain access simultaneously to alienated young adults, to unalien-ated young adults, to government officials, and to estate owners. I found myself frequently explaining to those of the unalienated group my time with the more alienated. Achieving a politically neutral presence is, however, easier in some set-tings than in others.

In the third situation, research participants overidentify with the researchers. In doing so, they may begin to act in ways that they perceive the researchers want them to act or in ways that impress them. Van Maanen (1983) cites the example of police he studied who used overly aggressive patrol tactics in an effort to increase their worth in the eyes of the observer. Gold (1969) suggests that the informant who becomes too identified with the fieldworker may even become an observer much like the researcher. In sum, friendship can affect the behavior of researchers or their others, with potentially detrimental consequences for complete data col-lection and analysis.

It appears, therefore, that you should establish rapport but avoid friendships in the research setting or, at least, as Zigarmi and Zigarmi (1978) suggest, with research participants. Most prescriptions are easier to say than to follow. Many researchers do form friendships during fieldwork, most frequently with those who play the special role of key informant (West 1980). In other cases, the nature of the research requires getting to know a small number of people well. Friendship often develops in the process. Hansen's work is illustrative:

> That I did not remain fully detached from the flow of Danish life might be seen as a failure in my role as objective analyst. Yet to understand the subtle dynamics of Danish behavior required as detailed a knowledge of the individual Danes as I had the capacity to acquire. Access to this information was made possible by friendship, and once established that relationship imposed standards of behavior at least as compelling (to me) as the rules of my discipline. (Hansen 1976, 131–132).

The work of Hansen and many others over the last twenty years challenges the traditional concern for detachment and objectivity. As a researcher, you need to examine the assumptions underlying your relationships with your research others. If "objectivity" is important, then friendship is a problem. Friendship entangles in that it conveys the impression that one has chosen sides, taken a stand, decided on preferences. Each such impression risks shutting down data sources or biasing the data collection process. From another perspective, however, friendship may be a goal that rapport helps to achieve. Friendship may assist you and research participants to develop new understandings in a negotiated fashion.

Research friendships flourish more easily in critical and feminist research where researchers adopt an ethic of advocacy on behalf of research participants. Such researchers have been instrumental in disputing the presumed necessary distancing of more traditional research: "Traditionalists tended to eschew 'politics,' to avoid 'total immersion,' and to be wary of 'going native,' all of which, in contrast, are elements of feminist methods" (Punch 1994, 86). Nonetheless, feminist researchers, in particular, puzzle over the meaning of relationship with their research others. As Behar (1993) states,

> Feminist ethnographers have found themselves caught inside webs of betrayal they themselves have spun; with stark clarity, they realize that they are seeking out intimacy and friendship with subjects on whose backs, ultimately, the books will be written upon which their productivity as scholars in the academic market place will be assessed. (297)

Friendship and intimacy is messy, emotional, and vital. No matter how much you try to practice "relational ethics" (Flinders 1992) with research others, no matter how much your friendships go beyond the research site and time, feelings of exploitation or betrayal may bubble up from time to time in either researcher or other. Yet, friendships in themselves do not always last forever, nor are they always without pain. Marleen Pugach (correspondence, 1995) writes of a research relationship that reminds us that our humanness is what is important.

> Last March first I drove north, ate my last green chile cheeseburger at the Owl Bar, spent a few hours in Albuquerque, and headed east, away from the mountains and toward my other home in Wisconsin. Today, my former landlady called to tell me, a year

to the day after I left, that a good friend of mine had died four days ago. She knew that my reading about this in the local paper would have been too much of a shock, and she called to ease the pain . . . and to catch up, to remind me that her son had had his first birthday last week (the birth I waited for so I could finally leave for home . . .). The shock is enormous—I am not ready for Carmen to be gone. She was the one who would not let me tape record our conversations, but she shared the most phenomenal stories about the community, the old "Hispanic" community from up on the river. . . .

She told me, before I met her face to face, that living "out of town" would be fine for the kids, that she had raised one in the city and one in the country. That comment gave me the confidence to rent our wonderful house amidst the yucca, mesquite, road-runners and rattlesnakes. I don't think she knew that. We used to meet for breakfast or lunch at my favorite hole-in-the-wall Mexican restaurant, the one run by the couple from Mexico City, whose nephew I used to interview from the bilingual program. I'm sure I never was able to get down enough of her real words; our meetings crossed the line between research and friendship, and I wasn't always able to write as fast as I needed to. . . .

We talked last in November, just before her son's wedding. I sent a Christmas card, I never found out if she read the copy of *Animal Dreams* I sent as a thank-you gift for having us all there in August. This is not research relationship. I went to Havens to learn enough to tell a story, but the real story is that you can't separate yourself from the people who welcomed you for all those months. What do I say about Lisa, who called to tell me that Carmen had died? This is not a research obligation, born out of my need to know about life on the border. And it's not a function of the hackneyed truism about "human as instrument of research." That is a term of obligation, of distance, of voyeurism. I want Carmen to be there because I liked her so much, because her vitality kept you up when you thought you might not be able to do any more. . . . I am left with the uncomfortable feeling that spending time in a place you want to study is a real liability if you're inclined to build real relationships. It's not a case of collaborative research for the purpose of action . . . It's a case of pure friendship, not cultivated over long years, but with instant depth because you recognize that you were meant to be friends even if the study had never happened; it was simply the occasion for a friendship that already should have been.

Bringing qualitative research into what is already your home territory releases you from this potential liability; you keep your friends, your social context, and you tiptoe only a little distance from where you always have been. Intensive fieldwork in a new location pushes the question. It is not an issue of power relationships that I'm trying to understand here. Instead, it echoes the things I've been wondering about for months: can you do ethnography without making wonderful, lifelong friends? Would you want to? Does "making friends" automatically put you into the feminist camp of qualitative researchers? Carmen helped me, to be sure, and it is only if I write well that I can properly acknowledge her contributions. But what I really wish is that she would still be there, on the ranch, telling me that whenever I return to Havens, my room there is ready. No one told me about this part of it.

Marleen's reflections demonstrate how research relationships can transcend the public realm into the private. Her story moves us to consider how we want to experience the multiple kinds of relationships that might enter into research. She suggests that we interact with openness, honesty, and respect; not with the masks that rapport can provide or with the walls of professional distancing. In effect, Marleen urges us to remain reflexive, but to be fully authentic in interactions and to honor the consequences of acting with genuineness. She also prompts us to be fully conscious of our emotions, a part of subjective awareness to which I now turn.

Subjective Lenses

"We cross borders, but we don't erase them; we take our borders with us." (Behar 1993, 320)

Subjectivity has long been considered something to keep out of one's research, something to, at the least, control against through a variety of methods to establish validity. It has had a negative connotation in the research world and has not traditionally been a topic for discussion in a research proposal or project.

In "Virtuous Subjectivity: In the Participant-Observer's I's," however, Peshkin (1988b) challenged the notion of subjectivity as something negative, as others (Denzin and Lincoln 1994; Oleson 1994; Wolcott 1995) also have done. Qualitative researchers, recognizing that subjectivity is always a part of research from deciding on the research topic to selecting frames of interpretation, began to claim the term. They discuss how subjectivity, once recognized, can be monitored for more trustworthy research and how subjectivity, in itself, can contribute to research.

Part of being attuned to your subjective lenses is being attuned to your emotions. Your emotions help you to identify when your subjectivity is being engaged. Instead of trying to suppress your feelings, you use them to inquire into your perspectives and interpretations and to shape new questions through re-examining your assumptions. "Ignoring or suppressing feelings are emotion work strategies that divert our attention from the cues that ultimately help us understand those we study" (Kleinman and Copp 1993, 33). For example, Tsing (1993) reports how she learned from her emotions, which flared when a research participant suggested that she did not work:

> Once Ma Salam's mother tried to flatter me by saying that I didn't work (*bagawi*) but only "traveled" (*bajalan*). My first thought was to take offense and argue for my industriousness; in the United States, to do no work is to be worthless. But I soon realized my mistake: for Meratus to "work" is to do repetitive caretaking activity, while to "travel" is a process of personal and material enrichment. (68)

It is when you feel angry, irritable, gleeful, excited, or sad that you can be sure that your subjectivity is at work. The goal is to explore such feelings to learn what they are telling you about who you are in relationship to what you are learning and to what you may be keeping yourself from learning.

The way to become aware of which subjectivities, of all the subjectivities that make up your autobiography, are being engaged in your research is to keep note. Watch for when they creep into your consciousness, be alert for how they take over the questions you ask, and write about them, continuing to look for them as your research progresses. Some hint of which subjectivities might be called into play during your research can be foreshadowed by reflecting on how your research is autobiographical. When I ask students to do this, I stress that I don't want their life story, but I want to know how their research topic intersects with their life. Why are their research questions, of all the research questions they could ask, of interest to them?

Kristina, whose interview questions were discussed in Chapter 4, planned to interview women from Africa about their perspectives on women's legal rights around marriage, divorce, and property. She thought she had chosen her topic because she was preparing to move with her husband to East Africa for several years and wanted to use her thesis requirement as an opportunity to learn something about the lives of African women. As she considered how her topic was autobiographical, however, she realized that her choice had deeper roots:

> My interest in women's rights began in ninth grade with a talk by a women's rights activist that I attended with my mother. The activist told her life story of being raised in the Mormon Church and her struggle to support the Equal Rights Amendment which eventually resulted in her excommunication from the Church of Latter Day Saints and her divorce. Until that evening, I had believed that discrimination against women was part of the past. I distinctly remember my mother saying to me, "You think that there aren't any more barriers for women, but you'll see." Her statement caught me off guard. I was a successful student; I was planning on going to a competitive college and pursuing a career in law or business. But I began to pay more attention to women's issues, especially those which highlighted inequalities between men and women.
>
> My parents' divorce a year after this event dramatically shaped my ideas about women and marriage forever. They had been married for 20 years and while both of my parents struggled after the divorce, my father recovered much more quickly, both financially and emotionally. My mother had somehow "invested" more of herself in the marriage and at the end found herself "bankrupt" with fewer resources to help her start her life over. I think the unequal responsibilities between my parents (Mom being primarily responsible for me, my brother, and the house), as well as her limited work experience, made it more difficult for her to create a new life. Since this time I have been acutely aware of the increased burdens women generally carry in many family situations and I think this awareness has helped me to focus my interests on African women's legal rights around marriage, divorce, and property.

By understanding the ways in which her topic is autobiographical, Kristina can become more aware of her emotional investment in issues of marriage, divorce, property, and women's rights as she begins her interviews with African women.

During his ethnicity study, Peshkin[3] began to reflect upon how different research situations engage different subjective lenses. When he did his study in Mansfield, a small Midwestern rural town, he became entranced by the sense of community there. He liked Mansfield and its people and he did not want them to lose their community feeling. His next school-community study was in the fundamentalist Christian setting of Bethany Baptist Church and Bethany Baptist Academy. While there, he did not feel moved to admire their sense of community because other subjective lenses were on high alert. He writes,

> I knew that I was annoyed by my personal (as opposed to research) experience at BBA. I soon became sharply aware that my annoyance was pervasively present, that I was writing out of pique and vexation. Accordingly, I was not celebrating community at Bethany, and community prevailed there no less robustly than it had at Mansfield. Why not? I was more than annoyed in Bethany; my ox had been gored. The consequence was that the story I was feeling drawn to tell had its origins in my personal sense of threat. I was not at Bethany as a cool, dispassionate observer (are there any?); I was there as a Jew whose otherness was dramatized directly and indirectly during eighteen months of field-work. (Glesne and Peshkin 1992, 103)

As Peshkin entered his next school-community study in urban Riverview where he planned to follow the play of ethnicity in school and community in order to learn how ethnicity operated in the lives of students and parents, he resolved to look for his subjectivity, noting the feeling and the circumstances. He incorporated his reflections into a set of six "Subjective I's." As in Mansfield, the "Community-Maintenance I" was present, but the Riverview research situation called forth "Subjective I's" that previous studies had not, such as what he terms his "Pedagogical-Meliorist I." About this "Subjective I," Peshkin states,

> This . . . is a defensive self. It is directed toward students, generally minorities, whom I observed getting nowhere in their classrooms. They were being taught by teachers who had not learned enough, often did not care enough, to make a difference in their students' lives. Class time for both students and teachers was an occasion for little more than marking time until the bell released both from their meaningless engagement. This circumstance, regrettably common, disturbed me more than I had ever been disturbed by the ineffective teachers I had observed at other schools. The difference at Riverview High School was that the students in such classes were usually minorities, those who came to school with two strikes against them. I found myself doing what I never before had done as I sat in the back of classrooms: hatching schemes that would alter the classrooms I was watching, schemes that were calculated to reorient instruction and make a difference in the lives of the students. (Glesne and Peshkin 1992, 105)

Tracing your subjectivities, as Peshkin did during his Riverview study, shows points on a map of yourself. These points do not create a complete map because no research evokes all of your subjectivity. Some "Subjective I's" surely will appear again in other studies; just as surely, new "Subjective I's" will appear in other studies. And most likely, no two people doing the same study would map the same subjectivities, although many educators and social service professionals in my qualitative research classes identify a "Justice I" and a "Caring I" when reflecting upon the subjective lenses involved in their research. Lorrie provides an example:

I view my inquiry into how physical therapists work with elders with dementia through several lenses. First, and most connected to me, is the **personal lens.** The personal lens comes from my past, derived from the relationship I had with my maternal grandmother. Secondly, I view this topic through a **justice lens.** I have seen elders treated unfairly by health care providers; they don't receive the same quality of treatment as younger people, even when they have the same problems. I want to work toward achieving equal treatment of elders by understanding what they need for successful treatments. Thirdly, I am looking at this research through a **caring lens.** I have a strong interest in having the elders in our society treated with the respect and dignity they deserve. I want everyone in society to know what resources exist in our elderly community members.

To address the **personal lens,** I must return to my experience as a child. I can never remember a time when I wasn't drawn to older people. My parents were older when I was born—the age of my peers' grandparents. Essentially, I skipped a generation. Consequently, I found myself surrounded by elderly people on both sides of the family. The most influential person was my grandmother. My grandmother had multi-infarct dementia. She was treated very poorly by an underqualified and undereducated staff in one of the local facilities. After she died, I knew that I had to work specifically with elders; it was something that I could not ignore, a calling.

The basis of my personal interest in geriatrics stems from my relationship with my grandmother and my observations of the care she received at the most vulnerable point in her life. However, I also see the personal lens linked with the **justice lens.** I have always been an advocate for equal treatment. I have always been sensitive to people who are oppressed or underprivileged. And I have been acutely aware of my own privileged lifestyle. The injustices in our communities affect me deeply. I believe that the elderly, especially those without financial resources and without advocates, are the most vulnerable members of our society. In many ways they are more vulnerable than children because most children have strong advocates, parents. Elders have multiple needs; far too often, they are neglected or taken advantage of.

Finally, I see my **caring lens** connected to both the personal lens and justice lens. Having spent many hours with elderly individuals, I am well aware of what they have to offer. I value elders. I see them as wise, interesting people with rich experiences. Elders deserve to be treated with a special dignity.

As a physical therapist who has practiced in this area for 8 years, I will have to consider my subjectivity regarding my relationships with research participants. They will also be my colleagues, many of whom I have worked closely with at one time. They have an image of me and my interest in this topic; and I have images of them. To avoid making assumptions, I will need to listen carefully and probe thoroughly. To avoid misinterpretations, I intend to seek feedback on the actual transcripts from each participant.

Just as having knowledge of the participants makes "objectivity" challenging, it also has advantages. The background knowledge I have of many of the participants may assist me in probing more effectively. Furthermore, my knowledge of the profession will be helpful in asking better questions and being able to interpret data. Having the same professional training as the participants will allow for our time to be spent on rich details of their experiences rather than superficial discussion of the profession.

Monitoring and Using Subjectivity

As Lorrie indicates in the previous example, awareness of your subjectivities can guide you to strategies to monitor those perspectives that might, as you analyze and write up your data, shape, skew, distort, construe, and misconstrue what you make of what you see and hear. Try to see what you are not seeing, to detect what you are making less of than could be made, so that you can temper as necessary the press of subjectivity.

Mark describes how monitoring his subjectivity helped him to see in new ways. He was researching attitudes of officers in corrective facilities toward the schooling of their wards.

> The most unexpected event during the research process was that I changed my mind. My original "Subjective I" and several field log entries identify my concern over my judgmental stance regarding officers. I recognized that I must be cognizant of this and had to be careful to place "no prior constraints on what the outcomes of the research will be" (Patton 1990, 41). In the field log, I reminded myself "that during this research I am not a reformer." What surprises me now is that I have come to respect more what the officers do in their day-to-day routines in the cellblocks. By their sharing their thoughts and experiences with me, I have been informed, and consequently reformed. In their own way, they are also involved in helping a rather difficult clientele overcome massive barriers and become better people. I am delighted.

Monitoring subjectivity is not synonymous with controlling for subjectivity, in the sense of trying to keep it out of your work. When you monitor your subjectivity, you increase your awareness of the ways it might distort, but you also increase your awareness of its virtuous capacity. You learn more about your own values, attitudes, beliefs, interests, and needs. You learn that your subjectivity is the basis for the story that you are able to tell. It is the strength on which you build. It makes you who you are as a person and as a researcher, equipping you with the perspectives and insights that shape all that you do as researcher, from the selection of topic clear through to the emphasis you make in your writing. Seen as virtuous, subjectivity is something to capitalize on rather than to exorcise.

Virtuous subjectivity should not be confused with subjectivism, however, which exalts personal feeling as "the ultimate criterion of the good and the right" (*Webster's* 1986). By means of your subjectivity, you construct a narrative, but it must be imaginable by others, and it must be verifiable by others. The worth of your narrative cannot rest on its goodness or rightness in some private sense. It cannot be illusion or fantasy that has no basis outside your mind.

Developing awareness of your subjectivity and monitoring when it is engaged is a productive undertaking. Although it is not possible to be complete in this mapping of self, you can learn enough that is consequential about the selves generated in a particular research situation to be able to make use of this knowledge and to be responsible in reporting those selves to the readers of your work. A reflective section on who you are as researcher and the lenses through which you view your work is now an expected part of qualitative research studies. How you pursue your own subjectivity matters less than that you pursue it; the means can be as idiosyncratic as the special, personal twist that all researchers give to the standard methods that they adopt to conduct their research. Reading, reflecting, and talking about subjectivity are valuable, but they are no substitute for monitoring it in the process of research.

INTERSUBJECTIVITY

The old people were genuinely proud of me, generous, and affectionate, but at times their resentment spilled over. My presence was a continual reminder of many painful facts: that it should have been their own children there listening to their stories; that I had combined family and a career, opportunities that the women had longed for and never been allowed. (Myerhoff 1979, 26–27)

Intersubjectivity is a term used to highlight the fact that the subjectivities that help to shape research are not those of the researcher alone. Rather, particularly in inquiry where researcher and research participants interact over a period of time, the subjectivities of all players guide the research process and content. As Myerhoff indicates in the above quote, her observations and interviews with Jewish elders activated emotions within her participants that, in turn, shaped their behavior.

In another example, Patti Lather and Chris Smithies (1997) observed HIV/AIDS support groups and conducted interviews with women in the groups. Their work, which spanned several years, became important to many of the participants as the following quotations indicate:

I'm really excited about you guys writing this book and I want you to get it published right away. . . . Going through the interviews and hearing everyone's story, a lot of this stuff, we don't talk about in group, we don't talk about like how do you really feel about that stuff. (xxvii)

When are you guys going to publish? Some of us are on deadline, you know. (169)

Lather, Smithies, and the women living with HIV/AIDS formed relationships, laughed, cried, and re-examined their lives through the project. And the women's urgency to get their story told pushed Lather and Smithies to desktop publish an early version of their book, *Troubling the Angels*.

As research relationships develop, the negotiation of subjectivities is ongoing, with the potential for values, attitudes, and understandings of both researcher and participants to be changed through the research process. Similar to monitoring subjectivity, reflecting upon the interplay between researcher and researched is essential for understanding how research relationships influence fieldwork and interpretation (Busier, Clark, Esch, Glesne, Pigeon, and Tarule 1997). As Welch (1994, 41) states, "We create our own stories, but only as coauthors."

Thinking about the subjectivity of your others can also assist you in data interpretation. Ask yourself how those in the research site would react to your interpretations, to your phrasings? Is your interpretation paternalistic in ways? Does it romanticize? Try to take on the role of a particular research participant and read your words thinking about their impact and meaning to you as someone who has been "researched."

Reading here about subjectivity and intersubjectivity is like reading about other aspects of the research process: It may represent the beginning of understanding, a necessary condition on the way to making your perspectives explicit and to grasping the place of subjectivity in your research. For this to occur, however, you have to engage in personal encounters with self and others throughout the research process. Aware that there is something to seek, to uncover, and to understand about yourself, you are ready to be informed through the research experience.

Rapport and Subjectivity

There is a connection between rapport and subjectivity: Your capacity and limitations for establishing rapport are affected positively and negatively by your subjectivity. Liking or not liking a person (or a place or event) presses you toward or away from that person, with the predictable consequence that you distort by under- or over-sampling. Being aware that you are so inclined suggests the need for moderation. Being aware that you are so disinclined suggests that you have an obstacle to overcome if you are successfully to pursue contact with people not to your taste. As observed earlier, friendship is not an essential condition for conducting research; being accepted and trusted is. Also essential is consciousness of your own subjectivity so that you can disabuse yourself of the fiction that, as the disembodied passive voice conveys, watching, listening, and reading are going on without a known human agent. Invariably, a sentient being does the watching, listening, and doing. It makes a difference who. The goal is to get as fully as possible in touch with the embodied self who performs the acts of research.

For more discussion on rapport, see Delamont 1992; Gans 1982; Glesne 1989; Gonzalez 1986; Kleinman and Copp 1993; and Mitchell 1993. Particularly useful references on subjectivity include Barone 1990b; Couch 1987; Eisner 1990; Jansen and Peshkin 1992; Krieger 1985; LeCompte 1987; Peshkin 1982b, 1988a, 1988c; Riley 1974. For sources that focus upon issues of intersubjectivity, particularly those that involve friendship relationships in the field, see Kulick and Willson 1995; Lewin and Leap 1996.

Exercises

1. Reflect upon the nature of the optimal research relationships in your study. What implications do such relationships have for developing and maintaining rapport?
2. Write a "Subjective I" section for your research project. In it answer the following questions:
   • In what ways is your research autobiographical?
   • Which "Subjective I's" are engaged by your research project?

- What can you do to make use of your subjectivity in your research project? How might it benefit your study?
- In what ways will you monitor subjectivity that might otherwise blind you to certain aspects of your research?

Notes

1. There are writers who presume to have nailed down the techniques for achieving rapport. From within the self-help literature, see Brooks (1989).
2. This section on rapport draws on "Rapport and friendship in ethnographic research" by Corrine Glesne, from *The International Journal of Qualitative Studies in Education*, 1989, vol. 2, no. 1, pages 45–54, published by Taylor & Francis Group.
3. Peshkin's reflections on subjectivity that are presented here are taken from the first edition of *Becoming Qualitative Researchers* and draw from Peshkin 1982b, 1988a, and 1988b.

Chapter 6

But Is It Ethical? Learning to Do Right

As a group of students entered their second semester together in a qualitative research methods class, they reflected on the role trial and error had played in their best-learned lessons. Ernie wondered, "Can you even consider the possibility of learning research ethics through trial and error?" With increased awareness of ethical issues, they deliberated over perceived ethical dilemmas and wondered about the unintended consequences of their work.

This group of students realized that ethical considerations should accompany plans, thoughts, and discussions about each aspect of qualitative research. Ethics is not something that you can forget once you satisfy the demands of institutional review boards and other gatekeepers of research conduct. Nor is it "merely a matter of isolated choices in crucial situations" (Cassell and Jacobs 1987, 1). Rather, ethical considerations are inseparable from your everyday interactions with research participants and with your data.

Of course, ethical decisions are not peculiar to qualitative inquiry. Guidelines for ethical conduct grew out of medical and other types of intrusive research and led to an emphasis on informed consent, avoidance of harm, and confidentiality. Different epistemological systems, however, give rise to different ethical concerns (Lincoln 1990; Scott 1996). The emphasis on separation between researcher and researched in positivist research "prescribes a set of attitudes toward research subjects which fosters believing—on both sides—that researcher knows best" and that "researchers are in the best position to determine, within certain guidelines, what constitutes ethicality in social science research" (Lincoln 1990, 290). In interpretive approaches, however, the researcher interacts with participants in order to understand their social constructions. This orientation "thrusts upon the respondent two new roles: that of agency, self-determination, and participation in the analysis and reconstruction of the social world; and that of collaborator in both the processes and products of inquiries" (Lincoln 1990, 290). What constitutes ethicality becomes something to be negotiated and heavily contextual.

Lincoln speaks of an ideal here; many qualitative researchers do not work collaboratively with their respondents. But when they do, as in action research and orientational research, other ethical issues arise. At one time, researchers doing action or intervention research took primary responsibility for trying "to bring about a good and document it" (Soltis 1990, 254), sometimes with unintended consequences for and unanticipated harm to participants. Today, in action research, " 'subjects' are seen as partners in the research process. To dupe them in any way would be to undermine the very processes one wants to examine" (Punch 1994, 89). In both feminist and critical research, choosing one's research topic may be an ethical issue itself, as Soltis (1990) observes:

> In critical research there seems to be the presumption that the very purpose of all human research is to raise our consciousness regarding ethically suspect arrangements embedded in the structure of our sociocultural world. This requires that researchers be ethical in the *purpose* as well as in the *process* of doing research. Perhaps this raises the most fundamental ethical questions of all: Should the fundamental purpose of human inquiry be directed primarily at securing the good of human beings? (255)

This chapter focuses on ethical issues that arise out of the researcher-other relationship in traditional qualitative research. It does not discuss those ethical issues generic to all types of research, such as falsifying results or publishing without crediting co-researchers. As in previous chapters, unequivocal advice on "right" or "wrong" ways to behave is difficult to provide. Rather, the issues raised here are meant to alert you to areas that need consideration and forethought, so that you can possibly avoid learning ethical lessons through trial and error.

Ethical Codes

Nazi concentration camps and the atomic bomb served to undermine the image of science as value-free and automatically contributing to human welfare (Diener and Crandall 1978). Medical research in the United States that resulted in physical harm to subjects (such as the Tuskegee Syphilis Study) and social science research that caused, at the least, psychological pain (such as the Milgram shock experiment) led to the formation of codes of ethics by different professional organizations and academic institutions. By 1974, the federal government had mandated the establishment of institutional review boards (IRBs) at all universities that accepted federal funding for research involving human subjects. Five basic principles guide the decisions of IRBs when reviewing applicants' proposals:

1. Research subjects must have sufficient information to make informed decisions about participating in a study.
2. Research subjects must be able to withdraw, without penalty, from a study at any point.
3. All unnecessary risks to a research subject must be eliminated.

4. Benefits to the subject or society, preferably both, must outweigh all potential risks.
5. Experiments should be conducted only by qualified investigators.

A research code of ethics is generally "concerned with aspirations as well as avoidances; it represents our desire and attempt to respect the rights of others, fulfill obligations, avoid harm and augment benefits to those we interact with" (Cassell and Jacobs 1987, 2).

Various professional groups created their own codes of ethics. The ethical guidelines adopted by the American Anthropological Association (AAA) address issues that qualitative researchers in general face. The AAA Code of Ethics has evolved through several versions, most recently amended and adopted by the AAA membership in 1998. The following portion is taken from their 5 page statement and focuses upon researchers' responsibilities to people and animals with whom they work and whose lives and cultures they study.

1. Anthropological researchers have primary ethical obligations to the people, species, and materials they study and to the people with whom they work. These obligations can supersede the goal of seeking new knowledge, and can lead to decisions not to undertake or to discontinue a research project when the primary obligation conflicts with other responsibilities, such as those owed to sponsors or clients . . . .

2. Anthropological researchers must do everything in their power to ensure that their research does not harm the safety, dignity, or privacy of the people with whom they work, conduct research, or perform other professional activities . . .

3. Anthropological researchers must determine in advance whether their hosts/providers of information wish to remain anonymous or receive recognition, and make every effort to comply with those wishes. Researchers must present to their research participants the possible impacts of the choices, and make clear that despite their best efforts, anonymity may be compromised or recognition fail to materalize.

4. Anthropological researchers should obtain in advance the informed consent of persons being studied, providing information, owning or controlling access to material being studied, or otherwise identified as having interests which might be impacted by the research. It is understood that the degree and breadth of informed consent required will depend on the nature of the project and may be affected by requirements of other codes, laws, and ethics of the country or community in which the research is pursued. Further, it is understood that the informed consent process is dynamic and continuous; the process should be initiated in the project design and continue through implementation by way of dialogue and negotiation with those studied. . . . Informed consent, for the purpose of this code, does not necessarily imply or require a particular written or signed form. It is the quality of the consent, not the format, that is relevant.

5. Anthropological researchers who have developed close and enduring relationships . . . with either individual persons providing information or with hosts

must adhere to the obligations of openness and informed consent, while carefully and respectfully negotiating the limits of the relationship.

6. While anthropologists may gain personally from their work, they must not exploit individuals, groups, animals, or cultural or biological materials. They should recognize their debt to the societies in which they work and their obligation to reciprocate with people studied in appropriate ways. (American Anthropological Association 1998, 2–3)

The AAA Code of Ethics includes directives on the researcher's responsibilities to scholarship and science, the public, students and trainees, and applied work. Many of the principles are general and open to interpretation; nonetheless, they provide a framework for reflection on fieldwork, sensitizing you to areas that require thoughtful decisions.

In light of today's codes of ethics, a number of studies from the 1950s and 1960s would never be approved. Generally, subjects were drawn from low-power groups; in some cases, they gave information only to have the findings used against their own interests by people in positions of power (Punch 1986). Ethical codes help to mitigate this occurrence. Nonetheless, some researchers object to ethical codes because they can also protect the powerful. For example, Wilkins (1979, 109) notes that prisoners' rights are rarely a matter of concern for authorities until someone wants to do research in prisons. In effect, authorities can protect themselves under the guise of protecting subjects. Institutions that require explicit consent often have elaborate screening devices to deflect research on sensitive issues. Galliher asks, "Is not the failure of sociology to uncover corrupt, illegitimate covert practices of government or industry because of the supposed prohibitions of professional ethics tantamount to supporting such practices?" (Galliher 1982, 160).

In addition, some aspects of ethical research codes may be culturally biased. Lipson (1994) points out how Western codes of ethics focus on respect for the individual and for individual rights, while "in many other cultures, 'personhood' is defined in terms of one's tribe, social group, or village" (341). She uses examples from her work with Afghan refugees to demonstrate how "Afghans do not think of themselves as individuals who have their own rights or autonomy, but as members of families" (342). That ethical codes may preclude certain kinds of research or that they may be culturally biased are not grounds for dismissal, but rather indicate how, in qualitative research, standards of ethicality may evolve as your research perspectives grow.

Informed Consent

Though informed consent neither precludes the abuse of research findings, nor creates a symmetrical relationship between researcher and researched, it can contribute to the empowering of research participants. The appropriateness of informed consent, particularly written consent forms, however, is a debated issue that accompanies discussions of codes of ethics by qualitative inquirers. Through informed consent, potential study participants are made aware (1) that participation is voluntary, (2) of any aspects of the research that might affect their well-being, and (3) that they may freely choose to stop participation at any point in the study

(Diener and Crandall 1978). Originally developed for biomedical research, informed consent is now applicable when participants may be exposed to physical or emotional risk. Sometimes the requirement of written consent is readily accepted, as in the case of studying young children by means of interviews. In other cases, however, the very record left by consent papers could put some individuals' safety at risk if discussing sensitive topics (i.e., crime, sexual behavior, drug use). If written consent were required for all research projects, then much of the work of the qualitative researcher would be curtailed. Written consent would also eliminate all unobtrusive field observations and informal conversations.

Margaret Mead stated that "anthropological research does not have subjects. We work with informants in an atmosphere of mutual respect" (in Diener and Crandall 1978, 52). Field relationships continually undergo informal renegotiation as respect, interest, and acceptance grow or wane for both researcher and other. As the relationship develops, the researcher may be invited to participate in ways he or she hoped for, but could not have sought access to in the beginning (from secret ceremonies to executive golfing rounds). When research becomes collaborative, cooperation, active assistance, and collegiality may exceed the demands of informed consent (Diener and Crandall 1978; Wax 1982). This sense of cooperation and partnership may be more relevant to the ethical assessment of qualitative fieldwork than whether or not informed consent forms were signed.

Researcher Roles and Ethical Dilemmas

In the beginning stages of research projects, novices tend to see their research role as one of data gathering. As they become more involved in fieldwork, they find themselves functioning in a variety of roles depending upon research problems and procedures, their own characteristics, and personal attributes of research participants. Some of the roles may worry the researcher while others may be attractive but perplexing in relationship to their data-gathering goal. This section addresses several roles that qualitative researchers easily assume: exploiter, reformer, advocate, and friend. Different ethical dilemmas accompany each role.

EXPLOITER

> Esperanza has given me her story to smuggle across the border. Just as rural Mexican laborers export their bodies for labor on American soil, Esperanza has given me her story for export only. . . . The question will be whether I can act as her literary broker without becoming the worst kind of coyote, getting her across, but only by exploiting her lack of power to make it to *el otro lado* any other way. (Behar 1993, 234)

Questions of exploitation, or "using" your others, tend to arise as you become immersed in your research and begin to rejoice in the richness of what you are learning. You are thankful, but you may begin to feel guilty for how much you are receiving and how little you seem to be giving in return. Take this concern seriously. Do researchers, as welcomed but uninvited outsiders, enter a new community, mine the raw data of words and behaviors, and then withdraw to process those data into a product that serves themselves and, perhaps, their professional colleagues? Research participants usually remain anonymous. In contrast, researchers may get status, prestige, and royalties from publications (Plummer 1983). Researchers sometimes justify their actions with trickle-down promises such as, "Through getting the word out to other professionals (special educators, nurses, social workers), we will be able to help other people like you."

Exploitation involves questions of power. If you are not engaged in collaborative research projects, then how do you decide if you are "using" your others? Mitzi began to interview homeless mothers about the schooling of their children. She agonized over questions of exploitation:

> What am I giving back to these homeless mothers that I interview? It seems so unfair that this middle class privileged person is "using" this needy population . . . Can someone in a shelter tell me they don't have time. Privilege allows my response [of no time] to others to be OK. For them, that response would be suspect.

Dick, in his study of first-year principals, felt he "used" his relationships, his contacts, and his friends all over the state to get data.

Although you may appreciate Mitzi and Dick's heartfelt sentiments, their interpretation of their own behavior may be too harsh. Take Mitzi's case. Her homeless mothers are among our nation's most unfortunate people. Mitzi's research will not bring them the security and support of a home, a job, and good schooling for their children. But did Mitzi make such promises? To do so would be unethical. Did she treat the mothers with respect and dignity? This is ethical. Did she listen carefully, taking pains to understand what she was hearing? This is ethical. Did she intend to incorporate what she learned into her own professional conduct? This is ethical. Did she drop her topic once her dissertation was complete, never writing or talking about it again? This may be unethical.

If the standard of ethicality is solving the problems of people from whom you collect data, and solving them right away, then much research is doomed never to begin. Were Mitzi to use the results of her research exclusively for her own good, she could be accused of being an exploiter. That Mitzi receives more good from her research—degree, job, status, income, attention—is not inevitable, but often it is unavoidable. When Mitzi's concern fastens exclusively on her personal gain, she is being unethical. When she writes honestly and cogently about the homeless mothers and the schooling of their children, sharing the knowledge that she gains, she is being ethical. Perhaps Mitzi should have conceived of a collaborative study with the mothers. That she did not do so, that she created and maintained a power imbalance, does not condemn her as unethical.

INTERVENER/REFORMER

Unlike the exploiter role, which researchers wander into but want to avoid, the intervener or reformer role is one researchers may consciously decide to assume. As a result of conducting research, researchers may attempt to right what they judge to be wrong, to change what they condemn as unjust. Through observations at a zoo,

Nancy grew increasingly concerned over what she considered to be inhumane treatment of certain animals and agonized over what to do with her information.

In the process of doing research, researchers often acquire information that is potentially dangerous to some people. Don was interested in the history of an educational research organization. As he interviewed, he lamented, "I'm hearing stuff that I neither need nor wish to know about attitudes and relationships." The process was complicated for Don because he was investigating an organization in which he himself was involved.

As I interviewed young Caribbean farmers about their practices, I unexpectedly learned about the illegal cultivation and marketing of marijuana. And as Peshkin interviewed students in his ethnicity study, he became privy to information like the following:

> You know about the corner store, right? No? Gosh. They sell alcohol to anyone. Anyone. My friend and I went there to buy some chips and the guy who was standing behind the counter said, "You guys drink? I'll sell you some wine coolers. I won't tell your parents. Don't worry about it. Want some wine cooler?"

When your others trust you, you invariably receive the privilege and burden of learning things that are problematic at best and dangerous at worst.

Your ethical dilemma concerns what to do with dangerous knowledge. To what extent should you continue to protect the confidentiality of research participants? If you learn about illegal behavior, should you expose it? If those of us in the above examples informed authorities of our knowledge, we would jeopardize not only our continued research in those sites, but also possible subsequent projects. None of us discussed our knowledge with other research participants, nor personally intervened. If what you learn relates to the point of your study, you must explore ways to communicate the dangerous knowledge so that you fully maintain the anonymity of your sources. Such advice is consistent with other researchers who suggest that continual protection of confidentiality is the best policy (Ball 1985; Fine and Sandstrom 1988).

In their book *Knowing Children,* Fine and Sandstrom (1988) discuss how preadolescents "not only behave in ways that are unknowingly dangerous, but also knowingly and consciously behave in ways that are outside the rules set by adults" (55). As trust develops between the researcher and children, words and actions of the children may pose ethical dilemmas for the researcher. A child may, for example, act as a bully or make a sexist comment. Fine and Sandstrom conclude that "children must be permitted to engage in certain actions and speak certain words that the adult researcher finds distressing. Further, in some instances, the researcher must act in ways that are at least tacitly supportive of these distressing behaviors" (Fine and Sandstrom 1988, 55).

The question remains, however, of how "wrong" a situation must be before you should intervene on the basis of your unexpectedly acquired knowledge. If, for example, as a researcher you suspect ongoing emotional abuse of a child, do you react differently than if your work puts you in contact with students being offered alcohol at the corner store? Could not the latter also be construed as a case of child abuse? How do you decide where the lines are between a felt moral obligation to intervene and an obligation to continue as the data-collecting researcher?

No definitive answers exist to the above questions and again, judgments are made on a mix of contextual elements and personal compulsions. Some preventative measures, however, will help avoid such dilemmas. Laurie, a nurse, conducted research in a hospital setting. She worried about what she should do if she observed malpractice while in her research role. Finally, she discussed her worries with her cohorts in a qualitative research methods class. By taking the worry seriously and putting it through a variety of configurations, the class urged Laurie to meet with her gatekeepers and with the nursing staff whom she was observing and interviewing to get their advice on how she should proceed if she observed malpractice. In the earlier example, Nancy also appealed to colleagues after witnessing behavior at the zoo which she considered "wrong." After much debate, the group agreed that she should continue collecting data and become an animal advocate after she published the data.

Developing some sort of support group to discuss worries and dilemmas is a valuable part of the research process. Some researchers build a panel of experts into their research design. A student's dissertation committee can serve this function, but expert panels and dissertation committees do not necessarily know how to deal with ethical questions that arise in qualitative research. Ideally, the researcher has a support group made up of others who, although perhaps involved in substantively different topics, are all struggling with similar methodological questions.

ADVOCATE

Advocates are like interventionists in that they decide to take a position on some issue that they become aware of through their research. Unlike interveners or reformers who try to change something within the research site, the advocate champions a cause. As Lynne interviewed university custodians, she was tempted to become an advocate:

> I keep asking myself to what extent the research should improve the situation for custodians. This is magnified somewhat by my feeling that I have been a participant in the process, raising issues with custodians that many by now have come to terms with or raising expectations that some good will result. Even though my research was for the purpose of understanding and not "fixing," how can one come so close to what is judged to be a very bad situation and walk away? I keep asking myself, "Do I owe them solutions or at least some relief?" My answer is always "no," but then I keep asking myself the same question, probably because I just don't like my answer.

Lynne's research heightened her concern for the well-being of the custodians she studied, and the "take-the-data-and-run" approach left her uncomfortable. Traditional qualitative researchers find that advocacy can take a variety of forms—presentations and publications among the most readily available. Lynne needs to decide whether such formats will serve her concern, or if there are others that are within her competency that would be acceptable to the custodians.

Finch (1984) experienced a dilemma over publishing data she collected through her study of play groups. She found that child-care standards differed among working- and middle-class women.

> This evidence, I feared, could be used to reinforce the view that working-class women are inadequate and incompetent childrearers. Again, I felt that I was not willing to heap further insults upon women whose circumstances were far less privileged than my own, and indeed for a while, I felt quite unable to write *anything* about this aspect of the play-ground study. (84)

Finch resolved her dilemma by distinguishing between the structural position in which the women were placed and their own experience with that position. This enabled Finch to "see that evidence of women successfully accommodating to various structural features of their lives in no way alters the essentially exploitative character of the structures in which they are located" (Finch 1984, 84). Thus, she described the child-care practices of the working-class women in a way that would support them in an unfair and unequal society. Finch did not alter her data; she did not explain away the differences she uncovered. Her ethical sensitivity led her to contextualize her findings, so that the behavior of the two groups of women was framed within the differential realities of their lives. This is not the politician's cynical "damage control," but the academic's commitment to effective interpretation.

FRIEND

Researchers often have friendly relations with research participants; in some cases, the relationship is one of friendship. Whether friendship or friendliness is the case, ethical dilemmas can result. You may gain access to intimate information given to you in the context of friendship rather than in your researcher role. Should you use such data? Both Hansen's (1976) exploration of Danish life and Daniels' (1967) investigation within a military setting relied on personal friendships as channels for information. Hansen (1976) expressed her discomfort with her role as researcher and her role as friend: "The confidential information I received was given to me in my role as friend. Yet, I was also an anthropologist and everything I heard or observed was potentially relevant to my understanding of the dynamics of Danish interaction" (Hansen 1976, 127). Hansen refers to a particular confidential story told to her by one woman:

> Later that day I would record this conversation, alone, without her knowledge, in my role as anthropologist. In my role as investigator the conversation became "data." Would she have spoken so frankly about this and other more intimate subjects had she understood that I listened in *both* roles, not only as friend? (129)

As she continued to gather data, Hansen grew concerned over how she would protect the anonymity of her interviewees and struggled with thoughts on whether public description of behaviors violates an individual's right to privacy. She and Daniels both experienced ethical dilemmas over publishing findings that would possibly discomfort their friends, if not betray their friendship relationships. In the light of research data and publications, their friendships appeared utilitarian, a characterization that is problematic for perpetuating friendship.

Both Hansen and Daniels need to ask, as do we all in similar circumstances, if their narrative truly needs to include all that their friends tell them. Will the narrative hold up if the troublesome bits are excluded? Can these troublesome bits be presented in less troublesome ways? In the end, should we not let our friends be judges, by submitting to them what we have written, and taking our lead from their decisions?

In an article on "Intimacy in Research" (Busier et al., 1997), the authors argue that intimacy can be a "route to understanding" (165) but that it carries with it responsibilities and considerations, including reflexivity on the nature and influence of the relationship, analysis of the role of power in the relationship, and attunement to relational ethics. In relational ethics "the derivation and authority of moral behavior [is located] not in rules and obligations as such, but in our attachments and regard for others . . ." (Flinders 1992, 106). Predicated on trust, caring, and a sense of collaboration, relational ethics is at the core of feminist research, a kind of research where the role of "friend" is quite accepted.

The Researcher-Other Relationship

No matter how qualitative researchers view their roles, they develop relationships with research participants. The relationships in traditional qualitative research, however, are generally asymmetrical, with power disproportionately located on the side of the researcher. Consequently, researchers must consciously consider and protect the rights of participants to privacy. They must reflect on and mitigate deceptive aspects of research and consider issues of reciprocity.

THE RIGHT TO PRIVACY

In discussions of the rights of research participants, privacy is generally the foremost concern. Participants have a right to expect that when they give you permission to observe and interview, you will protect their confidences and preserve their anonymity. Respect confidentiality by not discussing with anyone the specifics of what you see and hear. When a principal asks you what you are learning from the teachers, you respond with something like the following:

> I am really enjoying talking with your teachers. They seem to take both their jobs and my research seriously and are therefore helping me tremendously. It's too early yet to know what I can make of all the information I'm receiving, but a couple of themes have been emerging and I'd like the opportunity to discuss them with you. Do you have the time?

Such a response leads away from particular individuals and towards the discussion of general concepts, which respects the principal's interest in your findings without violating any of your commitments to teachers. Such discussions must balance your unqualified obligation to the teachers with your appreciation of the principal's natural interest in your findings. It also makes use of an opportunity for participant feedback or a "member check" (Lincoln and Guba 1985) on your analytical categories.

Researchers sometimes argue over whether unobtrusive methods, even in public places, invade rights of privacy. This discussion usually includes debates on the use of covert observation (to be discussed in the next section, "Deception"). One position is that covert observation in public places is permissible because people ordinarily watch and are watched by others in public places. Accordingly, social scientists should be able to observe as well. A counterpoint is that when such observations are systematic, recorded, and analyzed, they no longer are ordinary and thereby violate rights of privacy.

Similar arguments develop around less discussed means of unobtrusive data collection. Diener and Crandall (1978) describe a study in which researchers used both surveys and the contents of garbage bags to discover what people bought, discarded, and wasted in different sectors of Tucson, Arizona. The findings concluded that poor people waste less food than higher-income people, and that there is a marked discrepancy between self-reports on alcohol consumption and evidence from bottles and cans in the garbage. Although garbage content was not linked to particular households, the examined bags often included envelopes with names on them. Do such studies violate privacy rights?

The issue of privacy arises again during the writing-up phase of the qualitative inquiry process. To protect the anonymity of research participants, researchers use fictitious names and sometimes change descriptive characteristics such as age or hair color. Fictitious names, however, do not necessarily protect participants as demonstrated by two frequently cited cases: West's (1945) *Plainville U.S.A.* and Vidich and Bensman's (1968) *Small Town in Mass Society*. Despite made-up names, the towns were easily identified by descriptions of their characteristics and locations, and people in the towns easily recognized themselves in the descriptions of individuals. In both cases, research participants were upset by the portrayals of the towns and their inhabitants. Critics (see Johnson 1982, 76) point out that West, for example, focused on the negative, that he looked with an urban perspective, and that he used offensive and judgmental words such as "hillbilly" or "people who lived like animals."

Plummer (1983) states that although "confidentiality may appear to be a prerequisite of life history research; it frequently becomes an impossibility" (142). He cites several examples: fifty years after the original study, Shaw's (1930) Jack Roller was located for reinterview, and after a month of detective work, a reporter tracked down Oscar Lewis's (1979) *Children of Sanchez*. These studies and others raise a number of ethical questions around the publication of data: What obligations does the researcher have to research participants when publishing findings? If the researcher's analysis is different from that of participants, should one, both, or neither be published? Even if respondents tend to agree that some aspect of their community is unflattering, should the researcher make this information public?

Despite justified worry about protecting anonymity, researchers may also have to deal with anonymity declined. Jacobs (1987) tells of an anthropologist who wrote about a community in Melanesia; she disguised villagers and their location through use of pseudonyms. Three years later, she returned to the field to distribute copies of her manuscript to those who had been most helpful and to ask permission to conduct further study. People liked the book and felt the accounts were correct, but told her that she had gotten the name of the village wrong and the names of the individuals wrong. She was told to be more accurate in the next book. The author was faced with an ethical dilemma: Should she follow the wishes of the villagers or the conventions and cautions of ethical codes? When her second book was completed, she sent a copy to the village and asked for comments as well as whether they still wanted actual names used. When she did not get a direct reply to her question, she used the same pseudonyms in her second monograph.

Jacobs (1987) tells of another case of anonymity declined, this time within the United States. An applied medical anthropologist worked for three years in an urban African American community. Before she published her articles, she asked community members to read, comment on, and criticize them. They complimented her on her accuracy, but questioned her use of pseudonyms for the town, the health center, and the individuals who "struggle to improve the healthcare for our people" (in Jacobs 1987, 26). The anthropologist explained the reasons for privacy conventions and how disclosing names could result in possible harm. In the end, she omitted the actual name of the center and its location, but she acknowledged the names of staff members in footnotes. This decision was made collaboratively.

Scott (1996) distinguishes between *open autocratic research* and *open democratic research*. In the open autocratic case, the researcher is open with research participants about all aspects of the research and invites their feedback on research interpretations, but does not give the respondents the rights of veto. In open democratic research, participants have the right to control not only which data are collected, but also which data are included in the research report through a series of negotiations between the researcher and project participants. In the first situation, power resides with the researcher; in the second situation, community power and politics affect what gets reported.

DECEPTION

> It is interesting, and even ironic, that social scientists espouse some of the techniques normally associated with morally polluted professions, such as policing and spying, and enjoy some of the moral ambivalence surrounding those occupations. (Punch 1994, 91)

Chris was interested in researching the gay community on a university campus. He attended a meeting of the Gay/Lesbian Alliance as a participant observer, jotting notes unobtrusively. Because the meetings were open to the public, he originally saw no reason to proclaim his role as researcher. As that first meeting continued, however, he struggled with feelings of deception and guilt. Finally, he quit taking notes and decided to meet with the organization's officers and obtain permission to attend meetings in the role of researcher.

Conventionally, we regard deception as wrong. Nonetheless, its role in research is debated time and time again. Deception easily enters various aspects of research, and it can take the form of either deliberate commission or omission. For example, in covert studies, participants never know that they are being researched. Some researchers misrepresent their identity and pretend to be someone they are not; others present themselves as researchers, but misrepresent or do not fully explain what it is that they are researching. This latter practice is called omission or *shallow cover* (Fine 1980). The decision to deceive generally rests on a concern to ensure the most natural behavior among research participants.

Punch (1986, 39) raises two questions concerning the role of deception in research: (1) Are there areas in which some measure of deception is justified in gaining data? and (2) Are devious means legitimate in institutions that deserve exposure? These questions summarize the ongoing debate over the use of deliberate deception in research.

Covert research gets its strongest support from those who advocate research of the powerful. As in investigative journalism, access to the workings of some groups or institutions with power would be impossible without deception. Van den Berge says of his research in South Africa, "From the outset, I decided that I should have no scruples in deceiving the government" (in Punch 1986, 39). If you, like Van den Berge, view an institution as "essentially dishonorable, morally outrageous and destructive," do you ignore it and study something more publicly acceptable in order to avoid being deceptive? Jack Douglas, a strong supporter of the *utilitarian* or "ends justify the means" approach, states,

> The social researcher is . . . entitled and indeed compelled to adopt covert methods. Social actors employ lies, fraud, deceit, deception and blackmail in dealings with each other. Therefore the social scientist is justified in using them where necessary in order to achieve the higher objective of scientific truth. (in Punch 1986, 39)

From the utilitarian perspective, deception in research may be justified by benefits to the larger society. Ethical decisions are made on the basis that moral action is that which results in the greatest good for the greatest number. Critics of this position argue that although costs and benefits may be estimated, both are impossible to predict and to measure. Furthermore, they argue, who is to set the standards that determine when something is for the greater good of society? The decision maker in most studies is the researcher, who is never an objective participant, no matter what he or she claims.

Currently, the utilitarian position that one does what is necessary for the greater good is overshadowed by the *deontological* ethical stance, which posits that moral conduct can be judged independently of its consequences. The deontological framework holds up some standard, such as justice or respect or honesty, by which to evaluate actions. This position changes the nature of the researcher-researched relationship and readily makes it unethical for researchers to misrepresent their identity to gain entry into settings otherwise denied to them, to deliberately misrepresent the purpose of their research, or to leave research participants feeling cheated. Bulmer (1982), for example, argues that covert research is not ethically justified, practically necessary, or in the best interest of social scientists. He views the rights of subjects as overriding the rights of science, thereby limiting areas of research that can be pursued. Bulmer suggests that the need for covert methods is exaggerated and that open entry may more often be negotiated than is commonly supposed (Bulmer 1982, 250). (See Flinders, 1992, for an in-depth examination of qualitative inquiry from the perspective of four ethical frameworks: utilitarian, deontological, relational, and ecological.)

Even when you are as honest and open as possible about the nature of your research, you will continue to develop ethical questions concerning your fieldwork. Many of the questions will be context-bound, arising out of specific instances in each study. For example, informed consent regulations indicate that you should disclose to potential participants all information necessary for them to make intelligent decisions about participation. Yet doing so is difficult in qualitative research because often you are not fully aware of what you are looking for, among whom, or with what possible risks. "The researcher is in a perplexing situation," states Erickson. "He or she needs to have done an ethnography of the setting in order to anticipate the range of risks and other burdens that will be involved for those studied" (Erickson 1986, 141). Although the partial nature of your knowledge does not obviate the propriety of informed consent, it does make implementing it problematic.

Certain ethical standards could encourage researchers to eliminate whole sections of their findings because publishing them could harm the individuals or groups they studied. Is this, too, a form of misrepresentation? Colvard (1967) suggests that reporting statuses and pseudonyms instead of actual names, paraphrasing quotations rather than presenting them verbatim, and withholding information obtained in more personal than official roles neither protects privacy adequately nor preserves knowledge adequately. View Colvard's observations as cautionary. Always be aware of ways in which your work may be deceptive.

RECIPROCITY

In some kinds of research, reciprocity is assumed to be a matter of monetarily rewarding research subjects for their time. Although participants in qualitative research sometimes receive remuneration, the issue of reciprocity becomes more difficult because of the time involved and the nature of the relationships developed between researchers and their others. The degree of indebtedness varies considerably from study to study and from participant to participant, depending upon the topic and the amount and type of time researchers spend with their others.

Glazer (1982, 50) defines reciprocity as "the exchange of favors and commitments, the building of a sense of mutual identification and feeling of community." As research participants willingly open up their lives to researchers—giving time, sharing intimate stories, and frequently including them in both public and private events and activities—researchers become ambivalent, alternately overjoyed with the data they are gathering, but worried by their perceived inability to adequately reciprocate. As I wrote up my Caribbean work, I reflected:

> Cultural thieving is what ethnographers do if their written product is limited in its benefits to the gatherer and, perhaps, his or her community. Also known as "data exporta-

tion" or "academic imperialism" (Hamnett and Porter 1983, 65), the process is reminiscent of past archaeologists carrying stone, pottery, and golden artifacts away from "exotic" places of origin to the archaeologists' homeland for analysis and display. What is owed to the people observed is the question. Are the terms of trade more than glass beads? (Glesne 1985, 55-60)

Researchers do not want to view people as means to ends of their choosing. Nonetheless, in noncollaborative qualitative work, they invariably cultivate relationships in order to gather data to meet their own ends. In the process, researchers reciprocate in a variety of ways, but whether what they give equals what they get is difficult, if not impossible, to determine.

Equivalency may be the wrong standard to use in judging the adequacy of your reciprocity. What can you do for those teachers who let you spend hours at the back of their classroom, or for those students who come to your interview sessions week after week? Literally, their time is invaluable to you. Is there anything within your means to deliver that your research participants would perceive as invaluable to them? Probably not. Often they do not have a relationship with you that puts you in a position to have something that, typically, is of such consequence to them. What you do have that they value is the means to be grateful, by acknowledging how important their time, cooperation, and words are; by expressing your dependence upon what they have to offer; and by elaborating your pleasure with their company. When you keep duty teachers company, assist participants in weeding their gardens, or speak to the local Rotary Club, you demonstrate that you have not cast yourself as an aloof outsider.

The interviewing process particularly provides an occasion for reciprocity. By listening to participants carefully and seriously, you give them a sense of importance and specialness. By providing the opportunity to reflect on and voice answers to your questions, you assist them to understand some aspect of themselves better. If your questions identify issues of importance to interviewees, then interviewees will invariably both enjoy and find useful their roles as information providers. By the quality of your listening, you provide context for personal exploration by your interviewees.

Although researchers do not wittingly assume the role of therapist, they nonetheless fashion an interview process that can be strikingly therapeutic. Obligations accompany the therapeutic nature of the interview. Self-reflections can produce pain where least expected, and interviewers may suddenly find themselves face to face with a crying interviewee. Tears do not necessarily mean that you have asked a bad or a good question, but they do obligate you to deal sensitively and constructively with the unresolved feelings, without taking on the role of analyst. If appropriate, you might suggest people, organizations, or resources that may be of help. Follow up through letters or conversations to assist such interviewees in feeling comfortable with their degree of personal disclosure. When Dick interviewed first-year principals, one began to cry as he expressed his stress and frustration with the job. When Eileen interviewed students of color about their experiences on a predominantly white campus, a young man began to cry as he talked about leaving his home community. At first, both Dick and Eileen were stunned, but they sympathetically listened. Finally, they suggested people and organizations that might be of interest and assistance to the interviewees.

The closer the relationship between researcher and research participants, the more special obligations and expectations emerge. For example, Cassell (1987) tells of an anthropologist who, during her initial fieldwork and successive summers, was accepted as granddaughter of an elderly Southwestern Native American couple. Their children and spouses treated her as a sister. One summer, when the anthropologist returned to the reservation, she learned that her "grandfather" showed signs of senility, was drinking heavily, and was hallucinating. His children and their spouses left soon after her arrival saying that they had cared for him all year and that it was now her turn. Although his care took full time and her work did not get done, the anthropologist felt she had no choice but to honor her "occasional kin" status. She also felt, however, even more a part of the family and free to bring with her an emotionally and educationally challenged nephew the next summer. Her "kin" helped tremendously in dealing with him. In another example, biographer Rosengarten wrote about his work with Ned Cobb and the form of his reciprocity: "There was one special reason why Ned Cobb's family agreed to busy itself with me, apart from the feelings between us. My work with Ned revived his will to live" (Rosengarten 1985, 113).

Interviews and other means of data collection can contribute to raised expectations in less intimate relationships as well. When researchers spend days and months asking people about their problems and aspirations, they elicit voices of dissatisfaction and dreams. In the process, they may encourage people to expect that someone will work to alleviate their plight. If, as a researcher, you plan only to publish your findings, then you must find a way to make that clear to research participants throughout the data-gathering process. Through written reports, however, qualitative researchers frequently convey reciprocity by their tales of injustice, struggle, and pain. Reciprocity may also include making explicit arrangements to share royalties from publications.

No Easy Solutions

By their nature, ethical dilemmas defy easy solutions. Researchers continue to debate over whether or not some people or areas should be researched. They question whether or not fieldwork is inevitably deceitful. They argue over the role of conscious deception in fieldwork. They raise ethical questions over the issue of power in relationships, particularly with economically poor and "deviant" groups. And they question whether codes and regulations can successfully shape research ethics.

Plummer (1983) identifies two positions in relation to ethics: the ethical absolutist and the situational relativist. The absolutist relies heavily on professional codes of ethics and seeks to establish firm principles to guide all social science research. The relativist believes that solutions to ethical dilemmas cannot be prescribed by absolute guidelines but have to be "produced creatively in the concrete situation at hand" (141). Pointing out weaknesses in both positions, Plummer suggests a combination: broad ethical guidelines with room for personal ethical choice by the researcher. Ethical codes certainly guide your behavior, but the degree to which your research is ethical depends on your continual communication and interaction with research participants throughout the study. Researchers alone must not be the arbiters of this critical research issue. (For further discussion about ethics in qualitative research, see Burgess 1984; Ellen 1984; Eisner and Peshkin 1990; Guba 1990; Punch 1986; Rynkiewich and Spradley 1976; and Whyte 1984.)

Exercises

1. Choose one of the following ethical dilemmas (either individually or as a group in class) and reflect upon what you would do if you were the researcher.
   a. You are interviewing college women who are anorexic, but whose anorexia is no longer active, about their schooling experiences. You have arranged to interview each of your participants at least 5 times over 2 consecutive semesters. During the third interview with one participant, just after the winter holidays, you begin to suspect that her anorexia is active again because of her obvious weight loss and a few of her comments. When you ask her how her health is, she replies that she is feeling great. What do you do?
   b. You are working on an intellectual biography of a well-respected university president. Most of your interviews are with the president who has obviously consented to your request to compose an intellectual biography, including some attention to his formative years. You are reading all of his published works and interviewing some family members as well as significant colleagues. In the process, you uncover some potentially damaging or, at the least, unflattering information about his private life. What do you do?
   c. You are inquiring into a refugee resettlement program in a small southern city, with particular interest in educational aspects and community involvement. Through development of rapport and time spent volunteering with the program, you begin to learn how an early immigrant is seemingly taking finanacial advantage of recent refugees. He is charging for information and services that should be provided through the settlement program and people are going to him, rather than trying to get their needs met through the program. You want to protect the new refugees from exploitation and to report the behavior of the earlier immigrant, yet you also worry that perhaps you don't fully understand what is happening culturally. What do you do?
2. Reflect in your field log on potential ethical issues that might arise during your study. What can you do to minimize their potential? What would you do if faced with your ethical concerns? Discuss with at least one classmate.

Chapter 7

Finding Your Story: Data Analysis

I can no longer put off the inevitable. I've been home about three weeks now, and I've found as many distractions as I could to avoid coding. I've organized my files, I've set up the study and done a major reorganization so I can spread out the stacks that will soon pile up. I'm reading, I'm thinking, and as a way of really beginning, I took out the book prospectus I wrote in November. During the last months at my site, I put a few Post-it notes into the prospectus file with other BIG looming ideas, ones that showed me I would have to tinker with the planned structure. Today I thought I'd just print out a sheet of the tentative chapter structure to put up on the wall (and delay coding once again?). I began typing it, and what did I find? It's all wrong, it doesn't capture the way I've been thinking at all. The power of the shift hit me head on. I tried to reorganize the chapters, but I found that wouldn't work either. So instead I wrote out the big themes I have been thinking about in my sleep, while I drive, when I cook Passover food . . . and that's where I'll have to start. (Pugach, Correspondence, 31 March 1994)

Data analysis involves organizing what you have seen, heard, and read so that you can make sense of what you have learned. Working with the data, you describe, create explanations, pose hypotheses, develop theories, and link your story to other stories. To do so, you must categorize, synthesize, search for patterns, and interpret the data you have collected. (See also, Bogdan and Biklen 1992; Coffey and Atkinson 1996; Delamont 1992; Denzin 1989; Dobbert 1982; Fetterman 1989; Lincoln and Guba 1985; Merriam 1988; Miles and Huberman 1994; Patton 1990; Silverman 1993; Strauss 1987; Tesch 1990; Wolcott 1994.)

Early Data Analysis

Data analysis done simultaneously with data collection enables you to focus and shape the study as it proceeds. Consistently reflect on your data, work to organize them, and try to discover what they have to tell you. Writing memos to yourself, developing analytic files, applying rudimentary coding schemes, and writing monthly reports will help you to learn from and manage the information you are receiving.

MEMO WRITING

By writing memos (see Glaser and Strauss 1967) to yourself or keeping a reflective field log, you develop your thoughts; by getting your thoughts down as they occur, no matter how preliminary or in what form, you begin the analysis process. Memo writing also frees your mind for new thoughts and perspectives. "When I think of something," says Jackie, "I put it on a card. I might forget about the thought, but I won't lose it. It's there later on to help me think." Even as you become intimately familiar with your data, you can never be sure of what they will tell you until analysis and writing are complete. As you work with data, you must remain open to new perspectives, new thoughts. Gordon states,

> I have found that my analysis goes on even if I am not actually working with the data. Insights and new ways to look at the data arise while I am at work at other things. Probably the most productive places for these insights is on the long drive to class and during long, boring meetings when my mind is not actively engaged.

It is particularly important to capture these analytic thoughts when they occur. Keeping a battery-operated tape recorder in the car can help, as can jotting down your thoughts wherever you happen to be, day or night. The comments and thoughts recorded as field log entries or as memos are links across your data that find their way into analytic files.

ANALYTIC FILES

Analytic files (see Lofland 1971) build as you collect data. You may begin with files organized by generic categories such as interview questions, people, and places. These files provide a way to keep track of useful information and thoughts. As your data and experience grow, you will create relevant specific files on the social processes under investigation, as well as on several other categories such as subjectivity, titles, thoughts for introductory and concluding chapters, and quotations from the literature.

Each of these specific files serves a distinct purpose. The subjectivity file, for example, helps you to monitor and use your subjectivity (see Chapter 5). Given the bearing of your subjectivity on the way you perceive your data, you cannot meaningfully separate the two (although you can forget their relationship). But by keeping track of your subjectivity, you will become attuned to the outlook that shapes your data analysis.

The title file contains your efforts to capture what your narrative may be about (see Peshkin 1985). Although your research project has a stated central focus (per your research proposal), you do not really know what particular story, of the several possibilities, you will tell. Conjuring up titles as the data are being collected is a way of trying out different emphases, all of which are candidates for ultimately giving form to your data. The titles become a way of getting your mind clear about what you are doing, in an overall sense, although the immediate application may be to concentrate your data collecting as you pursue the implications of a particular focus. In short, your search for a title is an act of interpretation. Titles capture what you see as germane to your study; but as your awareness of the promise of your study changes, so do your titles.

Files related to introductions and conclusions direct you to two obvious aspects of every study—its beginning and its ending. Regardless of the particular name that you give to your introductory and concluding chapters, you frame your study in the former—providing necessary context, background, and conceptualization. You effect closure in the concluding chapter by summarizing, at the very least, and by explicating the meaning that you draw from your data as befits the point of your study. It is never too early to reflect on the beginning and ending of your work, much as the formal preparation of these chapters may seem a distant dream when you are caught up in collecting data. Ideally, the existence of these files alerts you to what you might otherwise miss in the course of your study; they stimulate you to notions that, like your titles, are candidates for inclusion in your forthcoming text. Until the writing actually is done, however, you will not know which will be the surviving notions.

The quotation file contains quotations from your reading that appear useful for one of the several roles that the relevant literature can play. Eventually, they will be sorted out among chapters, some as epigraphs: quotations placed at the heads of chapters because they provide the reader with a useful key to what the chapter contains. Other quotations will be the authoritative sprinklings that your elders provide as you find your way through the novel terrain of your own data. By resourceful use of quotations, you acknowledge that the world has not been born anew on your terrain. The quotation file, like other files, is meant to be a reminder that reading should always inspire the question: What, if anything, do these words say about my study?

Analytic files help you to store and organize your own thoughts and those of others. Data analysis is the process of organizing and storing data in light of your increasingly sophisticated judgments, that is, of the meaning-finding interpretations that you are learning to make about the shape of your study. Understanding that you are in a learning mode is most important; it tells you that you need not be all at once as accomplished as eventually you need to be to meet the challenges of data analysis. It reminds you that by each effort of data analysis, you enhance your capacity to further analyze.

RUDIMENTARY CODING SCHEMES

> This experience lends entirely new meaning to the term "fat data." I can't even imagine reading everything I have, but I know I need to. And coding it? And all the while you're writing, events are still evolving in the community and you really can't ignore that, either. . . . So you really don't stop collecting data, do you? You just start coding and writing. (Pugach, Correspondence)

Marleen Pugach was still at her research site when she wrote this letter, realizing her need to begin to organize the data she was acquiring. Sorting your data into analytic files is a place to start. Through doing so, you develop a rudimentary coding scheme.

As the process of naming and locating your data bits proceeds, your categories divide and subdivide. Learn to be content, however, with your early, simple coding schemes, knowing that with use they will become appropriately complex. In the early days of data collection, coding can help you to develop a more specific focus or more relevant questions. For example, Bob was looking at the role of a principal in a junior high. Although he kept a daily log of his activities, he often felt that he was "missing the forest for the trees." He was collecting a lot of data, but he kept wondering if they were adding up to anything. When he began to give code names to main points in his log, he became familiar with what he was finding and, accordingly, with what he was missing. Through this process, Bob narrowed and shaped a focus that was both definable and manageable.

Cindy provides another example. Interested in the role of school boards in small, rural communities, she began a pilot study by observing meetings of one rural school board and interviewing its members. After fifteen hours of data collection, she reread and began to code all of the data she had gathered. In the process, she reconceptualized her problem statement:

> My initial problem statement was so broad it was difficult to work with. The process of coding and organizing my codes has helped to determine an approach to solidify a new problem statement that will lead me in a focused exploration of two major areas of school board control—financial and quality education.

Unlike a squirrel hoarding acorns for the winter, you should not keep collecting data for devouring later. Rather, examine your data periodically to insure that your acorns represent the variety or varieties desired, and that they are meaty nuggets, worthy of your effort.

Establishing the boundaries for your research may be continuously difficult. Social interaction does not occur in neat, isolated units. Gordon reflected on his work:

> I have felt right along that it is questionable whether I am really in control of this research. As I immerse myself in the analysis of my data, I begin to be sure that I am not. I constantly find myself heading off in new directions and it is an act of will to stick to my original (but revised) problem statement.

In order to complete any project, you must establish boundaries, but these boundary decisions are also an interpretive judgment based on your awareness of your data and their possibilities. Posting your problem statement or most recent working title above your work space may help to remind you about the task ahead. Cindy used a computer banner program to print out her working title, which she taped to the wall over her desk. The banner guided her work whenever she lifted her head to ponder and reflect.

MONTHLY REPORTS

Throughout the data collection process, writing monthly field reports for yourself, for committee members, or for the funding agency is a way to examine systematically where you are and where you should consider going. Keep them short and to the point, so that they don't become a burden for you to write or for your readers to read. Headings such as those I call "The Three P's: Progress, Problems, and Plans," help you to review your work succinctly and realistically plan it. In reflecting on both the research process and the data collected, you develop new questions, new hunches, and, sometimes, new ways of approaching the research. The reports also provide a way to communicate research progress to interested others, keeping them informed of the whats and hows and giving them a chance for input along the way.

MAINTAINING SOME SEMBLANCE OF CONTROL

By the end of data collection, expect to be overwhelmed with the sheer volume—notebooks, note cards, computer files, manila files, and documents—that has accumulated. You truly have acquired "fat data"; their sheer bulk is intimidating. Invariably, you will collect more data than you need. The physical presence of so much data can lead you to procrastinate, rather than to face the seemingly endless task of analysis.

It may help to think of the amount of film that goes into a good half-hour documentary. Similar to documentary film making, the methods of qualitative data collecting naturally lend themselves to excess. You collect more than you can use because you cannot define your study so precisely as to pursue a trim, narrowly defined line of inquiry. The open nature of qualitative inquiry means that you acquire even more data than you originally envisioned. You are left with the large task of selecting and sorting—a partly mechanical but mostly interpretative undertaking, because every time you decide to omit a data bit as unworthy or locate it somewhere you are making a judgment. Gordon reflects on his experience with sorting data:

> Sorting the data is actually less difficult than I feared, and it certainly is not worthy of the apprehension I suffered before getting started or the procrastination growing out of the apprehension which has left me behind schedule. Before I began, the job seemed immense and endless. Once started, I found that it is not really one large task but more a series of small, discrete tasks. These tasks seem to be equal parts drudgery and intuition.

Dealing with fat data requires methodical organization. Keeping up with data organization during the collection process makes the bulk less intimidating and easier to manage, as Gordon further observes:

> Transcribe notes onto the computer after each interview and observation. This admonition has been prompted by my discovery that a fairly substantial part of my data is not in readily usable form. I have had to go back after three months and type my notes because I find it hard to use data that I cannot read easily. Drudgery . . . .

Keeping up with the data involves writing memos to yourself, making analytic files, and developing preliminary coding schemes.

At some point, you stop collecting data, or at least stop focusing on data collection. Knowing when to end this phase is difficult. It may be that you have exhausted all sources on the topic—that there are no new situations to observe, no new people to interview, no new documents to read. Such situations are rare. Ideally, you should stop collecting data because you have reached theoretical saturation (Glaser and Strauss 1967). This means that successive examination of sources yields redundancy and that the data you have seem complete and integrated.

Recognizing theoretical saturation can be tricky, however. It may be, for example, that you hear the same thing from all of your informants because your selection of interviewees is too limited or too small to get discrepant views. Often, data collection ends through less than ideal conditions—the money runs out or deadlines loom large. Try to make research plans that do not completely exhaust your money, time, or energy, so that you can obtain a sense of complete and integrated data.

Later Data Analysis: Entering the Code Mines

In the early days of data collection, stories abound. Struck by the stories, you tell them and repeat them. You may sometimes even allow them to assume an importance beyond their worth to the purposes of the project. Making sense of the stories as a whole comes harder. You do not have to stop telling stories, but in data analysis you must make connections among the stories: What is being illuminated? How do the stories connect? What themes and patterns give shape to your data? Coding helps you to answer these questions.

When most of the data are collected, the time has come to devote attention to analytic coding. Although you may have already developed a coding scheme of sorts, you must now focus on classifying and categorizing. You are ready to enter "the code mines." The work is part tedium and part exhilaration as it renders form and possible meaning to the piles of words before you.

Marleen's words (correspondence, 3 May 1994) portray the somewhat ambivalent psychological ambience that accompanies entering the code mines:

> I'm about to finish the first set of teacher transcripts and begin with the students. This will probably mean several new codes . . . since it is a new group. I hope the codebook can stand the pressure. One of the hardest things is accepting that doing the coding is a months-long proposition. When my mother asks me if I'm done yet, I know she doesn't have a clue . . .

Coding is a progressive process of sorting and defining and defining and sorting those scraps of collected data (i.e., observation notes, interview transcripts, memos, documents, and notes from relevant literature) that are applicable to your research purpose. By putting like-minded pieces together into data clumps, you create an organizational framework. It is progressive in that you first develop, out of the data, major code clumps by which to sort the data. Then you code the contents of each major code clump, thereby breaking down the major code into numerous subcodes. Eventually, you can place the various data clumps in a meaningful sequence that contributes to the chapters or sections of your manuscript.

Consider the example of the first edition of this book, which I wrote with Alan Peshkin. Before we discussed writing it, each of us had been developing and collecting notes on qualitative inquiry. In the prospectus we prepared for the publisher, we described the probable chapters of the book. These chapters—conceivable as large, general, analytic files—became our major working codes as we continued to collect data and make notes of our thoughts. Most of the material fell easily under major codes such as observation, interviewing, or analysis, but some of it at first did not seem to fit well. We therefore added major codes such as dissertation advice and miscellaneous, trusting that as we worked with the data we would figure out how to integrate, incorporate, or eliminate the information filed under these headings. Then, we reread the data scraps located in each major clump in order to develop minor code words or subcodes. Exhibit 7.1 presents examples of the subcodes generated by data we had filed under the major code data analysis.

Each data scrap received both a code name and number. For example, each data scrap under the major code of data analysis that was related to the subcode of coding was marked both "8.2" and "DA/COD, for data analysis code." As we worked through each major clump of data, we relocated some data scraps under other major headings. When we began writing, we continued the coding process: we merged, more finely divided, or relocated subclumps. Neither the assignment of a code nor the code name itself was inviolable; rather, we renamed and reassigned data as we saw fit to help us organize and manage the data. After all, except when working with a team of researchers (see Liggett, Glesne, Johnson, Hasazi, and Schattman 1994), both acts are personal inventions in the interest of facilitating understanding.

When you work with data gathered through qualitative inquiry, each major code should identify a concept, a central idea, though not necessarily a chapter or section of the final product, as in the book example. There should be as many major codes as needed to subsume all of the data, appreciating that more may develop than will hold up as separate codes. The blending of codes occurs over and over as you reread and reinterpret.

To facilitate developing and working with a coding scheme, make a code book. Assign each major code its own number and page, as shown in Exhibit 7.1. Below the major code, list the number assigned to the subcode, the subcode name, and an explanation of the subcode. Start the code book soon after beginning to collect data so that it will reflect the emerging, evolving structure of your manuscript. It is highly personal, meant to fit you; it need not be useful or clear to anyone else. Although there may be common features and a common intent to everyone's data analysis process, it remains, in the end, an idiosyncratic enterprise. The proof of your coding scheme is, literally, in the pudding of your manuscript. The sense your manuscript makes, how well it reads, depends, in large part, on your analytic framework.

Begin by reading through whatever data you have—your observation notes, log, transcripts, documents, and literature. Identify what appears to be important and give it a name (code). The length of the coded sections will vary from several sentences to several pages. Novice researchers are sometimes tempted to code in very small chunks, separating even clauses of sentences. They usually then have to spend time later on, returning to whole transcripts to understand the context of

───────────────── **EXHIBIT 7.1** ─────────────────
Subcodes of the Major Code "Data Analysis"

8. Data Analysis (DA)

1.	TRU	trustworthiness
2.	COD	coding
3.	STO	finding one's story, conceptualization
4.	GEN	generalizations as products of qualitative inquiry
5.	OUT	anything related to possible outcomes
6.	THE	theory
7.	DIS	data display
8.	PRO	continuous nature of analysis process
9.	SUB	implications of subjectivity for DA
10.	INTRO	introductory material
11.	STR	strategy for conducting; different forms
12.	COM	use of computer in data analysis

their data fragments. Leave as much content around each data bit as possible. Because coding is an evolving process, it is advisable in the early stages to use a pencil to mark both data scraps and the code book. Be overgenerous in judging what is important; you do not want to foreclose any opportunity to learn from the field by prematurely settling on what is or is not relevant to you. In marking sections and giving them a name, you make judgments about which items are related and therefore belong under the same major code. The same subcode (such as anxiety, or theory, or ethics, in the codebook for this book, for example) may appear under several major codes. This indication of themes that may run throughout the work alerts you to look for their presence or absence under other major headings.

When you have collected and coded all of your data scraps, keep your code book in front of you and proceed to the next phase of data analysis: arranging your major code clumps into a "logical" order by asking yourself which clumps, or parts of clumps, belong together in the final code arrangement for your manuscript. Through such analysis, you sort out what you have learned so that you can concentrate on writing up your data.

The coding, categorizing, and theme-searching process is not as mechanical as the previous description may make it appear. Rather, it is a time when you think with your data, reflecting upon what you have learned, making new connections and gaining new insights, and imaging how the final write-up will appear. Let's hear from Marleen (correspondence, 3 May 1994) again:

> I now have a regulation code book complete with several major codes and subcodes . . . and I see already, in the process of coding, how they stretch out and then collapse and then multiply again as you complete more and more of the analysis. I also realize that

you never really are in a pure mode of coding. It's a very strange dynamic. You find yourself in the midst of what seems to be a very technical process—drawing brackets, locating the number for the subcode, moving through the pages, and then you find yourself needing to write down some narrative to anchor a set of thoughts you didn't have before, or to pin down a new way of thinking about something. A good example for me is how the teachers talk about their own language learning capacity . . . these dialogues suddenly seemed much more important than I ever would have imagined when I was in Havens (the now official pseudonym). And they have their own rhythm, a rhythm I didn't know was there before. This is when I know things are going well.

The art of data transformation is in combining the more mundane organizational tasks with insight and thoughtful interpretations. (Also see Coffey & Atkinson, 1996, for an excellent discussion of coding.)

Following is a list of Marleen Pugach's 11 major codes along with brief descriptions and some comments on how the material eventually got used in her book *On the Border of Opportunity: Education, Community and Language at the U.S.-Mexico Line.*

1. *Immigrants/visitors.* A theme in the book is that it's hard to make the distinction between immigrants and daily crossers.
2. *Border.* This is about who crosses, for what purposes, crossing then and now, how border towns are characterized, and interior life in Mexico.
3. *Hispanic culture in the community.* I ended up not writing much about this, except insofar as it gets lost when language gets lost.
4. *Language.* This includes who uses Spanish, when, with whom, language learning and language loss, to whom language is important. One subcode is *language in the community.* This became a whole chapter (chapter 3), so that chapter has a lot of the other subcodes subsumed under it. *Language in school* is also another subcode, and it became chapter 4.
5. *Equality of opportunity/discrimination.* Context of the community, historical issues, segregated housing, etc.
6. *Havens as a changing community.* This category ended up with the category of community context and is presented in chapter 1 mostly. The changing nature of the town is part of the context. Community self-image is part of this.
7. *School programs, school context, solutions posed to school problems.* Mostly in chapter 5.
8. *"We all get along."* This theme kept coming up, so it ended up deserving a category, but I didn't play it up except in that "these are good kids and the town is a good place to live." It seemed more of an issue in terms of ethnic group relations, and that is where it came out in the book.
9. *Classroom and school dynamics.* This is chapter 5.
10. *Opportunity.* This was an idea early on, and it came up often. It ended up as some of the markers in chapter 6, as a major theme and as a metaphor.
11. *Teachers' language knowledge.* I separated this from general language knowledge issues, and it became part of chapter 4, an important part of it.

The following are reflections of Andrea and Jill, who, after ten to twenty hours of fieldwork, undertook the coding/analysis process for the first time. In their descriptive portrayals, you may see your own struggles, achievements, and realizations.

Andrea: I approached my first attempt at coding with the vivid analogy of being in "the code mines" in mind. Beginning the process was indeed like preparing to descend into a mine shaft. The thought of dropping into the dark, cold abyss of twelve interviews and countless reflections made me shrink from the task. Perhaps, in the lightless confusion of data, I would not be able to sort out any meaning to it all. Perhaps, after seven months of collection, I would find no gold nuggets of wisdom in the walls of my code mines. Perhaps, like the miner, I needed to better prepare myself for entering the bowels of my notebooks and field logs.

Hence I consciously entered into a series of avoidance tactics that kept me in the light of day as yet another week flew by. I finished transcribing my last three tapes. I backed up my disk. I reorganized my files. I considered reflecting more on my previous reflections. I even flipped through my Word Perfect manual, on the pretense that I might find an ingenious way to manage my codes, someday. I kept a fire going in the wood stove to ward off the cold I constantly felt in my bones.

Finally, the day came. I could put it off no longer; indeed, I was dreadfully remiss in waiting so long. I approached my first-semester notebook of interviews with images of Tolkien's Bilbo Baggins approaching the cave of Gollum. I must retrieve the precious ring, or never return to class and Professor Gandolf Glesne. I laid open my first interview next to my new, brightly colored coding notebook.

Anticipation far exceeds the event in the exploration of the unknown. Three pages of codes flowed from my pen from the first interview. They were familiar words, words repeated on paper, on tape, and in my mind throughout my whole study. Like the Hobbit with his ring on, I disappeared into my interviews for hours.

After the initial showering of codes, each interview added fewer to my list. That was comforting. I had a sense that the list would be manageable. The second interview added only one page of new codes, the third a half page. After that, each interview produced one new code and usually elaboration or clarification on some previous codes. Before I was done, the maze of words began organizing themselves in my mind. I flipped to a clean page and began jotting down umbrella phrases to collect subcodes under.

I am no longer a Pennsylvania coal miner dreading my life's work. I am no longer the Hobbit with but one precious ring. Today I am Smog the dragon sitting upon a mountain of jewels, stolen from my interviews. They lay, however, disheveled beneath me and hard to account for. So today my task is to organize my treasures that I might know what I have before I go on. The task is a bit easier because I made some notes as I was coding. I began clumping my codes into broader categories. They fall into neat piles, with only a few exceptions. These I place temporarily until I can consult with my fellow researchers. So ends, for me, the dreaded imagery of life-threatening mind shafts. I have much real work ahead, but I have dealt with the anxiety of passing the test.

Jill: I have reshuffled and reshuffled the cards. I have marked and arranged the deck carefully, so that when I lay my hand on the table, I will have played a winner.

First create the codes, the markings for the deck. Then mark the cards. It seemed straightforward at the start. Code the interviews; make the cards; deal out the marked hands. Only the marks kept shifting, and cutting and pasting to create the deck was tedious, not mindlessly relaxing as hoped.

It was not an auspicious start! I wasn't having a good time. In fact, by the time I was finished I was sure I never wanted to see, or shuffle, or deal those cards again. And worse, the Card King had betrayed me. The glory of index cards indeed! Eight-and-one-half × 11 slices of paper simply do not fit neatly on 5 × 8 index cards. I descended into the bowels of the code mines, where nothin' comes easy and canaries die a long, slow death.

But, the King wasn't all wrong. Once the cards were ready for play, I began to understand his game: build the deck and cut the cards so you can shuffle and deal, shuffle and deal, and then shuffle and deal again. So forgiving! A game of solitaire with more than one right way, and more than one chance to lay out the hands. In fact, about halfway through the play, when I imagined all my cards laid out on the table, I knew that the house was about to win the game. So I shuffled the deck, and dealt them out again.

The game makes sense now. The dealer groups and regroups the cards into playable hands. Sometimes she shuffles and deals it all out again. By the time she's done, the cards are not so crisp to the touch, but they sure play smooth and easy.

The game of qualitative research has general guidelines, but house rules vary, casino to casino. Solitaire is a dealer's game, after all.

Current house rules at the novice's casino are as follows:

1. One notion to a card. Peeling quote slivers off the cards slows the play of the game.
2. No color coding the cards. The whiteout budget is insufficient.
3. No multiple copies of passages from interviews. One quote to a card, one category to a quote. Forced choices speed the game, while the redeal option protects against premature folding.
4. No dealing hands to please subjective eyes. And one last rule that every good player should know:
5. "Know when to hold 'em, and know when to fold 'em."

This game calls for time and patience. For me, it is best played a few hands at a time, with time to ponder the cards in between. The trick, I think, will be not to let the deck get cold.

Jill refers to the problem of transferring 8-½ × 11 paper to 5 × 8 cards when using note cards for coding. It is a tedious matter, one that can be avoided by using computer programs to code and segregate data bits. Or the paper scraps can simply be cut and put into file folders. Cards are, however, easier to handle than slips of paper and not as apt to get lost or misplaced.

Displaying Data

Miles and Huberman (1994) have created a comprehensive text on using data display in the analysis of qualitative work. They describe data display as "an organized assembly of information that permits conclusion drawing and action taking." Making an analogy to "you are what you eat," they claim that "you know what you display" (Miles and Huberman 1994, 11). Matrices, graphs, flowcharts, and other sorts of visual representations assist in making meaning of data, as well as in exposing the gaps or the areas where more data are needed. Data display is, therefore, another ongoing feature of qualitative inquiry. It can be a part of developing the research statement, data collection, analysis, and final presentation of the study.

As you begin to conceive your research by working on the research statement and plans for data collection, data displays help you to identify the elements of your study. Expect the displays to change as you learn more. After data collection has begun, urge Miles and Huberman (1994), create diagrams that reflect some risk; that is, use one-directional arrows that indicate potential cause and effect. Doing so forces you to begin to theorize about the social phenomenon under study. Exhibit 7.2 "The Relational Work of Partner Teaming" is an example of a thematic data display by Penny Bishop (1998, 171). She created the diagram as a way to help her understand and present the major concepts evolving through her inquiry into effective partner team teaching in middle schools.

───────────────────────── **EXHIBIT 7.2** ─────────────────────────
The Relational Work of Partner Teaming

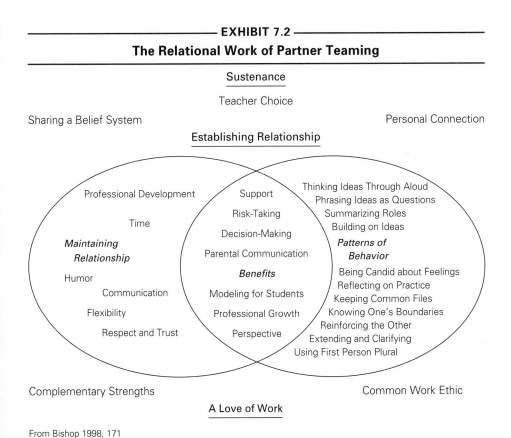

From Bishop 1998, 171

After becoming absorbed in using a computer graphics program to display her work, Andrea teased another student about her 61 pages of notes: "Want me to reduce it to one good graph?" Data display provides the skeleton of your work. Just as observing Earth from a satellite allows you to see the overall pattern of geologic structures and human adaptations to these structures, data displays help you to see the overall patterns in your research without getting lost in the details.

When thinking about displaying your data, experiment with a variety of forms. Tables provide detail, but bar and line graphs often portray patterns more vividly. If you are comparing two or more groups over time, line graphs are particularly useful. Matrices that use symbols such as + and 0 rather than numbers also can aid in uncovering patterns. For example, if investigating perceived constraints to effective education in six rural schools, you might, after a round of interviews, develop a table similar to Exhibit 7.3.

With the table before you, you would look for patterns and begin to form some hunches about what was going on, using your knowledge of each rural town and school. For example, you would notice that schools 2, 3, and 5 all perceive their tax base as a problem, but not their communication between school and community. Schools 1, 4, and 6 are just the opposite. Returning to your data, you would try to figure out possible explanations. Although the communities are similar in size, you would note that the communities that host schools 1, 4, and 6 have a sizable proportion of nonnatives who have moved to the area in recent years. The communities that host schools 2, 3, and 5 do not. You would then hypothesize that the newcomers are bringing more money into the towns and, along with it, strife in school governance decisions. In reflecting on possible reasons for the pattern of responses in the categories of access to information and access to experts, you would wonder whether distance from the state's largest city makes a difference. Developing a new matrix, you would then map your hunches as demonstrated in Exhibit 7.4. Such matrices-forming work serves to suggest both new questions and people or sites for investigation, as well as to make sense of the data collected.

──────── **EXHIBIT 7.3** ────────

A Matrix Example of Constraints to Effective Education in Six Rural Schools

School	Tax Base	Communication with Community	State Policy	Access to Information	Access to Experts
1	0	+	+	0	0
2	+	0	+	+	+
3	+	0	+	0	0
4	0	+	+	+	+
5	+	0	+	+	+
6	0	+	+	+	+

Key: + = perceived as a constraint by school personnel
     0 = not perceived as a constraint by school personnel

--- EXHIBIT 7.4 ---

A Matrix Example of Data Patterns and Researcher Hunches Regarding Constraints to Effective Education in Six Rural Schools

School	Tax Base	Communication with Community	Access to Information	Access to Experts
native/near city (3)	+	0	0	0
native/not near city (2, 5)	+	0	+	+
mixed/near city (1)	0	+	0	0
mixed/not near city (4, 6)	0	+	+	+

Key: + = perceived as a constraint by school personnel
     0 = not perceived as a constraint by school personnel

Borrowing from the natural sciences, cognitive anthropologists use taxonomies to assist in displaying social phenomena. In this approach, the researcher seeks to understand how others classify "cognitive domains" or salient aspects of the world. Structured interviews are used to elicit indigenous classificatory schemes. Each category is, in turn, probed for subcategories and sub-subcategories until the interviewee's categorization scheme is fully mapped. For example, Janet Davis (1972) investigated eighth graders for categories of the cognitive domain she called "things kids do at school." Through interviewing, she found that major categories included picking on other kids, sitting in classes, being nice to teachers, and acting up. Davis went on to investigate subcategories, such as all the ways that kids are "nice to teachers." She then probed for sub-subcategories such as how a student becomes a teacher's pet. Exhibit 7.5 is extracted from Davis's taxonomic chart of the domain of "things kids do at school" (Davis 1972, 115–116). Taxonomic charts help researchers to see what they know and don't know about a particular cognitive domain.

--- EXHIBIT 7.5 ---

Partial Taxonomy of the Domain "Things Kids Do at School"

Take tests

Sit in classes

Be nice to teachers:

Do what you're told
Turn in assignments
Talk nice, use good grammar
Don't talk out of turn
Don't talk during lectures

Try to become a
pet (get in with
teacher)   ┌─ Do extra stuff
           │ Volunteer
           │ Sweep floor
           └─ Kiss their butts

Adapted from Davis 1972, 115–116.

A student at the University of Vermont investigated the types of undergraduates enrolled there as defined and categorized by undergraduates. Although categories were not necessarily mutually exclusive, the interviewer found that, according to interviewees, there were preps, punkers, out-of-staters, Vermonters, granolas, squids, nerds, smarts, intelligents, and jocks. Many of these categories had subcategories such as both normal and progressive granolas or positive and negative jocks. Such information lends itself to a taxonomic chart that can then be used as a type of guide for discussion of the cognitive domain. (See Spradley 1970; Spradley and Mann 1975; Spradley and McCurdy 1972.)

Mathematics also can be useful in determining patterns. Regarding the use of mathematics in anthropology, Agar (1980) comments:

> Anthropologists, more than other social scientists, have mathophobia. One of my favorite wisecracks is to define mathematical anthropology as what happens when anthropologists number their pages. . . . Most of the points I need to make are made with simple frequency distributions. If that is all you need, stop there. . . . If you choose not to use statistical procedures in your systematic testing, it should be because you know enough about them to know they are inappropriate, not because the very thought causes you to break out in a rash. (132)

Simple frequency counts can help to identify patterns. For example, imagine that you have been inquiring into the attitudes of young people toward agriculture in the rural Caribbean. Through interviews with 85 persons, including 25 employed in town, 50 working in agriculture, and 10 living in rural areas but not working in agriculture, you receive mixed answers to the question "How do young people feel about working land?" Your first frequency distribution (represented by Exhibit 7.6) suggests that young people are not very interested in doing agricultural work. Yet, by listening to and rereading the interviews, you form the hunch that the attitudes are linked to land tenure. You go back to your interviews and rework the frequency counts, taking into account the relationship of each interviewee to the land. This time your frequency distribution demonstrates a definite pattern in the relationship between attitudes toward doing agricultural work and land tenure (see Exhibit 7.7). The numbers assist in shaping a more specific hypothesis about attitudes toward farming.

—————————— EXHIBIT 7.6 ——————————

Frequency Distribution of Perceived Attitudes toward Working the Land

	Positive Attitudes	Negative Attitudes
Town employees	4	21
Agricultural workers	21	29
Other rural people	0	10

—————————————————— EXHIBIT 7.7 ——————————————————
Frequency Distribution of Perceived Attitudes toward Working the Land by Dominant Land Tenure Situation of Interviewee

	Positive Attitudes	Negative Attitudes
No land worked	0	25
Agricultural laborer	0	13
Works family land	5	5
Shares crop/rent	2	17
Works land rent-free	10	0
Works own land	8	0

Using Computers

We have only recently begun to grasp the possibilities for computer use in qualitative research. Researchers primarily use the computer as a tool to facilitate what, in the past, they did manually. Many, however, are making use of the technology available to manage, make meaning, and present data. This section includes a brief overview of computer use in qualitative research and makes cursory introductions to some of the software that assists in handling qualitative data. (For more information, see Becker 1984; Conrad and Reinharz 1984; Pfaffenberger 1988; Tesch 1990; Weitzman and Miles 1995.)

AN OVERVIEW OF COMPUTER USE

Computers have revolutionized the handling and manipulation of quantitative data. Because qualitative researchers work with words and without discreet variables, they initially found it more difficult to use the machines efficiently in applications other than word processing. As computers have become more affordable, more transportable, and more usable through the development of software, more qualitative researchers regularly look to computers to assist in the research process.

Computers can play a role in most every aspect of qualitative research, even at the initial, participant selection stage. Penny used electronic mail, or E-mail, at the beginning of her work to consult a national panel of expert practitioners in order to develop a profile of effective middle-level partner teams. She went on to make initial contact with several of her research participants using E-mail as well. The use of E-mail not only facilitated the process, but also provided written documentation of the communication, something telephone use would not have done. E-mail can expedite communication between researcher and others throughout the research process.

Computers can assist in keeping a record of fieldwork activities. Forms can be developed for recording data collection dates, sites, times, and people interviewed or observed. In this way, an account is kept not only of progress in data collection, but also of gaps in data collection since one can easily see where and with whom time is spent. As with manual documentation, the researcher needs to take care in storing data and protecting the anonymity of participants. The computer makes it easy to change real names to pseudonyms wherever they occur within a file.

Computers can be used systematically to record field notes, interview transcripts, and observation notes. Some researchers carry their laptop or notebook computers into the field and eliminate taking observation and even interview notes by hand. The process of going over hastily typed notes or of transcribing interviews from tapes into the computer familiarizes researchers with the data and enables them to record new questions, thoughts, and hunches in files labeled as such. Because the computer forces the organization of data, it provides occasion for constant reflection. The data stored in computer files are easy to access for preliminary analysis that can further guide data collection. The concreteness and specificity necessary for computer use require researchers to be clear and explicit about their decisions, responding, in part to urgings by Miles and Huberman (1994) and others that qualitative researchers delineate their analytic methods. Computer use can therefore help to demystify qualitative analysis and contribute to its accountability.

Performing the tasks involved in data analysis is easier with data recorded on computer files than it is with data recorded through manual means. Computers assist in sorting, referencing, counting, coding, and displaying data. Various types of programs, including word processors, database managers, graphics, spreadsheets, and qualitative software, can be used. Beginning researchers should use caution, however, in using the quantitative facilities of computers inappropriately because computers make it nearly effortless to count. For example, one could easily compare how many times a particular word appeared in the interviews of two separate groups. This might appear interesting, but it may not be particularly meaningful.

Without dispute, computers make the writing and rewriting process easier. Excerpts from files in which data have been recorded or analyzed can be inserted into the report text without having to retype long sections. Computers can also make even the most preliminary sketch of ideas look polished and organized. This is advantageous in that printed drafts invite reading and can be easily edited and changed. It can also be disadvantageous, if one is lulled by the look of completion and prematurely ceases working. Pfaffenberger (1988) suggests minimizing this temptation when printing out drafts by using paper of lower quality or of a different color and using the plainest printing options, such as no right justification and a very plain typeface.

Computers are also allowing researchers to think about representation of their data in more experimental forms through hypertext and hypermedia. In ethnographies of the future, the "reader" may be able to interact with text, data, and applicable literature, moving at his or her desire from narrative to field notes to audio reproduction of an interview to images to methodological notes. By the click of a button, the reader would choose his or her own unique path through the research.

COMPUTER SOFTWARE

Qualitative researchers have appropriated existing computer programs, adapting them to their own purposes, and are increasingly developing new software programs to meet their needs. This section begins with examples of adapting other programs.

1. *Word processing programs* can be used (although inefficiently) to code and sort data. After reading the text and developing a code book, you can systematically code the text files by inserting code words or numbers where appropriate. The code should be a unique string of characters that would not normally appear in the text. For example, "tea" would not be a good code choice for "teacher issues" because, through search commands, you would get every instance of the three characters *t, e, a* in the text, including words such as "instead" or "tease." A better choice would be something like "TCHISS." Using search, block, and move commands, you could later sort your files according to your codes, making sure to identify source and data information for each datum as you do so.

2. *Database managers* are programs in which data are entered according to a structured format. Although best at handling numeric data, most programs will also accept a minimal amount of text data.

   The general idea behind database managers is that you design a form which simulates an index card marked by key words. After entering data on the form, you can sort by words or numbers (e.g., date, age, sex). Programs vary by how many characters are allowed per form. Some allow only one page, others up to ten pages. Also, depending on the software, it may or may not be easy to alter the format for recording data.

   Database managers are particularly useful for keeping records of fieldwork. You can create a form to record the fieldwork activities deemed important. For example, to keep track of interview procedures, you could record the number of the interview session, the date, the name (or pseudonym) of the interviewee, the time the interview took, the role of the interviewee, the date of transcription, and other information (see Exhibit 7.8). Such a format would help you to keep track of your research activities. With each interview, you would add a line. Depending on the program, you might even add columns as you discover helpful aspects to include.

EXHIBIT 7.8
Example Form for Keeping Interview Records

Date Number	Date Interviewed	Interviewee	Transcribed	Time	Role	Subject	Note
18	4/8/91	C. Perez	4/10/91	1.5	teacher	math	—
19	4/9/91	D. Brown	4/10/91	.5	admin.	—	late; not completed
20	4/9/91	M. Levine	4/20/91	1.0	teacher	history	—

3. *Spreadsheets* were initially developed for accounting tasks. Spreadsheet programs create tables in which you label each vertical column and each horizontal row, and fill in the resulting cells with data. These programs produce matrices, which can be useful in various stages of data collection and analysis. For example, in the planning stage of a study in group homes for adults with developmental disabilities, the rows of the matrix could be the three group homes you intend to visit. The columns could be characteristics of the group homes that are of interest to you, such as size, number of residents, use of recreational facilities, and involvement in meal preparation. As data are collected, you could add more columns of relevant characteristics. The matrix helps to summarize the data collected, showing similarities and differences among the cases and illuminating missing information.
4. *Graphics* packages assist you in creating charts, tables, graphs, and diagrams.
5. *Qualitative software* have been developed particularly for use with qualitative data. Each is used for coding, searching and sorting as a part of data analysis; each has different features. Here I briefly describe working with *The Ethnograph, HyperQual2,* and *NUD.IST,* but urge you to consult Tesch (1990) and Weitzman and Miles (1995) for more information on these and other programs. For example in *Computer Programs for Qualitative Data Analysis,* Weitzman and Miles review 24 computer programs and cluster them into 5 groups: text retrievers, text base managers, code and retrieve programs, code-based theory-builders, and conceptual network-builders.

Qualitative software programs are designed, in general, for assisting in descriptive and interpretive analysis and theory building. *The Ethnograph* and *HyperQual2* focus on enabling descriptive/interpretive analysis. When using *The Ethnograph,* the researcher transfers all field notes and data files from a word processing program to *The Ethnograph* program. The program numbers the lines in a file and formats the file with a large right margin. Reading and rereading the data, the researcher creates a code book and then, on a printed copy of the numbered file, begins to assign codes to chunks of text. Using *The Ethnograph*'s coding capability, the researcher then enters line numbers and the assigned code words into the program. More than one code word can be entered for the same start line number, allowing more than one code word to be assigned to the same segment or to overlapping segments. With code words and line numbers entered, the researcher can sort data files by codes or combinations of codes.

Many of these basic functions provided by *The Ethnograph* are also fulfilled by *HyperQual2,* for Macintosh users. Both are considered "code-and-retrieve" programs, in that each software tool provides a structure for organizing, coding, and sorting data. In *HyperQual2,* however, the researcher may choose to enter data directly into the program, rather than transferring word processing documents into it. *HyperQual2* also provides two different modes for entering and managing data within the program. The first mode works with structured data, such as responses to an interview format. The second mode works with continuous text such as field notes. Although more complex and powerful than indicated by these brief descriptions, these programs' main contribution is in the sorting of coded data.

NUD.IST is a software program designed for theory building or developing systematic relationships among code categories. An acronym for Non-numerical Unstructured Data Indexing, Searching and Theory-building, *NUD.IST* enables users to develop indexing systems, or sophisticated organizing structures of their codes, which become an integral piece of the researcher's analytic work. Such systems are created in the form of inverted tree structures and allow unlimited complexity. While *The Ethnograph* and *HyperQual2* permit codes and their attached text segments to be created and stored in their own files, *NUD.IST* provides a separate database to store the codes and to note their place and relationship in the overall structure (Tesch 1990). As with coding in *The Ethnograph* and *HyperQual2,* the arrangement of codes into complex structures by the *NUD.IST* program is not done automatically by the computer. The researcher must first specify the codes and their relationships.

In summary, the computer is a tool for executing the mechanical or clerical tasks of qualitative research. It can help to make the researcher's work less tedious, more accurate, faster, and more thorough. It does not, however, think for the researcher. The researcher decides what to enter into the computer, what to ask it to do, and how to use the results of the computer's mechanical manipulations. The products of computer-assisted analysis are only as good as the data, the thinking, and the level of care that went into them.

Making Connections

Qualitative researchers use many techniques (such as coding, data displays, and computer programs) to help organize, classify, and find themes in their data, but they still must find ways to make connections that are ultimately meaningful to themselves and the reader. Wolcott (1994) discusses *description, analysis,* and *interpretation* as three means of data transformation, or of moving from organization to meaning. Description involves staying close to data as originally recorded. You draw heavily on field notes and interview transcripts, allowing the data to somewhat "speak for themselves" (10). This approach answers the question, "What is going on here?" (12) and the narratives of descriptive analysis often "move in and out like zoom lenses" (17), selecting and portraying details that resonate with the study's purposes.

Furney (1997) researched the implementation of special education reform in several elementary public schools. She includes description throughout her text as one means to convey the findings in her cross-case analysis. The following example is from observations of Instructional Support Team (IST) meetings:

> Balancing their lunch trays on their knees (somehow that cafeteria smell of hot dogs, applesauce, and lukewarm milk never changes in schools), Andy and Danielle describe the positive things that have happened for Kevin over the last week. They tell us about the points he's earned for using good language, his recent triumph over a classmate in a computer game, and how they and Kevin resolved an issue on the playground. Kevin describes his recent trip to the Woolworth store in town where he and his friend George perused the aisles looking for ways that Kevin could spend the money he has been earning restocking the soda machines in the teacher's room at school. (97)

Furney's narrative includes carefully chosen details to place the reader in the context of an IST meeting in one of the schools.

Wolcott (1994) describes *analysis* as a second category of data transformation. Analysis, according to Wolcott, is the identification of key factors in the study and the relationships among them. This method typically extends description in a systematic manner. It entails identifying essential features and the ways in which the features interact. Detailed coding schemes, data displays, comparisons to a standard, and other means of identifying patterned regularities are all useful in analysis. Note that the use of the term *analysis* is a bit confusing here since researchers (myself included) often refer to description, finding patterns, and interpretation as data *analysis,* rather than data transformation. Nonetheless, Wolcott's (1994) discussion is useful and I recommend his text, *Transforming Qualitative Data: Description, Analysis, and Interpretation,* for a more in-depth discussion.

Furney's (1997) study provides many examples of analysis (as described by Wolcott) throughout the text:

> The evolution of the Instructional Support Teams (ISTs) in the three schools raises some interesting points. On the one hand, the three principals spoke during the original and follow-up interviews about the positive aspects of naturally occurring collaborative structures that appeared to lessen the need for the more formal IST structure. On the other hand, they viewed the somewhat more formalized versions of their ISTs that had evolved over time as being necessary and generally positive. (142)

This consideration of the principals' views of instructional support teams moves away from description towards identification of patterns or trends in the data.

Interpretation is Wolcott's (1994) third means of data transformation. He notes that interpretation occurs when the researcher "transcends factual data and cautious analysis and begins to probe into what is to be made of them" (36). He discusses several strategies for data interpretation, including extending the analysis, using theory to provide structure, connecting with personal experience, and exploring alternative means of presenting data.

Once more, Furney's (1997) research provides an example of this mode of data transformation:

> In brief then, the schools in this study of Act 230 have helped to confirm my belief that caring for students should constitute the central purpose of education and guide its efforts to change. . . . In placing students at the center of the agenda for school reform, a host of related changes become apparent. The challenge to care for students implies an agenda to promote social justice and deal with issues of diversity. . . . Placing care at the center of a school also seems to require the establishment of a form of leadership that is both visionary and participatory, and creates a sense of shared responsibility and an openness to change. (174–175)

In this example, Furney moves beyond description and analysis to probe into the framework of caring. As she asserts the role of caring as the central purpose of education, she presents an interpretation of her findings.

Data transformation is of course an invariable aspect of all types of research, qualitative or otherwise. It is the effort of researchers to manage and make sense of their data, to transform it from its acquired form—at which point it is perhaps more accurately called "information"—into a form that communicates the promise of a study's findings. These forms include (but are far from exhausted by) description, analysis, interpretation, evaluation, and theory, which researchers may develop, augment, or contradict.

Examples abound of esteemed work conducted by scholars in the fields of education (Heath 1983; Lightfoot 1983; Metz 1978; Schofield 1989; Willis 1977), anthropology (Behar 1993; Geertz 1973; Mead 1949; Myerhoff 1979), and sociology (Becker, Geer, Hughes, and Strauss 1961; Gans 1962; Macleod 1987; Mills 1951) that testify to the considerable breadth of outcomes from qualitative studies. Data transformation, accordingly, is the prelude to sensitive, comprehensive outcomes that describe, identify patterns, make connections, and contribute to greater understanding.

Trustworthiness of Your Interpretations

In his article on James Agee, author of *Let Us Now Praise Famous Men*, Hersey cites reviewers of Agee's book, concluding with a quotation from Mrs. Burroughs, a woman from one of the tenant families portrayed in the book: "And I took it home and I read it plumb through. And when I read it plumb through I give it back to her and I said, Well everything in there's true. What they wrote in there was true" (in Hersey 1988, 74).

James Agee would have been pleased to learn that Mrs. Burroughs affirmed his interpretations of her life. You want your interpretations to be trustworthy, to be affirmed by the Mrs. Burroughses in your research lives and also by your colleagues. Mrs. Burroughs may just be pleased that Agee understood her life. When your colleagues also believe this, they use your work in the range of ways that trusted outcomes can be used—to confirm, expand, and inform their own work—and thereby contribute to the accumulative nature of knowledge.

The credibility of your findings and interpretations depends upon your careful attention to establishing trustworthiness. Lincoln and Guba (1985) describe prolonged engagement (spending sufficient time at your research site) and persistent observation (focusing in detail on those elements that are most relevant to your study) as critical in attending to credibility. "If prolonged engagement provides scope, persistent observation provides depth" (304). With each, time is a major factor in the acquisition of trustworthy data. Time at your research site, time spent interviewing, and time building sound relationships with respondents all contribute to trustworthy data. When a large amount of time is spent with your research participants, they less readily feign behavior or feel the need to do so; moreover, they are more likely to be frank and comprehensive about what they tell you.

Continual alertness to your own biases, your own subjectivity (see Chapter 5), also assists in producing more trustworthy interpretations. Consider your subjectivity within the context of the trustworthiness of your findings. Ask yourself a series of questions: Whom do I not see? Whom have I seen less often? Where do I not go? Where have I gone less often? With whom do I have special relationships, and in what light would they interpret phenomena? What data collecting means have I not used that could provide additional insight? Triangulated findings contribute to credibility. As described in Chapter 2, triangulation may involve the use of multiple data collection methods, sources, investigators, or theoretical perspectives. To improve trustworthiness, you can also consciously search for negative cases. "I didn't confirm all of my opinions, which was nice," said Andrea in the final report of her community study. "Maybe there is some validity to what I found."

As you are planning, collecting and analyzing data, and writing up your findings, do not forget the invaluable assistance of others. Ask friends and colleagues to work with portions of your data—developing codes, applying your codes, or interpreting field notes to check your perceptions. To promote trustworthiness, Lincoln and Guba (1985) suggest a procedure for enlisting an outsider to "audit" fieldwork notes and subsequent analysis and interpretations.

You can also share the interpretive process with research respondents, as a form of member checking. Researchers, as a matter of courtesy, often give respondents copies of interview transcripts for their approval. Obtaining the reactions of respondents to your working drafts is time-consuming, but respondents may (1) verify that you have reflected their perspectives; (2) inform you of sections that, if published, could be problematic for either personal or political reasons; and (3) help you to develop new ideas and interpretations. For example, when Penny compiled her participant observation notes into a "day-in-the-life" of an effective, middle-level partner team, she shared the initial draft with team members. They reflected on the accuracy of the depiction, as well as noted patterns of behavior of which they were previously unaware. In her field notes (May 1997), Penny wrote:

> I'm glad I took the opportunity to share my writing with Liza and Hope. They really helped me feel confident that my perceptions of their relational work are an accurate representation by their standards as well. I think they got something out of it too, as they laughingly noticed their tendency to phrase ideas as questions, to unconsciously rotate the facilitation of class discussion, to be up front about concerns, and to finish one another's sentences.

By sharing working drafts, both researcher and researched may grow in their interpretations of the phenomena around them.

Part of demonstrating the trustworthiness of your data is to realize the limitations of your study. Your responsibility is to do the best that you can under certain circumstances. Detailing those circumstances helps readers to understand the nature of your data. Discuss what documents or people or places were unavailable to you. Discuss what is peculiar about your site or respondent selection that could show the phenomena of interest in some lights but not in others. Approach the description of your study's limitations as part of setting the context. Limitations are consistent with the always partial state of knowing in social research, and elucidating your limitations helps readers know how they should read and interpret your work.

Conclusions

Qualitative researchers must decide what the payoff of their research can and will be. Depending on the existing state of knowledge about their topic, they may make a contribution that includes a full range, from the descriptive to the theoretical. In *Cross Creek,* Rawlings writes that a person "may learn a great deal of the general from studying the specific, whereas it is impossible to know the specific by studying the general" (1942, 359). Qualitative inquirers look to the specific, both to understand it in particular and to understand something of the world in general. From the positivist's point of view, the respondent pool in qualitative research is too limited for development of generalizations. The particular case that you study in qualitative research, however, is likely to contribute to an understanding of similar cases, such that going beyond the case in your ruminations will not be farfetched. (See Wehlage, 1981, for more on making generalizations in qualitative inquiry.)

In short, researchers conduct qualitative studies not merely for their own sake, but rather in the reasonable hope of bringing something grander than the case to the attention of others. Researchers hope for a description and analysis of its complexity that identify concepts not previously seen or fully appreciated.

This chapter concludes with an excerpt from a paper written by Gordon. He had completed his course-based research project and was reflecting on the analysis process, of which writing—the next topic for discussion—was a part.

> The paper is written, the computer clicks softly to itself as it cools after its long ordeal, and my cards lie scattered over the floor and desk. The paper lies in my briefcase in its bright blue cover, ready to be read and reviewed. It is done! It is over! Now what?
>
> After filling every waking moment with analysis and writing, leisure causes a kind of withdrawal. What does one say to one's wife and family? What does one do with all that time? I feel compelled to turn on the computer, to fill the blank screen with words once more. My mind is locked into the analysis mode, examining menus, cereal boxes, and junk mail and placing them in precise matrices. I compulsively buy and hoard 5×8 cards and glue sticks. I need to break the cycle, to fight my way back to the normal life of the nonresearcher. What to do?
>
> What else can I do? I'll analyze the process.
>
> My first thoughts concern the holistic nature of the process. There really is no way to separate the parts of research from one another. Data gathering includes parts of analysis, analysis leads to more data, writing leads to a greater understanding of both analysis and data. The process is totally holistic, each piece absolutely necessary to the whole. I am reminded of this as I stoop to pick up my cards, the various coding categories scribbled off, edges bent, and the writing illegible. How do you analyze information you can't read? One thing seems to be certain: Next time I begin the analysis as I do the data gathering. To separate the two processes by three months doesn't work. All the soft nuances are gone, the tones and the shades of meaning are missing.
>
> Another interesting discovery is that the writing process actually is an important part of the analysis. A lot of my insights and much of the understanding I gained from my research data came through the writing process. For me, writing is the final organization of my thoughts. Next time I will begin writing sooner.

A final thought is that matrices really help. By organizing my data into matrices, I was able to see in two or three dimensions. I realized only at this point that my really profound data concerned peer pressure on children, not parental pressures. Next time I will use more matrices.

This is a small first step on my way back to reality. By this time next week, the hours of writing and preparation will only be a fond dream that fades ever into the dust of newer crises. And yet, if I could only rewrite page 7, I bet I could . . .

Exercises

CLASS EXERCISES

1. Return to the class *Research Practice* exercise (Chapters 2 and 4). With interview transcripts in hand, create a code book for the interviews. Begin in small groups, agreeing on major and minor codes. Then, as a whole class, look at the ways each small group coded the interviews. Discuss the different kinds of stories each coding scheme might tell. Eventually, come to an agreement on a class coding scheme. Then each student should code, with the class coding scheme, the interview that he or she conducted.
2. Take the coded interviews from the above practice exercise. Cut and sort by major codes. Divide the class into small groups, each group receiving the data from one or more major code. Groups then work with the data associated with their code/s: sorting by minor codes and looking for patterns, relationships, further categorizations. Make note of analytical findings. Hold onto these clumps of coded data for a future exercise.

INDIVIDUAL EXERCISES

1. Most likely you have not yet collected all your pilot data (the process of access, scheduling, and data collection is taking longer than you ever dreamed). Nonetheless, begin with what you have and start creating your own code book and keep note of analytical thoughts.
2. Remember the research diagram you did when working on your research statement? Without looking at it, diagram your research now, incorporating the sense you are making of observations, interviews, and other data. Compare the diagrams. Reflect in your field log on what you have learned about your topic, making notes of particular gaps or questions that remain.

Chapter 8

Writing Your Story: What Your Data Say

. . . one hopes that one's case will touch others. But how to connect? Not by calculation, I think, not by the assumption that in the pain of my toothache, or my father's, or Harry Crosby's, I have discovered a "universal condition of consciousness." One may merely know that no one is alone and hope that a singular story, as every true story is singular, will in the magic way of some things apply, connect, resonate, touch a major chord. (Pachter 1981, 72)

Writing gives form to the researcher's clumps of carefully categorized and organized data. It links together thoughts that have been developing throughout the research process. The act of writing also stimulates new thoughts, new connections. Writing is rewarding in that it creates the product, the housing for the meaning that you and others have made of your research endeavor. Writing is about constructing a text. As a writer, you engage in a sustained act of construction, which includes selecting a particular "story" to tell from the data you have analyzed, and creating the literary form that you believe best conveys your story (Denny 1978). It perhaps matters to some—but needs no resolution—whether the researcher's construction is more like that of an architect, proceeding from a vision embodied in a plan, or like that of a painter, whose vision emerges over time from intuition, sense, and feeling. For many, constructing a text is quite possibly some combination of both plan and intuition.

This chapter touches on intuition, but it focuses on strategies for writing, questions of form and style, and responsibilities of the writer.

Roles of the Writer

By the time we finish reading a good ethnography, adroit rationalization has made familiar what at first seemed strange, the other, and has estranged us from what we thought we knew, ourselves. (Shweder 1986, 38)

A woman once asked me to review and provide feedback on her dissertation work, which she was completing at another university. She had developed her interview questions (both closed- and open-ended) and had scheduled her interviews with a number of administrators throughout the nation, but had not yet collected any data. Nonetheless, she had compiled a document of nearly 200 pages, divided into five chapters: introduction to the problem, review of literature, methods, findings, and summary with recommendations. She had completed the first three chapters and much of the last two, leaving blank spaces for percentages and applicable phrases once the data were available.

I do not know how many dissertations and research reports are written this way; not many, I hope. Those that are cannot do justice to the data in that they forfeit interpretation. They neither show respect for the time and input of the respondents, nor call on the analytic and creative qualities of the writer. And they do not succeed in making the strange familiar or in estranging us from ourselves.

This section addresses three possible roles of the writer of qualitative inquiry: artist, translator/interpreter, and transformer. Although writers do not always play all three roles, they nonetheless should keep them in mind.

ARTIST

To make meaning of data, writers employ technical procedures that are to some extent routine and mechanical, but writers of good qualitative studies also are artists who create. In his edited book *Extraordinary Lives,* Zinsser states:

> [Research] is only research. After all the facts have been marshaled, all the documents studied, all the locales visited, all the survivors interviewed, what then? What do the facts add up to? What did the life mean? This was the central question for the six biographers, and to hear them wrestling with it was to begin to see where the craft crosses over into art. (1988a, 17–18)

Craft involves the strategies and procedures authors use to write their story. The form and style of the written presentation require artistic sensibilities, which seem to involve a mixture of discipline and creativity. As artists, qualitative researchers move into the murky terrain where others may regard them as journalists, fiction writers, or worse. As artists, they seek imaginative connections among events and people, imaginative renderings of these connections, and imaginative interpretations of what they have rendered. They do this not just in the worthy cause of making their work most accessible, but, in addition, to do full justice to what they have endeavored to understand. The next chapter focuses on artistic renderings in qualitative research.

TRANSLATOR/INTERPRETER

The qualitative researcher is sometimes described as a translator of culture. The researcher works to understand the others' world and then to translate the text of lived actions into a meaningful account. Although the translator metaphor suggests struggle with representing the nuances of meaning, it also implies that the researcher is an objective middleperson, rather than someone whose perspectives and personality affect the portrayed account. To the contrary, qualitative researchers are interpreters who draw on their own experiences, knowledge, theoretical dispositions, and collected data to present their understanding of the other's world. As interpreters, they think of themselves not as authority figures who get the "facts" on a topic, but as meaning makers who make sense out of the interaction of their own lives with those of research participants. "An ethnography," explains Shweder,

> begins with an ethnographic experience: with your eyes open you have to go somewhere. Yet a culture is never reducible to what meets the eye, and you can't get to ethnographic reality by just looking. A culture is like a black hole, those compacted stars whose intense gravitational forces don't let their own light particles escape. You can never know it's there by simply squinting your eyes and staring very hard at it. If it is real at all, you can know it only by inference and conjecture. (1986, 38)

Inference and conjecture are mainstays of the interpretive process. Inferences are made about the relationship of one thing to another, on the basis of carefully collected, carefully analyzed, trustworthy data.

Interpretations and their portrayal are limited by a number of factors that are increasingly acknowledged by qualitative researchers, but are not necessarily peculiar to them. In *Tales of the Field,* Van Maanen (1988, 4–6) discusses several of these limitations in depth:

First, in what ways does the experiential nature of the research process shape the final story? The experiences of the researcher with the setting and research participants form the basis for the interpretive account.

Second, how do political relationships shape the final interpretation? If the research is funded, what do sponsors want studied? What role does academic politics play? If the researcher has more power than the researched, what effect might the power relationship have on the data collected?

Third, what is the theoretical position of the researcher? Researchers all have a theoretical stance, although often somewhat implicit, which forms a lens through which they view social phenomena. They are also shaped by their disciplines and by academic trends and traditions. Their interpretations of social interactions and the readers' interpretations of their texts are limited or bounded by extant "structures of meaning" (see Clifford 1986; Marris 1974). If, for example, you view educational systems as "meritocracies," then you will interpret your data differently than if you see them through the conflict theorist's hegemonic eyes, a structure of meaning that is fairly recent to educational perspectives.

Fourth, how do narrative and rhetorical conventions limit the portrayal of the researcher's interpretations? Narrative and rhetorical conventions tend to be somewhat governed by the researcher's academic discipline. Political relationships may also play a role. For example, some dissertation committees may be reluctant to allow a doctoral student to write the work in any but traditional forms.

Fifth, in what ways does the lack of historical situating of observations and interviews limit the researcher's work? Culture does not stand still; it changes over time. An interpretive portrayal is often only several snapshots of a place and time and its people. It can be, however, a powerful and useful portrayal that focuses on processes that transcend static, descriptive accounts.

Sixth, and finally, how does the projected audience shape both the form and the substance of the researcher's product? The researcher may use tables and charts with one audience, but not with another. Or the researcher may use a disciplined-based language if writing for colleagues, but not for a more general group of people. Researchers tell different things in different ways to different people.

By being aware of forces that help shape your interpretations and their depictions, you can challenge some while simply acknowledging others. The point is to be as conscious as possible of both your prospects and your limitations.

TRANSFORMER

It is to the role of transformer—in the sense not of reformer but rather of catalytic educator—that writers of qualitative research rightfully aspire. As others read your story, you want them to identify with the problems, worries, joys, and dreams that are the collective human lot. By reflecting on themselves and their families, friends, and associates, they acquire new insights and perspectives on some aspect of human interaction. Although not your primary purpose, this process of learning about self through understanding others is a gift of qualitative research done well. Shweder (1986) states it poetically:

> Good ethnography is an intellectual exorcism in which, forced to take the perspective of the other, we are wrenched out of our self. We transcend ourselves, and for a brief moment we wonder who we are, whether we are animals, barbarians or angels, whether all things are really the same under the sun, whether it would be better if the other were us, or better if we were the other. (38)

Writing up your work so that it contributes to transformative experiences requires the application of disciplined procedures and artistic creativity to meaningful data. We now turn to the disciplined procedures of writing.

Strategies for Writing

GETTING STARTED

Most of us can find numerous excuses to postpone writing. We have to read more, see more, and talk more; we must recode and reanalyze; and, inevitably, we feel compelled to mop the floor, make a phone call, do anything to avoid sitting down and writing. That those who spend much of their life writing also experience anxiety over getting started may be of some comfort. The following words are Peshkin's, written January 18, 1988, while in the beginning stages of writing his ethnicity study:

The demons of escapism loom large, but I will not weaken, I say weakly. Also weekly. Also daily. Writing, it seems, is primarily a matter of dealing with demons. It is good to give the enemy a name so he can be dealt with, except if the demon is cleverly chameleonlike so that you never know what new form he will assume. Each day I come to this place where work and the demons abide. They always are together, like dust balls under beds. Each day I feel like I'm going off to war, though the previous day's battle does not necessarily prepare me for the next day's. Each new day brings a surprise: what form will the demon assume? Will he bring fatigue within twenty minutes of beginning; will he shunt my attention to a book only vaguely related to my work that I can't resist looking at; will he leave me staring at a particular note card, fixated for no obvious reason on a point that at any other moment would not claim ten seconds' notice? The demon is clever; outsmarting him demands energy that he leaves me short of by diverting my attention and effort to other matters. I backslide, lord of writing. I desert your hallowed ranks for lesser gods parading in irresistible forms. I yearn for faithfulness, while doubting my yearning. Perhaps tomorrow I will be a warrior of the pen—whoever heard of a warrior of the word processor?—wielding a mighty sword that vanquishes demons. But I know that when my pen becomes sword, the demon becomes liquid and my sword creates no more than a splash. From swish to splash is no way to subdue demons. Only writing is exorcism.

So, while the novice procrastinates (and, in the process, prolongs the anxiety), those with more experience write. As the Portuguese proverb goes, "When there is no wind, row."

It helps to know that writing, like data analysis, is not a discrete step in the qualitative research process. Ideally, and not at all unrealistically, you should write throughout the time of data collection and analysis. Long before you begin a phase of work that you can call "write-up time," you should be writing. In fact, it is useful to be conscious at the outset of a research project that it will culminate in words, sentences, paragraphs, pages, and chapters. Distant though it may be, this culmination will arrive. Aware that it will, you should look and listen, analyze and interpret, and be attuned to the prospect that the results will be words to be read. Your efforts to collect data and make something of them should be in the spirit of a quest for what will appear in written form.

If you follow this advice, then you will have stacks of field notes and research memos, many containing well-developed thoughts in usable paragraph form. A time will come, however, when more of your effort will be put into writing than anything else. This time is often preceded by feelings of intense anxiety manifested in a variety of ways and labeled "writer morassity" by a student research support group in Vermont for whom metaphors of bogs, swamps, and slow drownings recurred. Woods refers to the "pain threshold" of writing, asserting that researchers must be masochists who confront the pain barrier till it hurts as they rework ideas that seemed brilliant before exposed to paper. He likens the suffering that the writer feels to that of other artists, and urges them to view the anxiety as a rite of passage that "is as much a test of self as anything else" (Woods 1986, 171). The writer gearing up for writing is often unsociable and ill-tempered while sorting and resorting data, trying to organize thoughts for writing.

Writing is a lonely process. While writing about people and social processes, you paradoxically remove yourself from the world of human beings. This estrangement is functional in two ways: First, you need to be by yourself because you need time to concentrate on writing. Woods observes that "research may benefit teaching, but the converse does not apply" (1985, 88) because assisting others distracts one from focusing on one's own work. Those who try to write dissertations or other research reports while "on the job" are likely to agree. Most writers do best with daily periods of extended time set aside for writing.

Second, estrangement is also functional in that it separates you from the research site. The distancing helps you to approach writing from a perspective that is more global than situation-specific:

> If one does not distance oneself from them [research participants], then there is a danger of being unable to dismantle the data, select from them, and re-order the material. One is left in the position of someone who, when asked to comment on and criticize a film or novel, can do no more than rehearse the plot. The ethnographer who fails to achieve distance will easily fall into the trap of recounting "what happened" without imposing a coherent thematic or analytic framework. (Hammersley and Atkinson 1983, 212–213)

So writers withdraw, immersed in their data and thoughts about their others, intending to give form and meaning to that which they have observed and heard and read.

Several strategies can help you deal with the anxiety and alienation that accompany beginning to write (see also Becker 1986b; Lamott 1994; Murray 1986; Richardson 1990; Ueland 1987; Wolcott 1990; Woods 1985, 1986; Zinsser 1988b):

1. Develop a long-term schedule with realistic deadlines. Expect to spend as much time, if not more, in focused data analysis and writing as you spend in data collection. You need time to play with the data and your words, to share drafts with research participants and colleagues, and to rework drafts a number of times. You need time, as well, to do justice to the considerable investment you have made in planning your study and collecting your data.

2. Develop a short-term schedule. Figure out when you are most creative in your writing. If possible, make appointments with yourself to write for three to four hours, four to five days per week. Expand the hours when you can. Some authors, with more flexible schedules, set a number of pages to be written each day rather than an amount of time to work. Somewhere around five double-spaced typed pages a day is a reasonable amount, unless you have nothing else to do but write.

3. Set aside a place for writing where you will be as free as possible of interruptions and distractions. When you go there, do not make phone calls, or write letters, or read books. Write.

4. Be prepared to write at other times and places. Many days become fragmented, with numerous short periods of unproductive time. Keep a notebook (or note cards) with you and stay open to ideas concerning your pro-

ject. Jot down your thoughts when they strike you, whether in the midst of a boring meeting, or riding the bus home, or working on something else. Murray (1986) suggests using fragments of time to make lists, notes, and diagrams; collect quotes; sketch outlines; and draft titles and key paragraphs.

5. Begin by editing yesterday's writing. Writers tend to need a gearing-up period before getting started. They find that editing what they wrote the day before helps them get into the new day's work, keeps the flow consistent, and assists in producing a better draft. Beginning by editing yesterday's writing not only lets you know exactly where to start today, but also allows you to revise that which seemed perfectly clear as it was written but may appear obscure a very short time afterward.

6. When stuck, read your work aloud. Reading aloud reveals the rhythm, flow and tone of the piece and often helps to form the thoughts and words that will follow.

7. When stuck, write. Write without concern for syntax, coherence, or logic. Write to work out ideas and thoughts; play with form and style later. It helps to acquire the right "first-draft mentality," that is, the state of mind in which you give yourself permission to write without concern for appearances. You write this way knowing that you will revise later and clarify what may be very messy indeed. You write this way appreciating that it is best to produce a draft of any quality rather than be held back by premature concerns for form and style. A great obstacle to writing is holding inappropriately high standards for the quality of your early drafts, particularly your first draft. A standard that is too high will put you on the road to the paralysis of writer's block. Better to settle for a draft of *any* quality, trusting in revision to produce order, style, and worthy words.

Murray finds that taking the attitude of conversing with one's peers facilitates the flow of words:

> No publication is the final theological word on a subject. Too many academics believe they have to write *the* article or book on their topic. That is impossible. Each publication is merely a contribution to a continuous professional conversation. I was paralyzed by the idea that I had to deliver the Truth—Moses like; I began to write when I realized all I had to do was speculate, question, argue, create a model, take a position, define a problem, make an observation, propose a solution, illuminate a possibility to participate in a written conversation with my peers. (1986, 147)

The written-conversation idea is easily extended by choosing a person that you know—a friend, relative, or colleague—and writing with that person in mind.

8. When the written-conversation idea fails, don't underestimate the power of engaging in dialogue. Getting together with another person and talking through the statement "What I am really trying to say in this section is . . ." will often enable you to move beyond your sticking point.

9. Establish or join a writing group. Not only does this kind of interaction provide ongoing feedback; it helps to establish regular deadlines. As well-intentioned as you are in setting your own short- and long-term due dates, there is

nothing like having to be accountable to others to help you meet those deadlines.

10. Finally, immerse yourself in exemplary ethnographies and qualitative studies, as well as in novels, poetry, and great works of literature (during non-writing hours). Your reading provides models and sources of inspiration. "Read widely as well as deeply," advises Murray (1986, 149).

Once you have started writing, keep at it. The clumps of notes carefully organized and segregated by paper clips and rubber bands are the makings for the qualitative researcher's text. As your "to do" clumps shrink in number and your "done" box fills, you have evidence of progress.

KEEPING AT IT

In Beryl Markham's conception of progress,

> A word grows to a thought—a thought to an idea—an idea to an act. The change is slow, and the Present is a sluggish traveler loafing in the path Tomorrow wants to take. ([1942] 1983, 154)

You should not wait until you know exactly what the words, thoughts, ideas, and acts should be before beginning to write. Writing "helps people generate, develop, organize, modify, critique, and remember their ideas" (Fulwiler 1985, 23). British historian Sir Steven Runciman emphasizes the role of writing in forming ideas: "When I'm writing, I'm dealing with something being revealed to me all the time. I get the insight when I'm actually having to try to put it into words" (in Plante 1986, 78). Writing helps to develop your thoughts and ideas and to discover what you know and how much more there is to know. Therefore, it is best to begin sooner rather than later.

Although you may begin writing with an overall organizational plan in the form of chapters, the act of writing is likely to reshape the plan, reorganize the pieces, subsume some sections, and add others. For example, the process of writing restructured Peshkin's outline for his ethnicity book:

> I am thinking I see benefits of being immersed. I think being immersed in writing is like being immersed in anything—you are never far from the work, you have continuity, thoughts get thought that might not get thought at all or not until much later. The latest appearance of a gain—breakthrough would be too strong—was the relegation of what was to be an entire chapter, Chapter 5, to a *part* of a chapter, Chapter 1. A chapter on the "town today" struck me as more fitting for the introductory stuff I have put in Chapter 1.
>
> So thinking, when I want to arrange the clump of notes, I was thinking small—part of a chapter, rather than big—an entire chapter. So thinking, I discarded lots of data that I'd originally put in the "town today" clump. Which is to say, I have a lot less to write and can look forward to soon getting on to real Chapter 5, which now looks to be "education today," having done "education history" in Chapter 4. What is becoming clear is that my

chapter outline, made when I had finished all coding, holds up only until I prepare to write a new chapter. Then, in light of the previous chapters done, I know whether the new one will fit next as the chapter, fit elsewhere as a chapter, fit somewhere as a part of a chapter, or fit nowhere at all. (Peshkin, personal notes, 24 May 1988)

Writing up data is a continual process of organizing and reorganizing the data as you work through what they are telling you. Begin on a macro-level: after coding all of your data, work with the codes to make an overall outline. The outline organizes the data and assigns data clumps (the coded bits of paper, note cards, computer printouts, and documents) to chapters or major sections. Somewhat like the Russian doll within a doll, your organizational steps should be repeated within each chapter and then within each chapter subsection.

Once your writing begins, the bits of paper within the carefully sorted clumps will look different. No longer homogeneous, they must be sorted into subclumps that make up each subsection of the text. For example, suppose you have a major code on "resolving conflict" for a study of first-year principals. Under "resolving conflict," you further categorize the data by techniques used, such as "holding meetings," "using humor," "turning the matter over to others," and "ignoring the situation." Now suppose that within the subclump "turning the matter over to others," you learn that first-year principals sometimes turn budget conflicts over to the school board, but personnel conflicts over to the superintendent. Your data scraps could be arranged accordingly. To write up your data, you must continuously, progressively code.

All data scraps do not necessarily end up where originally filed. As you work with the data, you may move individual pieces to a place that makes more sense now that you are writing; or you may relegate them to a miscellaneous pile that you scan at the beginning and end of each chapter or major section to see if something fits. Or you may file them in a discard box, concluding that they really are tangential to your story. Through this progressive coding process, you increasingly impose order on your data. Yet, at the same time, the order is flexible; it continuously changes, shaped by the ideas that your writing generates.

Not only are you imposing order on your data at this stage, but also you are engaging in the analytical process of selecting which data of all the data you collected to use in the text. Wolcott (1990, 18) describes this as "the painful task" of letting go of data. "The trick," he states, "is to discover essences and then to reveal those essences with sufficient context, yet not become mired trying to include everything that might possibly be described" (35). Ask your committee members to describe the most wearisome qualitative research paper or dissertation they have read. Most likely they will depict reports where authors felt compelled to insert seemingly every quote collected in list-like fashion with little interpretation or analysis. Kvale (1996) provides eight guidelines for reporting interview quotes (266–267). I emphasize three: (1) Quotes should not make up more than half the text in any descriptive or analytical chapter; (2) quotes should be kept short, ordinarily no more than half a page; and (3) quotes should be interpreted with the researcher clearly stating what perspective they illuminate (266). Of course, these are not hard and fast rules. A whole chapter, for example, may be primarily the edited words of an interviewee. As guidelines, however, they may assist you to let go of some of your data.

Discussing the organizational procedures of your writing is relatively easier than discussing what makes it more than a linear report of what you did and what you found. Your writing must develop how you interpret what you found by carefully integrating themes that support a thesis and create or augment theoretical explanations. No mechanical procedure exists for doing so. Rather, you must be so immersed in your data that you are open to those flashes of insight that come when least expected. Such moments make connections and provide perspectives that allow the pieces to fall into place.

DRAFTS AND REVISIONS

Expect your work to go through a number of drafts before it reflects the polish of a well-crafted manuscript. The first draft of your manuscript is like a roughly hewn form emerging from a block of wood as a sculptor works. To make the form a work of art, the sculptor carefully continues to shape the form, creating details, smoothing rough spots, and polishing the overall piece. Successive drafts do the same for the author's words. When your first draft is completed, read it for overall cohesion and then add, move, or eliminate sections as needed. In another reading, focus on the clarity of your theories and descriptions. With more readings, tighten, sharpen, and brighten (Trimble, in Jeske 1984) your work: Tighten by eliminating unnecessary words. Sharpen by reworking passive statements and employing precise and lively words. Brighten by simile and metaphor, by wit and lively description. Grammar, spelling, and punctuation should also get a turn.

Do not overlook the contribution of a reading that attends to subheadings. Subheadings benefit both author and reader. Scan your subheadings to check the order of the parts within each chapter. Try listing all of your subheads on a separate page, then reconsider their most effective, most logical order. In addition, name any previously unnamed sections; then reexamine the content and the order of paragraphs and pages within that section. Although unnamed sections may be easy for you to make order of—easy because the words are yours and you are familiar with them—that is not the case for the reader. With only two subheadings to structure thirty-eight typed pages, for example, too much of your chapter is left unstructured.

Artisans sometimes have assistants who help in certain stages of crafting a work. Qualitative researchers have colleagues or peers and research participants who play invaluable roles in polishing the final product. Enlist them to respond to your interpretations, ideas, and forms of expression, and allow time for such input in the shaping of your manuscript. Choose someone who is comfortable enough with your relationship to be honest and direct with you.

The Text: Questions of Style

VARIETY IN TEXT ORGANIZATION

Marleen Pugach spent a year doing her ethnography of a school in a town on the border between United States and Mexico. In considering questions of text organization, Marleen pondered how, out of the many possible ways to tell her story, she was going to frame her data:

> The analogy, it seems to me, is the making a movie analogy . . . that you need miles and miles of film to edit it down to something respectable. And I need all of this "stuff," my transcripts, field notes, newspaper clippings, and documents so I can figure out how to use the best of it all wisely, and set it within a framework that makes sense . . . and that I create. This is the challenging and scary part . . . the framework. Of course the transcripts and the rest of the data tell the story, but in reality I tell the story and these data, while they are the guts of the story, are used in the service of the framework. I'm not suggesting that the framework comes out of nowhere, or is just a creation of my fertile imagination, but just that the great subjectivity of it all is very much on my mind. This balancing of the data and one's own view is really at the heart of the task, isn't it? We gloss it over by reminding people not to get "wedded" to their categories too quickly, to let the story "emerge" from the data. But in a way these are very glib attempts to describe what is a terrifically delicate process—writing a real story, a consistent story, a true-to-the-data story that makes sense both to the local population and to the readers who have never been there. As the researcher, you have been there. And you are in a very powerful position in terms of how you frame all of the data you are now in possession of. This is VERY hard work. (personal correspondence, 1994)

Creating the frame for your data is hard work and, as Marleen observes, it is not just a matter of what your data "say," but of what you *and* your data say. The researcher's frame, however organized, generally falls into one of several ethnographic conventions. Van Maanen (1988) discusses, in particular, the realist, confessional, and impressionist conventions in his book *Tales of the Field*. The next chapter expands upon forms of writing-up inquiry. To some extent, the type of tale determines the voice and style of writing. To a lesser extent, it shapes text organization, the focus of this section.

Hammersley and Atkinson (1983) identify several strategies that authors use to organize their presentation of qualitative research. These strategies are useful starting points for thinking about text organization; you may choose to use more than one of the strategies within the same text, or use other organizational techniques altogether.

In the *natural history* approach, the text re-creates the fieldwork process of exploration and discovery. Through this technique, the author can dramatically portray a sense of people and place and their interactions with the researcher (typical of impressionistic tales). The natural history approach is not useful, however, for description and analysis of research themes.

In the *chronology* technique, "the pattern follows some 'developmental cycle,' 'moral career,' or 'timetable' characteristic of the setting or actors under investigation" (Hammersley and Atkinson 1983, 217). If the passage of time is particularly critical to the study, then the chronology technique is appropriate. For example, Peshkin's (1982a) book *The Imperfect Union* chronicles the struggle between a village and a school board over the closing of the village's only remaining school.

Another technique involves narrowing and expanding the focus. The author moves from descriptive detail to theoretical abstraction or vice versa. Like a zoom lens, the text glides through various levels of generality. Spradley advocates this technique when he identifies six levels of statements that he believes should be a part of ethnographic writing. The levels range from universal statements about human beings and their cultural or environmental situation to incident-specific statements (Spradley 1979, 207–210). The writer, says Spradley, must move back and forth through the various levels. Accounts written only at the more general levels will be dry and dull with no examples to ground theoretical statements. In contrast, those written at the more specific levels may make for interesting reading, but fall short of analyzing the cultural significance of the data.

Yet another organizational technique is to separate narration and analysis, as in Willis's (1977) *Learning to Labor*. He first engages the reader with a narrative account of the research setting that is rich in dialogue, events, and interaction. Then the writing style changes dramatically as he develops his theories with detailed analysis of the data.

Probably the most frequently used technique is organization by themes or topics. By analyzing the data, the researcher generates a typology of concepts, gives them names or uses "native" labels, and then discusses them one by one, illustrating with descriptive detail.

Some writers have found that amalgamations are useful to present certain descriptive data. Researchers who have spent months "shadowing" a few people may amalgamate the observed activities into a "typical day" for each participant (see Flinders 1987; Peshkin 1972). Ashton and Webb (1986) analyze interview and observation data from a number of people, discover categories or types of respondents, and then develop descriptive portraits of each type through amalgamation.

Glaser (1978) emphasizes the need to focus on the concepts and processes relevant to the study. Places, people, and their interactions are constantly changing, but concepts and processes have duration and are the building blocks of developing theory. Related to Glaser's ideas is the question of how to handle case studies. Barbara, for example, prepared four case studies of persons who had chronic lung disease. Her research question related to compliance with prescribed medical regimens. Should she organize her data to devote a separate chapter to each case; should she identify major concepts and processes from each case and devote a separate chapter to each; or should she do both, to some extent? An answer, such as there may be to these questions, would consider what is gained and lost by each of these three approaches. On one hand, the cases kept intact might illuminate understandings and insights about the process of compliance that would be lost if they were sliced up into corroborating data for general points. On the other hand, the general points about compliance might be what represent the greatest potential contribution of the cases. Beyond the agreement that research must make a contribution, neither Barbara nor the rest of us have the luxury of an agreement that specifies what that contribution must be and what organizational procedure for writing thereby follows.

Data display in tables, charts, or graphs can supplement text by introducing or summarizing categories discussed in detail in the text. Exhibit 8.1, adapted from my work in the Caribbean, exemplifies one way of illustrating theme categories that grew out of interviewees discussing their occupational desires for their children. (See Miles and Huberman 1994 for numerous examples of the graphic displays.)

However the substantive sections of a work are organized, they conventionally include an introduction and an ending. The introduction usually states the pur-

--------------------------------- EXHIBIT 8.1 ---------------------------------
Example of Theme Categories and Illustrative Responses

Occupational Desire Category and Illustrative Response	Number Who Agree
Something good (economically or in self-satisfaction) "Any kind of occupation that gives them satisfaction and joy."	10
It's up to them "I would not choose for my children."	10
Schooling first "Right now they must first further their education."	6
A life unlike mine "I want to bring him up so he doesn't have to hustle as I do, and let him have an open mind so he can learn easily without having to lie or fool anybody."	4

pose of the paper or book, presents the problem of inquiry, gives a general context to the problem, and foreshadows what is to come. Since many authors do not know with sufficient certainty what is to come until after they have written it, they often write the introduction last.

The ending should be a conclusion, which is quite different from a summary. "A summary is redundant and an affront to those readers who have actually read the paper, and a cop out for those who have not read it, however useful to them" (132). Summaries reiterate what has been said; conclusions deal with the "so whats." They stimulate thought and transcend the substantive content presented earlier. Glaser recommends using the conclusion as an opportunity to show the contribution of the work to formal theory by "brief comparative analysis with data from experience, knowledge and the literature, and by raising the conceptual level" (Glaser 1978, 133). Wolcott also emphasizes the importance of the concluding section. He cautions the writer to "recognize and resist the temptation of dramatic but irrelevant endings or conclusions that raise issues never addressed in the research" (1990, 56). And instead of trying to tie everything up into neat, understandable packages, Wolcott suggests that you leave yourself and readers "pondering the essential issues" (56).

Often, the concluding chapter gets short shrift because the author is exhausted from all that precedes it and feels pressed for time. The writing well runs dry just when it should be at its fullest. When authors fail to deliver adequately on the promise of their data, they fail to do justice to their investment in their research project. The concluding chapter then becomes the weakest production rather than the jewel in the writing crown that it should be.

Begin by appreciating the significance of your concluding chapter. Take care to schedule time for its completion—more time, in fact, than you may want to believe is necessary. Review all preceding chapters as preparation for writing the conclusion. Review your research questions so that you are certain to address all of them, and take note of what emerged as consequential that was not anticipated by your questions. And, finally, worry yourself continually with the questions: Am I doing full justice to what I learned? Am I saying enough for readers to appreciate what I intend as *my* contribution to the matter under study?

When you have completed your concluding chapter, read it and your introductory chapter together. Have you done in the end what you announced in the beginning that you meant to do? Have you discussed all of the questions you raised? If not, why not? Your opening chapter presents readers with expectations that they anticipate will be met in the course of subsequent chapters, and that will culminate in the final chapter.

Finally, pay attention to how you end your report, to the last sentence the reader reads. Delamont (1992) analyzed examples from the endings of ethnographies and other qualitative works. She found that some had academic "essence" statements, others pointed forward to the next project, and yet others, often the ones most journalistic in style, left the last word with a research participant. Pulling several favorite ethnographies from my shelves, I end this section with last sentences from Munoz, Tsing, and Myerhoff:

Academic Essence Example

Working together means taking on the risks and vulnerabilities of exploring the places where something catches: the unsettled and unsettling *fronteras* where the unfinished stories of identity are lived. (Munoz 1995, 257)

Looking Forward Example

Uma Adang's poem speaks to both Indonesians and foreigners within shifting and limited frames of meaning. This—not timeless truth—is the power of all creative work. We reread and write today to draw from this heritage and move beyond it. (Tsing 1993, 301)

An Imaginary Conversation with an Informant who had Died—Myerhoff Speaking

I still don't know Hebrew or Aramaic or Yiddish or Torah or Talmud. Neither do I know the prayer, nor can I light the fire or find my way to the place in the forest. But now I have been told about these things and perhaps this will be sufficient. (Myerhoff 1979, 272)

SPECIFICS OF STYLE

As with the overall form of your work, no absolutes govern the shaping of your style. The closest you can get is to apply what guides "good writing" in general to your writing of qualitative research.

The following five guidelines for good writing seem specifically applicable to qualitative research writing (for more complete discussion see Becker 1986b; Strunk and White 1979):

1. Make sentences active. Give passive statements an actor and avoid "it is" and "there are" constructions.
2. Make images concrete. Use descriptive words.
3. Avoid the jargon trap. "It is a way to strike a pose as a smart, well-versed, current member of a hot and influential in-group. But more than one hot and

influential in-group within ethnographic circles has become over time a cold and impotent out-group" (Van Maanen 1988, 28).

4. Use enough words to make your point.

5. Avoid wordiness. For example, the sentence "There is some question as to whether he is the person who should be in charge of running the school owing to the fact that he rarely reads or utilizes educational research findings" is better written, "Because he rarely uses research findings, some people question his role as principal."

Try reading your draft with a mind set for "making sentences active" and edit appropriately. Then read it again, but this time concentrate on clarity and concreteness of images and examples. Then read (and edit) for jargon, trite metaphors, and wordiness. With each reading, you shape your work, eventually forming a product that is worthy of your and your reader's time.

Schooled to write reports in a passive and authoritative manner with little, if any, of the researcher showing, some of you may experience some confusion as you let go of old habits. Even when students find some joy in their writing, as they work to write up qualitative research they are often overwhelmed by questions that they have not had to ask before. Following are some of the commonly asked questions. In response, I offer thoughts toward answers. In practice, a number of factors may influence the answers, including the demands of funding agencies, the expectations of supervising committees, the author's theoretical disposition or research tradition, and the degree of risk that the researcher is willing to take with experimental forms of presentation.

1. *Question:* Is it ok to use "I"?

   Answer: Writing in the first person singular fits the nature of qualitative inquiry. When reporting research methods, your "I" is particularly appropriate. The researcher conventionally becomes less visible, however, as he or she focuses on descriptive analysis of the data. The presence of your "I" in your text reflects your presence in your research setting. Your "I" says that yours is not a disembodied account that presumes to be objective by virtue of omitting clear reference to the human agent who lived through a particular research experience and lived with other people in the course of that experience. Avoid the obtrusive "I" that says, "Look at me," because, after all, the story you tell is not, usually, foremost about yourself. Use "I" in the sense of saying that you were present; it is well for both writer and reader to remember this fact. Moreover, it would be foolish for you to hide behind veils of awkward sentence construction, particularly when your ideal is graceful, clear, and cogent writing.

2. *Question:* When I am describing and analyzing what I saw and heard, do I also evaluate what I experienced?

   Answer: In discussing her biographical work on Alice James, Strouse states, "Getting brave enough to venture my own views was really what writing the book was all about" (1988, 190). Scholarly work is interpretive; to pretend otherwise is to fool yourself but perhaps very few others. Nonetheless, the purpose of qualitative research in general is to increase understanding, not to pass judgment. There may be a fine line between finding fault and finding meaning. Taking heed of this line is worthwhile. Tell the story that the data tell; do not use data to tell the story that a priori you want told.

3. *Question:* Can I tell a "story" in a dissertation, or do I have to follow the conventional format of problem statement, literature review, research methods, findings, and conclusion?

    Answer: The qualitative researching student has an advisor and committee whose judgments may set the guidelines and orthodoxy for the student's writing. In general, however, qualitative research has no conventional organizational format; I hope that none will develop. But telling a story, or following any particular chapter arrangement, is likely to be a matter of negotiation with your overseers, a negotiation that should be undertaken early. I do not personally endorse the conventional dissertation format because it is not congruent with the openness of qualitative inquiry and the variable forms that may best suit the stories to be told.

4. *Question:* Should I include a section titled "literature," or should I integrate the literature throughout the text?

    Answer: Depending on your study and audience, you may find both useful. It is accepted practice to integrate the work of others with your own. As Glaser (1978) stresses, however, novices tend to turn to the literature as the source of an idea or theory even when their thoughts developed out of fieldwork. The attitude toward existing literature, advises Glaser,

    > should not be one of adumbration, volume or reverence. It should be one of carefully weaving . . . theory into its place in the literature. . . . It is amazing how many authors try to find their best ideas in previous work in order to legitimate using it, as borrowed or derived as if they could not be allowed to generate it on their own. The proper attitude is simply to accept having discovered ideas. (137)

    Since your work may build on and extend the theories of others, you should make due reference to these other works, but do not allow them to overshadow your own thoughts and ideas.

5. *Question:* What use should I make of historical and current documents pertaining to sites other than the one I am investigating? For example, in a study of a one-room schoolhouse, Jody collected numerous historical documents pertaining to both her site and similar sites, including diaries of one-room schoolmarms. Can she use the documents from the similar sites? If so, how?

    Answer: Use whatever materials, however collected, that enhance your cause. The question is not where the material came from, but whether it will help.

6. *Question:* If I am focusing on one school in one community, how do I reference local documents if I have been using pseudonyms for the school and community?

    Answer: Use the pseudonym consistently in all citations so that confidentiality is respected, but explain to your readers that you are altering the citation.

7. *Question:* When quoting informants in the text, should I reference my interview notes? If so, how?

Answer: I never do, but your faculty overseers may insist that you do. It seems meaningless to provide such references when no one but you has access to your notes. In addition, such referencing interrupts the flow of the text.

8. *Question:* If in a quote the interviewee uses the name of a person or place, do I change the names to provide anonymity? If so, do I use brackets or some other means to demonstrate that the name has been changed?

   Answer: If by naming the person or place you will breach your commitment to anonymity, then the answer is clear: use pseudonyms. A general footnote at the beginning of your work can clarify your intent to alter names and places as needed. Thereafter, I see no need to call attention to the changes you make in the interest of preserving anonymity.

9. *Question:* When quoting someone, should I leave in every "umm," "you know," and other unconscious patterns of speech?

   Answer: Use your judgment. Leave in enough of such sounds and words to capture the person's speech, authentically but not so much as to impose on a reader's patience. Authenticity can be overdone; how many "you know's" and "umm's" should readers suffer?

10. *Question:* How do you assure confidentiality and anonymity to a person who plays a major role in a study and whose position is singular and central to the study (e.g., a school principal or superintendent)?

    Answer: "When total confidentiality or anonymity cannot be guaranteed, the issue becomes, in part, one of ongoing communication and agreement . . . between the investigator and research participants" (Johnson 1982, 85). This is a sensitive matter. You may feel particularly constrained in what you say because you cannot safely disguise the person's identity. My suggestion is to begin by saying all that you would like to say. Then reread what you have written as if you were that person. Finally, send a copy of your prose to that person and take your cue from his or her reaction.

11. *Question:* How do you describe and report unfavorable attitudes toward a person, program, or site when that person, program, or site is identifiable by research participants and by others in nearby areas?

    Answer: Ask yourself if it is at all necessary to report anything negative about persons and places that are identifiable. A commitment to scholarship does not provide a license to injure those who allow you access to their words and deeds. If your research, however, has a clear evaluative component and that component is a negotiated aspect of your entry arrangements, then the matter of negative findings assumes another perspective.

12. *Question:* Should I use precise counts, or imprecise terms such as "a few," "almost all," or "a majority"? For example, if I interviewed twenty persons, how much do I count when analyzing and reporting the data?

    Answer: Although some reference to frequency may contribute to your presentation, keep in mind that numbers do not play the same role in qualitative research that they do in quantitative research. Qualitative research has the potential to make many useful contributions, but these do not include generalizations derived from sampling in the quantitative tradition. When to count and in what ways to count are judgments that you make. To rule out all counting is to shut down a possible way of presenting your data that is fully warranted by your intent. To count as a basic way of structuring your data is to insert the rationality of the positivist paradigm where, ordinarily, it does not belong. Nonetheless, counting not only may be useful, it also may be necessary, as Erickson and Mohatt (1982) clearly demonstrate in their study of two classrooms of Native American students. Their study exemplifies several methodological techniques, including microethnography and linguistic analysis.

13. *Question:* Should I end my written report with a list of recommendations? Education is an applied field of study; shouldn't I be prescriptive?
Answer: The need to be useful is both understandable and desirable. Useful outcomes, however, do not always take the form of prescriptions. You must ask yourself: Have I designed my study for the purpose of being prescriptive? If so, then prescribe. If not, then the prescriptions, although interesting, are bootlegged onto a study designed to do other things. Do what you set out to do, and do it as well as you can. Attend to the matter of prescriptions when it is clearly suitable to do so. To focus on them when they are not integral to your design is to take effort away from where you planned it to be.

This set of questions and answers covers some of the practical considerations that arise in bringing a research process to fruition. They are important but secondary considerations, preceded in priority by commitments: to collect the best data you can; to have something to say—a matter of analysis, imagination, and boldness; to be enthusiastic about your topic; to intend to write well; and, not least, to revise and revise and revise.

Responsibilities of the Writer

Writing is a political act: carefully think through both the intended and the unintended consequences of your words. Your first responsibility is to your research respondents, those persons whose cooperation is the basis of your research. Ask yourself whether your choice of words results in judgments rather than in descriptions of a place and its people. Note the difference between saying the "community is backward" and "10 percent of the adult population can neither read nor write" (Johnson 1982, 87). Nagel, a biographer, also gives good advice: "Writing about another person's life is an awesome task, so one must proceed with a gentleness born from knowing that the subject and the author share the frailties of human mortality" (1988, 115). As a researcher, strive to understand the complexity of social phenomena. In doing so, you will most likely discover that research participants are as human as you are—neither saint nor sinner. Portray that humanness, neither disguising it with a hidden agenda of your own, nor overlaying it with emphases and highlights that gild—or wound, damage, and denigrate.

Central to the responsibility to research participants is the following question:

Are we placing research participants and their site(s) at undue risk because of our inter-actions with them? We should imagine a scenario in which the location(s) and their par-ticipants are revealed and ask ourselves what the possible consequences of that discov-ery would be. (Johnson 1982, 87)

How could the information be used either positively or negatively? Would individu-als be subjected to unwanted publicity? Would the disclosure of data about identifi-able individuals or groups with little power be exploited by others who have power? Are there things that should be omitted?

Another consideration is your responsibility to the larger community of social scientists. Ask yourself whether your portrayal will preclude another study at the same site, by you or by someone else. Will participants be reluctant, if not adamantly negative, about allowing another researcher in? If so, what harm have you done to scientific opportunities and fellow researchers, in addition to research participants?

You must also be responsible to yourself. Your research discoveries can have political ramifications for your job and your interactions with "superiors," particu-larly if researching in your own backyard. Bonnie, for example, gave a copy of her final report to the nursing supervisor who was both the gatekeeper to her research participants and her "boss." The supervisor was unhappy with the report findings and told Bonnie that if she published them, she could not return to work in the hospital. You must consider the consequences of your words on yourself as well as on your others.

How do you avoid the research complications that may disrupt your own life as well as those of research participants? The surest way is to anticipate complications and to work them out along the way by collaborative arrangements with research supervisors and research participants. Anticipate to whom findings of any but the most obviously laudatory type could prove disagreeable and include those persons in the preparation of the "controversial" sections. That is, treat your findings as ten-tative; discuss them in very general terms, not as *the* results. Solicit reactions to your words from research supervisors and participants. In addition, look for colleagues who will read your manuscript for examples of judgment, criticism, and potential ethical and political problems. The idea is to avoid complications, rather than have to get out of them.

Research is a political act, involving power, resources, policy, and ethics. Throughout the research process, the political context is generally limited to the re-search site(s) and the researcher's relationships with participants and, sometimes, with their supervisors (as well as the researcher's supervisors). Writing extends the complexity of research politics because it invites in a third party—the reader—with all the ramifications that inclusion of this invisible but vital participant may gener-ate for both researcher and researched. The next chapter, Chapter 9, delves more deeply into the politics of writing through examining the role of language in con-veying meaning—particularly how language and form connote and transfer values.

For more on the techniques of writing up qualitative research, see Becker's (1986b) *Writing for Social Scientists,* Richardson's (1990) *Writing Strategies,* and Wol-cott's (1990) *Writing Up Qualitative Research.*

Exercise

Return to the *Research Practice* exercise (last visited in Chapter 7). In the same small groups that worked on data analysis, begin to write up your section of a group report. The purpose of this exercise is to practice making decisions about how to express themes, patterns, and descriptions; what to use as supporting evidence; and which interviewee words to include and which to leave out. In your own individual research (or in an actual group project), you would want to be fully acquainted with all the data and the relationships among them as a whole. For this practice exercise, however, work only with the data for your section.

After each group has shaped a written report for its section, decide on a seemingly logical order for the combined report. Then, group by group, read the "class report." Discuss the ways in which different groups reported their data.

Chapter 9

Improvising a Song of the World: Language and Representation

Our knowledge is contextual and only contextual. Ordering and invention coincide: we call their collaboration "knowledge." The mind is a blue guitar on which we improvise the song of the world. (Dillard 1982, 56).

I became interested in alternative forms of presenting research when, with tenure achieved and then a subsequent sabbatical, I had time to play with creative writing. I was not sure of what form to pursue nor how to incorporate it into academic life, but during the sabbatical, I wrote extensively in a journal and, upon return to the university, I began taking poetry classes. Around that time, I read several articles by Richardson (1992, 1994a) in which she transformed interview transcripts into poetry. Delighted and inspired, I began searching for more work that supported my inclination to combine the humanities and arts with research presentation. I discovered that others were on journeys similar to mine.

Sandelowski (1994) locates qualitative research "at the meeting place between art and science" (55). Until recently, however, most social scientists desired to be perceived as scientific, not artistic. Since science was associated with fact and objectivity, social scientists used language considered objective, precise, neutral, and nonmetaphoric (Richardson 1990; Stewart 1989). The song of the world could be reported, but not sung. Some anthropologists wrote poetry for literary journals and others published field memoirs (often under a pseudonym), but usually they did not mix direct discussion of their field experiences, personal reflections, and poetic compositions with their ethnographic writing (Bruner 1993).

In these postmodern times, the contextual nature of knowledge along with the role of language in creating meaning has become a focal point of thought and debate. Some critical, feminist, and interpretivist scholars highlight, in particular: (1) how the research tale cannot be separated from the teller, the researcher;

(2) how the language the writer chooses carries with it certain values; and (3) how all textual presentations are "fashioned" and, thereby, in a sense, fictions. There are no "true" representations. As discussed below, these ideas have influenced how I, and others, think about writing up qualitative inquiry. They have also helped to open a space for experimenting with form in research representation, a topic also addressed in this chapter.

Reflexivity: The Researcher and the Researched

Researchers have always told stories to friends and colleagues of research relationships, dramatic field events, and day-to-day drudgery, but tended to omit such stories from written reports. They also left out discussion of subjective lenses through which they viewed their research. Rather, they presented their research with an authoritative "this is the way it is" stance (Van Maanen, 1988).

Qualitative researchers today ask how social science and self are "co-created" (Richardson 1994b). From this perspective, what you know about your research—reflected in your interpretations—is intertwined with what you know about yourself. Therefore, authors increasingly write themselves into their texts, acknowledging that they have always been there, creating meaning. How authors reflect upon their work and inscribe themselves into their texts, however, varies in degree and style.

A text (all of it or a section) may take the form of what Van Maanen (1988) calls a "confessional tale." In confessional tales, the point of view is not that of "natives," but that of fieldworkers, reflecting upon themselves as researchers. Authors of confessional tales often portray themselves as human beings who make mistakes and blunders, but who eventually "learn the rules" and come to see things in new ways. Accompanying the confessional tale is the "simple assertion that even though there are flaws and problems in one's work, when all is said and done it still remains adequate" (Van Maanen 1988, 79).

Rebecca wrote a confessional tale about her early stages in exploring adolescent girls' friendships. Passages within the tale convey her sense of insecurity and naiveté as she ventured into the "field":

> I move to a desk situated in front of the row the girls have claimed and set down my backpack. As I begin to unpack my materials I wonder how I should begin. "Hi, my name is Rebecca and I'm here to tell you a little bit about my study that you agreed to be a part of." All of the girls stare at me in silence, some with shadows of apprehension on their faces. I sit down on the desk behind me and adopt a stance and manner I hope minimizes my authority role.

After the introductory meeting with the girls, Rebecca felt relieved to have completed her first research "act." Despite her awkwardness, she encouraged the girls to talk, and she left excited by what was to come.

Linden (1993) states that "[f]ieldwork confessions abound, yet reflexive accounts of how other cultures and cultural 'others' act on field workers are rare" (9). Reflexive accounts, for many researchers, demand more than personal tales of research problems and accomplishments. They require thought about the researcher's position and how the researcher is affected by the fieldwork and field relationships, as Linden (1993) exemplifies in *Making Stories, Making Selves: Feminist Reflections on the Holocaust:*

> Writing this book has compelled me, repeatedly, to turn inward. Over and over again, I have examined the impress of the Holocaust on my Jewish consciousness. My self-reflections became an integral component of my research, inseparable from the book "about" Holocaust survivors I had initially planned to write. This process transformed my Jewish identity, and the book tells that story as well. (2)

In the text, Linden presents her own memories, family stories, and evolving sense of identity along with the narratives of the Holocaust survivors.

In *Translated Woman*, Behar (1993) addresses socioeconomic class differences between herself and Esperanza, the Mexican woman with whom she conducted research for several years. Behar also reveals details of her family life as she was growing up that she perceived influential in her research interpretations. Ever reflexive, she later discusses the effects of having written about her family. Her mother, angry with Behar's exposure of the family's "dirty laundry," asks her, "If you had to ask Esperanza for permission to write about her, why don't you have to ask permission to write about us?" (Behar 1995, 72). Since we are relational beings, exposing lives of those around us is a potential hazard of reflexivity.

Another potential risk of reflexivity is to use research as a kind of self-therapy or to focus as much on self as on other. Cynically referred to as ethno-narcissism, some reflexive accounts appear to be ways for people to make more of themselves than of the world around them. As a researcher, you are inseparable from your findings. A reflexive section is now an expected part of ethnographic writing. Just what to write about yourself in the text—and how much—remains, however, an issue worthy of consideration.

The Researcher's Language

Whatever reality is, besides existent, our sense of it . . . comes inevitably out of the way we talk about it. (Geertz, 1995, 18)

Meaning is more complex than the definition of words. The very choice of the language you use—whether clear and coherent, complex and disruptive, removed and formal, or personal and evocative—tells a story in addition to what you mean it to say. For example, consider researchers who pepper reports with *utilize, finalize,* and other *ize*-ending words instead of shorter terms such as *use* and *finish*. By their word choice, they take on the air of academic pretension, but not necessarily that of good writers, as Strunk and White (1979) remind us.

For another example, in crafting this book, I want to write in a style accessible to those of you who are novice researchers, to use clear, expressive language and examples that engage. But what meaning does my language choice produce? What messages do I re-produce? Certainly, I simplify much and simply ignore more. I gloss over historical catalysts and social philosophies. I do so, not because they don't matter to me, but because my primary intent is to welcome in those of you new to qualitative research. I trust that you will go on to read, discuss, and discover elsewhere variety and complexity in research perspectives and methodologies. In doing so, however, am I inviting you into a seemingly intriguing and engaging process without warning properly of all the hidden alleys and curves ahead? Am I encouraging "bad science" (and art) if some of you read this text and think that you now know all about being qualitative researchers? I don't want to deceive, or provide a false sense of "knowing," but both may be possibilities because of the language I choose.

The role language plays in assigning value is a focal point in the postmodern critique of social research. "Language does not 'reflect' social reality, but produces meaning, creates social reality" (Richardson 1994b, 518). For example, passive, disembodied sentences ("The study was conducted . . .") convey a sense of objectivity where the researcher and his or her actions (excitement, worries) disappear. For another example, return to my discussion of writing this text and my intent to use clear, accessible language. Lather (1996) states that such "plain speaking" can imply "a mirroring relationship between the word and the world" (527). She argues that sometimes we need to read and not easily understand in order to move our thinking beyond the taken-for-granted. Tsing (1993) takes a similar perspective, referring to her own ethnographic writing strategies as "guerrilla tactics of multiple, uneasily jostling theories and stories. . . . in which curiosity is not overwhelmed by coherence" (32–33). In essence, Lather and Tsing push me to ask questions of language use in this text, and I urge you to do so as well, not only of this text but also of your own.

The Researcher's Representations

A life as lived is what actually happened. . . . A life as told, a life history, is a narrative, influenced by the cultural conventions of telling, by the audience, and by the social context. (Bruner 1984, 7).

A life as told is a re-presentation of that life; the life and the telling are not the same thing. Rather, the narrative—the telling or the writing—is always an interpretation of other peoples' lives, an interpretation that qualitative researchers struggle with representing.

The realist tale (Van Maanen 1988) has been the dominant form of ethnographic representation. In this traditional form of reporting research, authors minutely document details of the lives of people studied, using closely edited quotations to portray participants' points of view. The researcher, however, is absent from much, if not all, of the text, taking a position of "interpretive omnipotence"

(Van Maanen 1988, 51) where the life is told, but in a way that assumes that the life and the telling are practically the same. In other words, the representation seems to be *true* to life.

Liebow, in his 1967 book *Tally's Corner,* explored the lives of "streetcorner" men who hung out on Tally's Corner in inner-city Washington, D.C., in the early 1960s. Liebow discusses, among other things, his own background and issues of class and race (he is white; the streetcorner men are black) in an appendix. In the text, however, he primarily presents descriptions of what he heard and saw, words of people with whom he spoke, and generalized interpretations such as the following:

> A crucial factor in the streetcorner man's lack of job commitment is the overall value he places on the job. *For his part, the streetcorner man puts no lower value on the job than does the larger society around him.* He knows the social value of the job by the amount of money the employer is willing to pay him for doing it. In a real sense, every pay day, he counts in dollars and cents the value placed on the job by society at large. (Liebow 1967, 57)

Liebow's writing is clear, descriptive, and engaging. In his portrait of a group of inner-city African American men and their relationships with work, women, children, and friends, Liebow provides the reader with a sense of "this is the way it really is."

Lincoln and Denzin (1994) describe qualitative research as in a crisis of representation, in which researchers ask, among other things, whether they can "ever hope to speak authentically of the experiences of the Other" (577). Giving up an authoritative stance means that you no longer can profess to know everything, but you can claim to *know something.* Your knowledge, however, is always partial, situated in a particular context with specific historical understandings (Richardson 1994b). That your understanding is incomplete does not make it unimportant, nor does it mean that you scatter methodological discipline and rigor to the wind. You may, however, want to experiment with representational form, making even more explicit your role as co-creator of research tales, improvising order on blue guitars.

The Art of Re-presentation

If we learn to "read" and "write" in a manner similar to the way the painter paints, we may well be able to sensualize prose which represents others so that our books become the study of human beings as well as human behavior. (Stoller 1989, 40)

"Experimental forms" and "alternative forms" are the current catchall phrases for the variety of nontraditional ways in which qualitative researchers have begun to represent their inquiry. "One practice these experiments have in common . . . is the violation of prescribed conventions" (Richardson 1994b, 520). Using traditions of artistic expression as guides, some researchers seek to combine the "strengths of science with the rewards of the humanities" (Stoller 1989, 9). To do so, they draw upon literary traditions such as drama, poetry, and narrative to represent their work; a few have begun to experiment with nonverbal forms such as photography, dance, and painting.

Eisner (1997, 8) discusses five reasons for choosing alternative forms of representation: (1) creating a sense of empathy for research participants; (2) providing a sense of particularity and authenticity; (3) generating insight and attention to complexity; (4) increasing the kinds of questions that researchers can ask as they think within new mediums; and (5) making better use of the variety in researchers' representational abilities. Rose (1993) sees ethnographies of the future as multigenre constructions, made up of many voices, and inclusive of emotional reactions as well as analytical descriptions. This description fits a number of recent ethnographies such as Lather and Smithies (1997) *Troubling the Angels: Women Living with HIV/AIDS* and Anna Lowenhaupt Tsing's (1993) *In the Realm of the Diamond Queen: Marginality in an Out-of-Way Place.*

Agar (1995) likens the "new ethnography" to creative nonfiction. Creative nonfiction writers want, he says, "to blend factual content and fiction form, to play the roles of both observer/reporter and textmaker, to commit equally to artistic and empirical truth, and to research fact not as an end in itself but as a means to art" (117). Agar worries, however, that ethnographers who experiment with form may put emphasis on form over content:

> Textuality as a consciousness-raising concept is long over-due. But textuality as the primary focus for what ethnography is all about is, I think, a mistake. . . . a move to new textual forms without more attention to the research processes that ground them would be a serious ethnomistake. (128–129)

Similarly, Eisner (1997) warns, "We also need to be sure, if we can be, that we are not substituting novelty and cleverness for substance" (9). I agree that, as researchers, you need to take these cautions seriously. Learn to represent your work in more traditional ethnographic forms and then give yourself license to play with form, to expand your repertoire of expressive modes. As you become familiar with different forms of representation, you will be able to more critically reflect on the appropriateness of the form.

Experimenting with form is as much (or more) about the process as the product. After a semester course focused on data analysis and writing, including an emphasis on experimental forms of writing, I asked students what they learned about their research and themselves through writing their work in more creative ways. Their answers suggested, in particular, that using experimental forms is a *freeing* experience that accesses feelings and encourages broader perspectives:

- It allowed me to get at feelings, and my relationship with others, in ways that I could not possibly have done in another form. It also allowed me—*freed* me—to think about what might have been, what might be now.
- It magnified the learning which happens during the writing process. It *freed* up my perspective to envision and construct meanings that go beyond my usual monophonic world.

In terms of what students learned about themselves, they usually mentioned something about the process of writing as in this response from Glen who worked hard with drafts and redrafts all semester: "I learned that my writing could be more interesting for me to write and for others to read."

Writing in different modes helps you to think about data in new ways. When creating drama or reader's theater, for example, you tend to focus on dialogue and how people's words support and challenge each other. When developing a short story, you are more likely to focus on observations, writing descriptively of the setting and actions as well as using words of research participants. Exploring ways of representing data, therefore, "forces [you] to think about the meanings and understandings, voices, and experiences present in the data. . . . Analytical ideas are developed and tried out in the process of writing and representing" (Coffey and Atkinson 1996, 109). When writing up data as a play, poetry, or narrative, you still code, analyze, and interpret data, but which chunks of data you select and how you order them will vary with form, stressing, in the process, different issues. The same data tell different stories, depending upon the form you choose. Experimenting with language and form is also an avenue for encouraging a spirit of discovery and creativity within you as you work.

The following sections highlight autoethnography, poetic transcription, drama, and short story as creative forms of representation. Examples are presented to encourage you to try experimenting with form. Some experiences may be best expressed in a particular form, but this presupposes that you are familiar with and versed in a wide range of expressive styles. As you experiment with form, however, continually reflect upon what the mode of representation allows you and the reader to know about research participants, you as researcher, and the meaning you are making.

Autoethnography

Each time I have attempted to do theoretical work it has been on the basis of elements from my experience . . . (Foucault, cited in Rajchman, 1988, 108).

The term *autoethnography* is used in a variety of ways: to describe narratives of a culture or ethnic group produced by members of that culture or ethnic group; to describe ethnographies of the "other," but one where the writer interjects personal experience into the text as in the confessional tale; and, more akin to autobiography, to investigate self within a social context, whether it be your own or that of another culture (Reed-Danahay 1997). Here, I am using *autoethnography* to refer to the kind of writing that inquires into the self as part of a sociocultural context.

Autoethnography begins with the self, the personal biography. Using narratives of the self, the researcher goes on to say something about the larger cultural setting and scholarly discourse, taking a sociological rather than a psychological perspective. For example, colleague Carolyne White has been using a kind of autoethnography that she calls *mystory* as a way for her graduate students to explore social constructions of ethnicity—especially whiteness. An excerpt from graduate student Mark Storz's "mystory" helps to exemplify ways in which White's students began to develop skills of social critique grounded in their own "situated and embodied knowledge" (White, Andino-Demyan, Primer, and Storz 1996, 61):

> ... I thought I had my act together regarding my perceptions of myself, race and racism. . . . I had grown up in a family who had some very definite prejudices against people who were different from us, African Americans in particular, but Italians and Poles and others as well. And somehow, by the grace of God, I didn't hold to those racist sentiments that I was brought up with. At least I didn't think so. In fact, I thought, having just finished seven successful years as a white principal of a predominately African American school in the inner city of Flint, Michigan, that I would have something to offer my peers [in the class].
>
> . . . . I'm on a journey back through the last seven years of my life, looking for evidence of unacknowledged privilege and unconscious oppression. Revisiting those times when parents of my students called me a racist, and I in my arrogance dismissed the accusations as the reaction of an unhappy parent. Now I wonder what in my words, actions, or body language, may have given that impression. I wonder, as principal when I was the only male on the staff, if gender bias was an unconscious aspect of my daily interactions with professionals whom I greatly respected. I even look back beyond the past seven years, when I traveled in a predominately white world, and wonder how my unconsciousness of whiteness may have contributed to the oppression of others. (White, Andino-Demyan, Primer, Storz 1996, 59–60)

In autoethnography, researchers approach themselves as subjects, as Mark does when he begins to explore race and the social construction of whiteness. Autoethnographers often use literary writing techniques to portray dramatically their experience. The reader may be asked to "'relive' the events emotionally with the writer" (Richardson 1994b, 521). Yvette does this as she takes the reader through her first exposure to her doctoral program. Yvette presents her account as a way to introduce concepts of adult education, particularly the role of a cohort of peers in adult learning—the focus of her dissertation research (Pigeon 1998).

> The space was animated with movement and social posturing. Doctoral core faculty members were working the room, chatting with people they appeared to know. As someone who didn't know anyone there, I had the distinct and uncomfortable feeling of being an outsider, wondering if I'd been sent an invitation by mistake. I tried not to stare as I postulated who these people were and what might be the socioeconomic range, not to mention the political affiliations of this somewhat conservative looking group. Did we have anything in common other than arriving in the same place at the same time? . . .
>
> "Let's get started," commanded the director. "We'll begin with introductions. Tell us your name, area of study, and why you have chosen to be in the doctoral program." Silence immediately spread through the room and everyone had a similar look of masked fear and deep concentration on their faces. It was apparent that most of us had not publicly divulged the details of our planned area of study since we had written it in our applications months ago. "Where should we start?" the director asked as he smiled.

I didn't know whether it was a smile of compassion or of sadism as he probably could sense the cohort's level of nervous anticipation. The group on the couch volunteered while the rest of us rehearsed in our mind what we would say when it inevitably became our turn in the introduction ritual. . . .

More than half way through the introductions, the Dean appeared at the door to welcome us. It was at that moment that all my fears and insecurities about being an adult thrown back into the role of student surfaced. Based on my past educational experience she represented authority and personified the esteem of the doctoral degree. As a student and a woman I had learned to genuflect when in the presence of either and here I was daring to achieve both. Self-doubtingly I thought, "Who am I trying to kid? What am I doing here?". . . .

I was abruptly jarred from my introspective stupor by the program director. "We are really here to support you," he said, "and we are invested in increasing our program completion rate." For some reason, this piece of news did not sound encouraging. "Oh and also, be sure to make use of your cohort for support. For instance you can study for the comprehensive exams together," he added. It struck me as odd that I hadn't taken my first course yet and he was talking about exams. This, along with the fact that I wasn't sure what "the cohort" was left me wondering if I had missed something . . . .

Autoethnographic accounts relieve the writer (or give a reprieve) of speaking for the other (Richardson 1994b). In contrast, poetic transcription—the next experimental form to be discussed—depends heavily on the other's words with the researcher snipping and snipping, as Behar (1993) describes her work with Esperanza's historias, only to "patch together a new tongue" (19).

Poetic Transcription

In poetic transcription,[1] the researcher fashions poem-like pieces from the words of interviewees (Glesne, 1997). The writer aspires to get at the essence of what's said, the emotions expressed, and the rhythm of speaking. The process involves word reduction while illuminating the wholeness and interconnectedness of thoughts. Through shaping the presentation of the words of an interviewee, the researcher creates a third voice that is neither the interviewee's nor the researcher's but is a combination of both. This third voice disintegrates any appearance of separation between observer and observed.

Exhibit 9.1 shows some of the process I used in making a poetic transcription from transcripts of over ten hours of interviews with a Puerto Rican educator, Dona Juana. The left column contains a portion of actual interview transcript. The right side begins with a poetic rendering of the transcript in chronological order. The chronological rendering continued with other sections of the transcript that seemed related. Then I began eliminating words and moving them around to create the poem found in Version 2 on the right side of the figure.

Students in Vermont have created poetic transcriptions from their research in ways that range from developing poetic "subjective I" pieces from reflective journal notes to compilations of interview voices. Penny Bishop (1998) created *Safety in*

(*Continued on p. 185.*)

───────────────── EXHIBIT 9.1 ─────────────────

The Making of a Poetic Transcription

Transcript	Poetic Narrative
C: If I asked you to use a metaphor to describe yourself as a professor, what would you say you were like? Someone I asked said that she was a bridge and then she told me why. What metaphor comes to mind for you? J: **I would be a flying bird.** C: A flying bird. Tell me about it. How are you a flying bird? J: Because **I want to move so fast.** C: Mm-hmmm. Cover a lot of territory. J: Yes. Yes. C: Are you any kind of bird or just any bird? J: Well, any bird because I don't want to mention some birds, some birds here are destructive. C: Are what? J: Are destructive. They destroy and I don't want to . . . C: No, you don't want to be one of them. No. You're just a bird that moves fast. J: That moves fast and sees from the tops of trees. **So I can see quickly.** C: See quickly, see everything. J: **Everything.** J: So you can see me? C: I can. I can see you, a flying bird. J: **I wish I could look at the world with the eyes of God.** C: With the eyes of what? J: Of God, of that spiritual power that can **give strength.** C: That can give strength? Strength? J: Yes, **to those that need.**	Version One: Chronologically and linguistically faithful to the transcript. **I would be a flying bird.** **I want to move so fast** **so I can see quickly, everything.** **I wish I could look at the world** **with the eyes of God,** **to give strength to those that need.** Version Two: Draws from other sections of the interviews, takes more license with words. **I am a flying bird** **moving fast, seeing quickly,** **looking with the eyes of God** **from the tops of trees.** **How hard for country people** **picking green worms** **from fields of tobacco,** **sending their children to school,** **not wanting them to suffer** **as they suffer.** **In the urban zone,** **students worked at night** **and so they slept in school.** **Teaching was the real university.** **So I came to study** **to find out how I could help.** **I am busy here at the university,** **there is so much to do.** **But the university is not the island.** **I am a flying bird** **moving fast, seeing quickly** **so I can give strength,** **so I could have that rare feeling** **of being useful.**

From Glesne 1997, 207.

Numbers using a process similar to the one I used with Dona Juana's transcript. Penny was studying exemplary partner team-teaching in middle schools. *Safety in Numbers* is a poetic transcription from interviews with one teacher.

Safety in Numbers
by Penny Bishop (1998, 37)

There is safety in numbers.
The kids in our class
know if they cut class
one of us will come and find them.
They know they have two people who care
instead of one.

There is safety in numbers.
A kid in our class
was being abused
and she got a very bad report card
and she was scared to go home.

So we decided to show up
at the trailer where
her father was
so we could talk with him
about her very bad report card
before he lit into her
before he beat her
or whatever.
And when we showed up
where her father was
her father was loaded.

Alone,
I think I would have put myself in danger.
Alone,
I think being there
would have been a mistake.
But as there were
two of us,
it was a lot safer.

There is safety in numbers.
The kids in our class have two people who
care,
instead of one.
It is twice as powerful—
the power of two.

In contrast to Penny's poetic transcription, Katie Furney (1997) compiled the voices of elementary school children to create a poetic transcription in which the children describe their school. At times, she changed tenses and pronouns, added lines at the beginning of the stanzas to give them some structure, and used conjunctions to hook similar comments from individual students together. Otherwise, the words are those the students spoke. Katie was researching practices in schools with a reputation for excellence in inclusion. She states that as she worked with the words of the students, "[I] heard echoes of the voices of teachers and administrators. I heard talk of engagement, caring relationships, students as active learners, and students who felt accepted and prized. I heard a sense of self-worth: the kind that comes from being cared for" (119–120). Her poetic transcription portrays a school in which students, parents, and educators can take pride.

School Is Fun—and You Learn a Lot Too
by Katie Furney (1997, 120)

I love school because it's cool
and I have lots of friends in school.
I have a lot of friends to spend time with
and they like school too.
If you didn't go to school you wouldn't know
as much as if you did go to school.
You learn stuff that you never knew before.

The teachers
usually listen to what you have to say.
They never ignore you and they let you
explain your own feelings.
They let you choose your own books
and your own topics in reading and writing.
They help us read and spell,
and they combine the stuff
that we are learning.

Sometimes you need help:
If you raise your hand quietly and ask
a question, your teacher will usually help you
get the right answer.
Our teachers help us work out and solve
our problems—
we can talk to our teachers.

Our teachers listen to us and respect
our privacy.
You don't just sit there all the time,
you get to do projects.
I like doing things with my hands,
like math on the computer,
helping other kids on the computer,
cleaning the classroom,
drama, breaks, recess,
my job.

There are some things that aren't so great:
there's never enough time to finish projects,
or to do math, reading, art, music and
library activities.
There's never enough food
or time to eat lunch.
The water fountain should be colder.
I hate getting into trouble and
I didn't like it when I broke up
with my girlfriend.

If I could change anything, I'd have
more projects, longer math and science classes, and
a longer school day to finish my work.
I'd like a bigger library with bigger books
and
a bigger bathroom for the teachers.
I would like more homework
(but I don't want any!)
I'd like a bigger playground, more sports,
a longer recess.
We should have more food, seconds every day.
I'd like them to put a different color of paint
on the walls—maybe something brickish.

Kids should run the school!
We would learn about space every day,
we'd watch Power Ranger videos,
and have pizza at every lunch.
All of the kids could pick up trash outside
of the school and get paid for it.

I like school—
I usually like all of my teachers
and they like me for how I am and I like that.
It's a cool school,
people should stay in school and be cool.

Poetic transcription is similar to poetry in its form and use of concentrated language, but it may or may not arrive at the artistic sensibilities of a good poem. The process, however, can assist you as a writer and ethnographer to focus on what is essential to the story and to juxtapose items and concepts that you would not put together otherwise. Poetic transcription, as with drama, the next creative form to be discussed, also asks you to approach your data with an artistic eye, to let "ordering and invention coincide" (Dillard 1982, 56).

Drama

In representing data through dramatic portrayals, the researcher crafts interview transcripts into dialogue and observation notes into scenes and stage settings.

"Reader's Theater" is the term used by Donmoyer and Yennie-Donmoyer (1995) to refer "to a staged presentation of a piece of text or selected pieces of different texts that are thematically linked" (406). Rather than act, presenters read text selections individually, and sometimes in chorus. Staging is simple, usually involving chairs or stools and perhaps a few props. The Donmoyers used data from eighth-grade students reflecting upon how they write to script a Reader's Theater piece titled, *In Their Own Words*.

Mienczakowski (1995) also used drama as the form for representing research data. Through participant observations and interviews with different groups of participants (health care workers, persons with schizophrenia, and persons dependent upon alcohol), Mienczakowski created "ethnodramas," that were performed by actors in a variety of theater spaces. The intent was to create "a form of public-voice ethnography that has emancipatory and educational potential" (Mienczakowski 1995, 364) by providing a forum for research participants to tell others about their health concerns. Whether Reader's Theater or ethnodrama, the narratives are actual ones, although editorial license is generally taken to construct scenes or imply conversations among people who were not necessarily together.

The following example is excerpted from Pam Kay's (1997) Reader's Theater script entitled *Whose Child Is This? Reader's Theater Exploring the Sociocultural Tensions Experienced by a Parent and a Teacher Around a Child's Emotional and Behavioral Issues* which she and colleagues presented at an American Educational Research Association conference. The script examines the relationship between a teacher and the parent of a first-grade boy experiencing emotional and behavioral difficulties. Data for the script were taken from a case study that was part of a multisite investigation into the prevention of serious emotional disturbance, funded by the U. S. Department of Education. The cast of characters includes Nancy, the parent; Carol, the teacher; and Pam, the researcher. Two brief excerpts are presented here:

Pam (to the audience): We had our second parent-teacher action research meeting. Carol came in a little late, and she was upset.

Nancy and Carol face each other. Carol speaks angrily to Nancy.

Carol: Why aren't you giving Doug his medicine in the morning before he comes to school?

Nancy (quietly): We are all out of it. I was going to see Dr. Dave on Friday, but he is away for a week.

Carol (still angry): The school nurse called the pharmacy, and the pharmacy says you should have 12 days supply left!

Nancy: Well, I don't.

Carol and Nancy turn away from the audience. (Kay 1997, 15)

Pam sits down and turns to face Nancy and Carol, who again face each other.

Carol (speaking carefully): Nancy, may I bring up what Doug told me the other day?

Nancy: Sure.

Carol (explaining to Pam): There was trouble on the playground again. Doug got very angry. After he had calmed down, he told me that his father is dying.

Nancy (in a low, husky voice): The doctor has said that he can't do anything more for Walter. He can make him comfortable, that's all. I am always very honest with my children, so I told them how sick their father is. Also, Amy and her two babies have moved home because her boyfriend was abusive. So there is lots of anger in our house these days.

Carol: He has had several bad days lately; he just wasn't Doug.

Nancy: He really interrupts me a lot and with the two little ones there, he has been jealous. He'll climb up on the table and jump off at me when I am holding one of the little ones. Of course, then I have to pay attention to him. *(Kay 1997, 16–17)*

Kay (1997) formed her script by sorting and selecting data gathered through individual interviews with Carol and Nancy, her field notes from team meetings, notebooks kept by Carol and Nancy, and field notes kept by a parent liaison employed by the project. Carol and Nancy's words are verbatim excerpts from the data. Pam used her own voice as narrator and stage director as a way of furnishing explanations and transitions.

Reader's Theater is a way to juxtapose the voices of research participants, to present multiple perspectives together, and to exemplify the complexity of a phenomenon. To be sure, the researcher/writer shapes the drama, but constructs it so that readers might understand more fully what it means to be, for example, the teacher *and* the parent of a child like Doug.

Short Story

In ethnographic drama and poetic transcription, writers artistically shape their representations, but they stay close to the data. In the ethnographic short story, researchers combine ethnographic insights and understandings with their own imaginations to tell good stories, drawing upon literary techniques such as flashback, characterization, dialogue, internal monologue, and action. For example, in *Drinkers, Drummers, and Decent Folk: Ethnographic Narratives of Village Trinidad,* John Stewart (1989) presents a series of ethnographic short stories that had their roots in his fieldwork in Trinidad. Stewart (1989) states that writing up his research as short story allowed him to focus on an "anthropology of the inside":

In an ethnography of the outside, that objective field to which most ethnographers are still grounded, social and cultural "structures" are the central concern. Not people. In an anthropology of the inside, how people fashion such "structures," how they manipulate, manage or are controlled by them, become the focus. (13)

Phil Smith, a doctoral candidate at the University of Vermont, is also seeking an anthropology of the inside. Working to understand issues of power and control in the lives of people with developmental disabilities, Phil is writing up some of his research as short stories. The following is an excerpt from "Food Truck's Party Hat":

He looks at me again, grinning again, his head moving, his whole body, really, in constant motion, he never entirely stops, some part of him always racing beyond the rest of him, beyond his own body even, moving moving moving on, tapping swinging gliding always in continuous seamless never-ending can't-make-it-stop not-even-in-sleep motion. "Boy use jug," he says, and laughs, eyebrows raised, a question.

No one knows, now, how Food Truck came to that phrase, or to the name Food Truck that he calls himself. He lived for over forty years at Langdon Training School, where they used to lock up all the people they called morons imbeciles epileptics retards. Remember those words? Growing up, in school, some kid sitting next to you in class would do something dumb, drop their pencil and then step on it, break it, and you'd lean over so old Mrs. Whatever-her-name-was wouldn't hear, and whisper, "What a 'tard!" just loud enough so all the kids around you could hear and laugh. "You're such a retard!" and grin, the funniest thing you had said in weeks, beaming at your own joke. I said it lots of times, impugned my brother's intelligence if he walked in my room without knocking, or broke my model airplanes, or read my science fiction books without asking. "You retard!" I'd say angrily, the worst thing I knew to call him. I didn't know Food Truck then.

Food Truck grew up at Langdon, mostly. He spent his early childhood with his parents, and then they couldn't take care of him anymore, I think, or the family doctor said—as a lot of them did back then—"Well, you know, you really should send him off to Langdon, he'll be much happier there, with his own kind." So he went off to live at Langdon as a young boy, and that was his whole life, that's really all he's known, the back wards. Course he's out now, been out for four or five years, they're all out.

The ethnographic short story prompts the writer and the reader to seriously consider not only their line between shaping and fictionalizing, but also the purpose of the telling, the intent of the researcher/writer. If the intent of the writer is to re-present the sense and feel, the complex emotions, and the dilemmas of everyday life, then the ethnographic short story can be an effective vehicle for entering that world.

Taking Risks

Meratus say that when God handed out the Holy Book, the Meratus ancestry ate his and thus ensured both internal inspiration and its essentially unarticulated script. (Tsing 1993, 245)

While forms of writing dominate this experimental field, some researchers play with nonverbal representation as well. Blumenfeld-Jones (1995) describes using dance. Clark (1998) is exploring painting as one way to synthesize data from her research with academic women from working-class backgrounds who were of the first generation in their families to attend college. Munoz (1995) uses photography as a form of representation. In these modes, as in creative verbal representations, the "essences (as understood by the artist) are extracted and represented in concrete, condensed forms" (Blumenfeld-Jones 1995, 392).

Yet other researchers are experimenting with "textual strategies" and the layout of text on the printed page. Ronai (1995) writes in a format she calls "the layered account" that, through the use of blank space or a row of periods or asterisks, allows the writer to integrate "abstract theoretical thinking, introspection, emotional experience, fantasies, dreams, and statistics" (395). Through writing short passages, the writer moves from one thought to another in a condensed way that requires the reader to supply transitions.

Lather and Smithies (1997) also play with textual form, using multiple genres and a split-text format to represent research with women living with AIDS. They split the page so that they can write different kinds of text, "a text at multiple levels, a double-coded text that is both broadly accessible and fosters brooding about the issues involved" (Lather 1995, 48). The top of the page focuses on the women and their stories, on dialogue between interviewee and interviewer, and social and cultural issues raised by AIDS; across the bottom of much of the book is commentary by Lather and Smithies regarding their experience doing the research. They also insert what they describe as "factoid" boxes of information about AIDS, plus various forms of writing by some of the women.

Researchers that use creative forms and these textual strategies are creating new kinds of ethnographies that attempt to counter many critiques of traditional ethnographies—that they are boring or written for specialized audiences; that they do not evoke emotions and the senses; that they ignore the role of researcher; and that they neglect the political. "Take risks," urges Ellis. "Write from the heart as well as the head" (in Bochner and Ellis 1996, 42). Through experimenting with form, researchers seek to be open to how the medium is at least part of the message. Different mediums allow you to say (and to see) different things about the lives you seek to represent. Whatever the forms of writing you use, help your readers understand enough, in a way that engages them, that they want to know more.

For more discussion on forms of representing inquiry, see Behar and Gordon (Eds.) 1995, *Women Writing Culture;* Benson (Ed.) 1993, *Anthropology and Literature;* Ellis and Bochner (Eds.) 1996, *Composing Ethnography: Alternative Forms of Qualitative Writing;* Reed-Danahay (Ed.) 1997, *Auto/Ethnography: Rewriting the Self and the Social;* Richardson 1997, *Fields of Play: Constructing an Academic Life;* Tierney and Lincoln 1997, *Representation and the Text: Re-framing the Narrative Voice;* Van Maanen 1995, *Representation in Ethnography,* and 1988, *Tales of the Field.*

Exercises[2]

1. Choose a journal article that reports a qualitative study. Reflect upon how authority is established in the article. What conventions of social science writing are used? What do you learn about the researcher through the article? What do you learn about the researcher's relationship to research participants?

2. Explore some aspect of your research topic by writing a short autoethnography in which you use dramatic recall and images from your own life to situate your research in the personal and the social. Reflect upon what you learned about your topic, your research participants (even though they were not present in your story), and yourself through this exercise.

3. Work with interview transcripts from one person and create a poetic transcription. Use only the words, phrasings, and speaking rhythms of the inter-

viewee. Reflect upon what you learned about your topic, the interviewee, and about yourself through poetic transcription.
4. Work with interview transcripts from several interviewees plus observation notes to create a Reader's Theater piece. Reflect upon what you learned about your topic, about the interviewee, and about yourself through writing up your data as drama.

Notes

1. This section draws from my article "That Rare Feeling: Re-presenting Research through Poetic Transcription" published in 1997 in *Qualitative Inquiry.*
2. Laurel Richardson (1994) suggests a series of writing practices in her chapter "Writing: A Method of Inquiry" in *Handbook of Qualitative Research,* including variations of those presented here. Anyone interested in alternative forms should read her chapter.

Chapter 10

The Continuing Search

The Road goes ever on and on
Down from the door where it began.
Now far ahead the Road has gone,
And I must follow if I can.
Pursuing it with weary feet,
Until it joins some larger way,
Where many paths and errands meet.
And whither then? I cannot say. (Tolkien 1965)

Becoming Qualitative Researchers: The Personal Context

Qualitative research investigates the poorly understood territories of human inter-action. Like scientists who seek to identify and understand the biological and geo-logical processes that create the patterns of a physical landscape, qualitative re-searchers seek to describe and understand the processes that create the patterns of the human terrain.

Research demands near total absorption. In speaking of being a naturalist, a student-in-training in Alaska said, "Somehow you've got to put your heart and soul into it—not just for personal reasons, but to really understand what's going on. The more you allow yourself to fall in love with a place, the more you see the con-nections" (Wilson 1989, 17). Similarly, qualitative researchers find their lives con-sumed by their work as they seek understanding and connections. Personal com-mitment, trust, and time are key to rich data and useful interpretations. Few anticipate the exacting demands of their research endeavors. For example, Toni set out in a pilot project to interview wives of medical interns about their sense of self. Six months later, she exclaimed:

> This project has really become bigger than me! It is everywhere. We talked about it in our social psych brown bag as we discussed feminist methodology. It comes up for me in almost all of my readings, at a conference I attended, in conversations . . . I have so much in my head and noted down somewhere that I have not had time to think about. . . . This project has consumed my life to the exclusion of almost all else.

Another student agreed: "I went to a conference the other day and kept taking notes for my research, and the conference was on a topic not even close to my project." Although, most likely, many of you do not have lives that adapt easily to the demands of qualitative research on your attention, it is when you find your "problem" everywhere that you can be assured you are getting somewhere.

As with any kind of exploration of the unknown, entering qualitative terrain can be lonely. Even though you may discuss your work with colleagues, friends, and research participants, in traditional qualitative research you are alone—unless, of course, you are part of a team. You are alone in the role of researcher at your research site, alone with the ultimate responsibility of fitting the pieces together and finding meaning in the whole. Toni reflected on the loneliness of her work:

> Talk about isolation! I'm feeling it in many realms. One is working with the data, being overwhelmed by it all. I feel isolated at times when I talk about this [lives of spouses of medical interns] because people seem to get uneasy as though I am saying something I shouldn't about medicine. Additionally, I am wondering about how the women [interviewees] will react when they see it . . . and how I will react to how they react.

As Toni suggests, qualitative research can raise self-doubts. You worry that people won't want to talk with you or won't let you observe. You wonder if you are asking the right questions. You suddenly panic over whether your towering stack of notebooks, note cards, and computer disks really tells you anything and, even if these records do, whether you are capable of putting the data bits together in a meaningful way. And you worry that perhaps you will not like what you bring to light.

That you do not know exactly what you search for contributes to periods of confusion and frustration. In the midst of analyzing data on a school in a rural transitional community, Carlton sighed, "I'm not sure if the data confuse me or if I confuse the data." Both surely occur in research projects. As surely, research projects require courage and integrity.

These discontinuities, the disturbing pieces that do not "fit," are actually what may give you clues to your more interesting realizations. You will need to learn to live with confusion, if not welcome it into your life—to see it as a harbinger of new mysteries to unravel. Mary Catherine Bateson (1984) recognized this in the work of her parents, Margaret Mead and Gregory Bateson:

> Both Margaret and Gregory developed a style that involved collecting observational material in the expectation that, however rich and bewildering it might seem at first, they

would arrive at points of recognition when things would "make sense" and fall into place. In the search for such moments of insight they would be dealing with points of congruence within the culture they were looking at and also points of personal response. (163)

Understanding involves getting at participants' perspectives, but it is more than that. It is reaching some collective understanding that includes self, the researcher, and those researched.

Although the research process is often exciting and meaningful, it can also be tiring. Exhaustion seems to hit hardest when one is trying to make sense of the data. Tina wrote,

> I felt extreme fatigue when the interviews were over. That fatigue made transcribing even more deadly. I remember many nights falling asleep for a few minutes at my computer during the transcribing process and thinking that I would never get to the last page. Somehow I did, but it was always a temptation to leave it until the next day.

Despite nights when you fall asleep at your computer, you will have moments of insight, if not stretches of profound contentment. Holly described what the process of writing up research meant for her:

> I have discovered that writing, an integral component of qualitative research methods, is my mind's lover. Transforming my thoughts into words not only allows me to reflect upon who I am and who I am striving to become, but also invites the reader to connect; to form a kind of relationship with me through the printed page.

It is to the printed page and other outcomes of your research that I now turn.

Applications of Qualitative Research: The Outcomes of Your Search

When teachers conduct a study of new students' adaptations to middle school, when mothers map their families' past, or when students challenge the university food service, they all engage in research for a reason. The applications of research are as varied as the researchers and their sundry studies. When people talk about applying research, they generally refer to making use of the final report or manuscript: the research *product*. The research *process*, however, also has its own applications.

USING THE RESEARCH MANUSCRIPT

Research manuscripts or texts can take you places that you have not had opportunity to go, exposing you to other cultures and to unique aspects of your own culture. They also help you to adopt new perspectives, to see something from a different point of view, and to reexamine your own theoretical constructs.

Barone cautions against thinking of the text as a tool: "A text of qualitative inquiry is . . . better viewed as an occasion than as a tool. It is, more precisely, an occasion for the reader to engage in the activities of textual re-creation and dismantling" (Barone 1990a, 306). If you view the text as a tool, then you may too easily accept it as fact and ignore what went into the research process, including values of the researcher and problems in research design.

Instead of responding to research findings as though they represent an absolute truth, use the findings as an opportunity to think about the social world around you. Like the English teacher who said, "The beauty of a good story is its openness—the way you or I or anyone reading it can take it in, and use it for ourselves" (Coles 1989, 47), a good qualitative text invites you in. It encourages you to compare its descriptions and analyses to your own experiences and to, perhaps, think differently about your own particular situation.

Lorna was working on a study concerning the inclusion of children with special needs into public school classrooms. In the midst of analyzing and writing up her work, she reflected upon her text as an occasion for drawing others in, even though not every problem was "solved":

> There are so many questions I am leaving unanswered. Resisting the urge to delete the last half of my paper, I opened the day's *New York Times* magazine. I was drawn to an article about a single mother with AIDS searching for a new "mother" for her only child. In the midst of my tears, I couldn't help but recognize this as qualitative research, as a case study. The power and depth were apparent. And this author also left many questions unanswered.

Scheper-Hughes (1992) describes how the text can be an occasion for *witnessing*, for giving voice to those who have been silenced or for providing a history of "people often presumed to have no history" (29):

> So-called participant observation has a way of drawing the ethnographer into spaces of human life where she or he might really prefer not to go at all and once there doesn't know how to go about getting out except through writing, which draws others there as well, making them party to the act of witnessing. (xii)

Witnessing sets the stage for conversations, dialogue, and systemic change. As Geertz (1988, 147) observes, "It seems likely that whatever use ethnographic texts will have in the future, if in fact they actually have any, it will involve enabling conversation across societal lines—of ethnicity, religion, class, gender, language, race . . . ."

Qualitative research texts also assist in academic pursuits (i.e., hypothesis generation and theory development) and in creating solutions to practical problems. Toni's work with wives of medical interns extends a theory that explains the development of self in relationship to others. Her descriptive stories may also serve as a mode of support and awareness-raising for research participants and other wives of interns. As with many research texts, Toni's work has both theoretical and practical applications.

Undoubtedly, countless reports find their way into the forgotten corner of office shelves rather than become moving, transforming works, yet research reports have changed lives. Willis's (1977) research in England drew attention to the role of resistance in shaping the lives of working-class "lads" both in and out of school. Gilligan's (1982) work with the moral development of women paved the way for exploring the gender bias that had permeated theories of human development, which, for the most part, had been generated from male data. These studies are not without their problems, yet they and others have contributed to how we perceive and interact with the world.

USING THE RESEARCH PROCESS

Unlike the research text, which may be meaningful to people living thousands of miles away from the research site, the usefulness or application of the actual process of doing research is more limited to those involved. This, however, does not detract from its significance and contributions to improving practice, evaluation, policy, and understanding.

Unless asked to participate in someone else's funded research project, you will generally find yourself researching something within your academic or applied discipline (e.g., special education, nursing, social work, educational leadership). As you conduct research, you will invariably learn things that will improve your practice. Dorothy, with nearly twenty years of experience in clinical nursing, stated that she already knew "the value of a carefully placed 'go on,' a contemplative 'uh huh.' " Nonetheless, in her study of the process of committing a loved one to institutional care, she discovered that her interviewees "seem to yearn for a listening ear." Her open-ended, probing questions allowed participants to tell their stories. "For some," she stated, "I have the sense I am the first health professional to listen." In her research role, Dorothy learned more about her clients than she had in her nursing role. Seeing that her clients appreciated an extended opportunity to discuss difficult issues, Dorothy planned to incorporate longer, more probing interviews into her practice. (Similarly, Aamodt, 1989, discussed using qualitative interviewing techniques with children who have cancer in order to provide more personally meaningful care.)

Dorothy also reflected on how the process of participant observation in qualitative inquiry expanded her concept of the potential usefulness of observation in nursing:

> Documenting observations comes as naturally to a nurse as listening. Attention to subtle detail is essential to comprehensive patient assessments. In nursing, however, the areas for observation are clearly prescribed. I know that observing the rate and depth of respirations along with the color of fingernails and mucous membranes will allow me to reach conclusions about lung function. But what specific observations must I record to eventually understand family decision making? Would posture, level of enthusiasm, appearance of fatigue all be useful information? I now consider what I see in general. I describe the apparent uneasiness with which a son relates his inability to keep his dad out of the hospital . . .

By conducting qualitative research, Dorothy learned both skills and knowledge applicable to her nursing practice. Similarly, practitioner-researchers in other disciplines learn skills and knowledge that assist them in carrying out their practice, conducting program evaluations, and shaping policy.

In traditional ethnographic research, the participants may learn something about the conduct of inquiry. Also, the interview and observation process propels participants to become more reflective on aspects of their lives. In participant-oriented research (such as action research and often, critical and feminist research), the research process is intended to assist participants. This kind of inquiry focuses upon issues of concern to those researched. The participants seek particular and localized solutions to some question or allow a researcher to work with them to address inequities or problems of some sort. The participants sometimes become co-researchers and learn not only how to carry out a research project, but also new ways to view or change their lives. When, for example, economically poor and isolated rural Vermont women in "Listening Partner" groups received the opportunity to regularly dialogue and collaboratively problem solve with women in similar situations, they began to look at and live their lives differently; and the relationships they formed through the learning circles rendered them less isolated (Belenky, Bond, and Weinstock 1997). The research *process* is as important as (or more important than) the *product* in participant-oriented research.

USING QUALITATIVE RESEARCH TO LEARN ABOUT YOURSELF

"I reached the wall," Charlie said. "I could not write another piece about the classroom. We were both tired—I of being there, and she of having me there." Charlie was in the midst of research on a multigrade classroom. He had been observing the classroom; interviewing children, parents, and school personnel; and discussing his thoughts in intense meetings with the teacher. After a short break, he returned to the classroom and was welcomed by the teacher and students; in the meantime, he had learned something useful about the process of doing research. Charlie began to schedule different kinds of breaks—reflective breaks that allowed him to take stock of his work, and absolute breaks that gave him a complete rest from the researcher role and gave his participants relief from the intrusion that a researcher, no matter how loved, represents.

The act of researching teaches you about yourself as a researcher. You may take pride in the way that you carefully listen and ask probing questions, but you may also realize that you are not as observant as you had hoped. You may need to develop better strategies to record and remember unspecified interactions. In addition to learning about yourself as a researcher, you may also learn more about yourself in general. Jill reflected, "By looking at what problems interest us and at what questions we ask, we may discover an avenue that leads us to a better understanding of what is important and of meaning to each one of us." Your research is autobiographical in that some aspect of yourself is mirrored in the work you choose to pursue. Figuring out where your interests lie leads you to a greater understanding of your core values and beliefs. Such understanding, in turn, can provide greater direction for future undertakings.

Concluding Words

A naturalist said, "You can love a landscape for a lifetime, and it will still have secrets from you" (Wilson 1989, 18). Whether researching a village in Brazil, a Christian school, or the superintendency of a rural school district, you will never understand it all, but you will know where next to look, what new questions to ask, and what sense it might have for yourself and others. As Lorna reflected upon her pilot project, she stated:

> When I go back and look at my original purposes, I believe that I made some slight progress, small mini-steps, both in terms of understanding inclusion, and learning about and how to use qualitative research. I feel like I cracked open the door, and peeked inside. (It's an enormous room!) The vastness of what is left to explore is simultaneously intimidating and exhilarating. Trying not to feel overwhelmed, I'll remember what one teacher said, "You work and work and work and work and work. And . . . the child makes slow gains." I think she meant that mini-steps count.

Each step, no matter how small, contributes to understanding. Scheper-Hughes (1992) calls for the practice of a "good enough" ethnography, accepting that understandings always will be only partial. We can, however, "struggle to do the best we can with the limited resources we have at hand—our ability to listen and observe carefully, empathetically, and compassionately" (28).

Qualitative inquiry is a search that leads into others' lives, your discipline, your practice, and yourself. You cannot be sure of what you will find, but you invariably get caught up in the search and make steps forward. Andrea's words convey the empathy, compassion, and respect that accompanied her work:

> There is so much I want to know. I feel as though each interview is a rosebud handed to me. As I take them home and transcribe them, they begin to bloom, and each petal is a new idea or a deeper understanding. Here I stand with three beautiful flowers in one hand and my other hand out-stretched. Tomorrow another bud.

True research does not end. Instead, it points the way for yet another search.

Exercises

1. Reflect upon the possible significance of your research. In what ways might it contribute to theory, policy, and/or practice? Write up these thoughts.
2. After completing your pilot project, return to your research statement, your research design, and your interview questions. What modifications would you make?
3. Develop a research proposal and step forth onto the inquiry road.

Appendix

Web Resources[*]

Web Pages

- Association for Qualitative Research:
    http://www.latrobe.edu.au/www/aqr/index.html
- International Institute for Qualitative Methodology:
    http://www.ualberta.ca/~iiqm/
- The Qualitative Report:
    http://www.nova.edu/ssss/QR/index.html
- Qualpage:
    http://www.ualberta.ca/~jrnorris/qual.html
- Readings in Qualitative Analysis:
    http://www.iat.unc.edu/guides/irg-55.html
- Sociological Research Online:
    http://www.socresonline.org.uk/socresonline

Qualitative Research Email Resources

See this website for a number of different email lists related to qualitative research:
http://www.hud.ac.uk/schools/human+health/behavioural_science/socinfo/
otherlin/qualreslists.html

---

[*]This list is not comprehensive. Other websites exist where issues of qualitative research are presented. This list is, however, a place to begin for those of you interested in this form of communication.

References

Aamodt, A. 1989. "Ethnography and epistemology: Generating nursing knowledge." In *Qualitative nursing research: A contemporary dialogue,* edited by J. Morse, 29–40. Rockville, MD: Aspen Publishers.

Adler, P., and P. Adler, 1994. "Observational techniques." In *Handbook of Qualitative Research,* edited by N. Denzin and Y. Lincoln, 377–392. Thousand Oaks, CA: Sage.

Agar, M. 1973. *Ripping and running: A formal ethnography of urban heroin addicts.* San Diego: Academic Press.

———. 1980. *The professional stranger.* New York: Academic Press.

———. 1995. "Literary journalism as ethnography." In *Representation in ethnography,* edited by J. Van Maanen, 112–129. Thousand Oaks, CA: Sage.

American Anthropological Association. 1998. *Code of ethics of the American Anthropological Association.* (6 pages) Http://www.ameranthassn.org

Anderson, G., K. Herr, and A. S. Nihlen. 1994. *Studying your own school: An educator's guide to qualitative practitioner research.* Thousand Oaks, CA: Sage.

Ashton, P., and R. Webb. 1986. *Making a difference: Teacher's sense of efficacy and student achievement.* New York: Longman.

Ball, S. 1985. "Participant observation with pupils." In *Strategies of educational research: Qualitative methods,* edited by R. Burgess, 23–53. Philadelphia: Falmer Press.

Barone, T. 1990a. "Using the narrative text as an occasion for conspiracy." In *Qualitative inquiry in education: The continuing debate,* edited by E. Eisner and A. Peshkin, 305–326. New York: Teachers College Press.

———. 1990b. On the demise of subjectivity in educational inquiry. Paper presented at the annual meeting of the American Educational Research Association, Boston.

Bartunek, J., and M. R. Louis. 1996. *Insider/outsider team research.* Thousand Oaks, CA: Sage.

Bateson, M. C. 1984. *With a daughter's eye.* New York: Morrow.

Becker, H. 1984. Field work with the computer: Criteria for assessing systems. *Qualitative Sociology* 7(1–2):16–33.

———. 1986a. *Doing things together: Selected papers.* Evanston, IL: Northwestern University Press.

———. 1986b. *Writing for social scientists.* Chicago: University of Chicago Press.

Becker, H. S., B. Geer, E. C. Hughes, and A. L. Strauss. 1961. *Boys in white: Student culture in school.* Chicago: University of Chicago Press.

Behar, R. 1993. *Translated woman: Crossing the border with Esperanza's Story.* Boston: Beacon Press.

———. 1995. "Writing in my father's name: A diary of *Translated Woman's* first year." In *Women writing culture,* edited by R. Behar and D. Gordon, 65–82. Berkeley: University of California Press.

———. 1996 *The vulnerable observer: Anthropology that breaks your heart.* Boston: Beacon Press.

Behar, R. and D. Gordon, eds. 1995. *Women writing culture.* Berkeley: University of California Press.

Belenky, M., L. Bond, and J. Weinstock. 1997. *A tradition that has no name: Nurturing the development of people, families, and communities.* New York: Basic Books.

Benson, P., ed. 1993. *Anthropology and literature.* Chicago: University of Illinois Press.

Berg, B. 1995. *Qualitative research methods for the social sciences.* Boston: Allyn & Bacon. (Orig. published 1989)

Berg, D., A. Gordon, and R. LeBailly. 1985. "Anxiety in research relationships." In *Exploring clinical methods for social research,* edited by D. Berg and K. K. Smith, 213–228. Beverly Hills: Sage Publications.

Bernard, R. 1988. *Research methods in cultural anthropology.* Newbury Park, CA: Sage Publications.

Bishop, P. 1998. Portraits of partnership: The relational work of effective middle level partner teachers. Unpublished doctoral dissertation, University of Vermont, Burlington.

Bissex, G. 1987. "Year-long, classroom-based studies." In *Seeing for ourselves: Case-study research by teachers of writing,* edited by G. Bissex and R. Bullock, 31–39. Portsmouth, NH: Heinemann.

Bissex, G., and R. Bullock, eds. 1987. *Seeing for ourselves: Case-study research by teachers of writing.* Portsmouth, NH: Heinemann.

Blumenfeld-Jones, D. 1995. Dance as a mode of research representation. *Qualitative Inquiry* 1 (4): 391–401.

Bochner, A., and C. Ellis. 1996. "Introduction: Talking over ethnography." In *Composing ethnography: Alternative forms of qualitative writing,* edited by C. Ellis and A. Bochner, 13–45. Walnut Creek, CA: AltaMira Press.

Bogdan, R. 1972. *Participant observation in organizational settings.* Syracuse, NY: Syracuse University Press.

Bogdan, R., and S. Biklen. 1992. *Qualitative research for education,* 2d ed. Boston: Allyn and Bacon.

Bottorff, J. 1994. "Using videotaped recordings in qualitative research." In *Critical issues in qualitative research methods,* edited by J. Morse, 244–261. Thousand Oaks, CA: Sage.

Brady, J. 1976. *The craft of interviewing.* Cincinnati: Writer's Digest.

Brooks, M. 1989. *Instant rapport.* New York: Warner Books.

Bruner, E. 1984. "Introduction: Opening up of anthropology." In *Text, play, and story: The construction and reconstruction of self and society,* edited by E. Bruner, 1–16. Washington, DC: American Ethnological Society.

———. 1986. "Experience and its expressions." In *The anthropology of experience,* edited by V. Turner and E. Bruner, 3–30. Urbana: University of Illinois Press.

———. 1993. "Introduction: The ethnographic self and the personal self." In *Anthropology and literature,* edited by P. Benson, 1–26. Urbana: University of Illinois Press.

Bruner, J. 1960. *The process of education.* Cambridge, MA: Harvard University Press.

———. 1979. *On knowing: Essays for the left hand.* Cambridge, MA: Belknap Press.

Bryant, I. 1996. "Action research and reflective practice." In *Understanding educational research,* edited by D. Scott and R. Usher, 106–119. New York: Routledge.

Bulmer, M., ed. 1982. *Social research ethics: An examination of the merits of covert participation observation.* London: Macmillan.

Burgess, R. 1984. *In the field: An introduction to field research.* London: Unwin Hyman.

Busier, H. 1997. Beyond the yellow brick road: Educational portraits of anorexic women. Unpublished doctoral dissertation, University of Vermont, Burlington.

Busier, H., K. Clark, R. Esch, C. Glesne, Y. Pigeon, and J. Tarule. 1997. Intimacy in research. *The International Journal of Qualitative Studies in Education* 10 (2): 165–170.

Caro, R. 1988. "Lyndon Johnson and the roots of power." In *Extraordinary lives: The art and craft of American biography,* edited by W. Zinsser, 199–231. Boston: Houghton Mifflin.

Carr, W., and S. Kemmis. 1986. *Becoming critical: Education, knowledge and action research.* London: Falmer Press.

Carspecken, P., and M. Apple. 1992. Critical qualitative research: Theory, methodology, and practice. In *The handbook of qualitative research in education,* edited by M. LeCompte, W. Millroy, and J. Preissle, 507–553. San Diego, CA: Academic Press.

Casagrande, J. B., ed. 1960. *In the company of Man: Twenty portraits by anthropologists.* New York: Harper & Brothers.

Cassell, J. 1987. "Cases and comments." In *Handbook on ethical issues in anthropology,* edited by J. Cassell and S. E. Jacobs, 37–75. Washington, DC: American Anthropological Association.

Cassell, J., and S. E. Jacobs, eds. 1987. "Introduction." In *Handbook on ethical issues in anthropology,* 1–3. Washington, DC: American Anthropological Association.

Clark, K. (1998). Moving beyond recognition: The voiced renderings of women academics that have experience being first-generation college students from poor and working class backgrounds. Unpublished doctoral dissertation, University of Vermont, Burlington. Manuscript in preparation.

Clifford, J. 1986. "On ethnographic allegory." In *Writing culture: The poetics and politics of ethnography,* edited by J. Clifford and G. Marcus, 98–121. Berkeley: University of California Press.

Cobb, A., and J. Hagemaster. 1987. Ten criteria for evaluating qualitative research proposals. *Journal of Nursing Education* 26(4):138–143.

Cochran-Smith, M., and S. Lytle. 1993. *Inside/outside: Teacher research and knowledge.* New York: Teachers College Press.

Coffey, A., and P. Atkinson. 1996. *Making sense of qualitative data: Complementary research strategies.* Thousand Oaks, CA: Sage.

Coles, R. 1977. *Eskimos, Chicanos, Indians.* Boston: Little, Brown.

Coles, R. 1989. *The call of stories: Teaching and the moral imagination.* Boston: Houghton Mifflin.

Collier, J. Jr., and M. Collier. 1986. *Visual anthropology: Photography as a research method.* Albuquerque: University of New Mexico Press.

Colvard, R. 1967. "Interaction and identification in reporting field research: A critical reconsideration of protective procedures." In *Ethics, politics and social research,* edited by G. Sjoberg, 319–358. Cambridge, MA: Schenkman.

Conrad, P., and S. Reinharz, eds. 1984. Computers and qualitative data: Editors' introductory essay. *Qualitative Sociology* 7(1–2):3–15.

Couch, J. 1987. Objectivity: A crutch and club for bureaucrats/A haven for lost souls. *Sociological Quarterly* 28:105–110.

Creswell, J. 1998. *Qualitative inquiry and research design.* Thousand Oaks, CA: Sage.

Crisler, L. 1958. *Arctic Wild.* New York: Harper & Brothers.

Dalton, M. 1959. *Men who manage.* New York: Wiley.

Daniels, A. K. 1967. "The low caste stranger." In *Ethics, politics and social research,* edited by G. Sjoberg, 267–296. Cambridge, MA: Schenkman.

Davies, K. 1996. Capturing women's lives: A discussion of time and methodological issues. *Women's Studies International Forum* 19(6): 579–588.

Davis, J. 1972. "Teachers, kids, and conflict: Ethnography of a junior high school." In *The cultural experience: Ethnography in complex society,* edited by J. Spradley and D. McCurdy, 103–120. Chicago: Science Research.

Delamont, S. 1992. *Fieldwork in educational settings: Methods, pitfalls and perspectives.* Washington, DC: Falmer Press.

Denny, T. 1978. Storytelling and educational understanding. Paper presented at the national meeting of the International Reading Association, Houston.

Denzin, N. 1988. *The research act,* rev. ed. New York: McGraw-Hill.

———. 1989. *Interpretive interactionism.* Newbury Park, CA: Sage Publications.

————. 1997. *Interpretive ethnography: Ethnographic practices for a 21st Century*. Thousand Oaks, CA: Sage.

Denzin, N., and Y. Lincoln, eds. 1994. *Handbook of qualitative research*. Thousand Oaks, CA: Sage.

Dickens, D., and A. Fontana, eds. 1994. *Postmodernism social inquiry*. New York: The Guilford Press.

Didion, J. 1988. Interview on "Fresh Air" program, 19 Jan. 1988. National Public Radio.

Diener, E., and R. Crandall. 1978. *Ethics in social behavioral research*. Chicago: University of Chicago Press.

Dillard, A. 1982. *Living by fiction*. New York: Harper and Row.

Dillon, D. R. 1989. Showing them that I want to learn and that I care about who they are: A microethnography of the social organization of a secondary low-track English-reading classroom. *American Educational Research Journal* 26:227–259.

Dobbert, M. L. 1982. *Ethnographic research: Theory and application for modern schools and societies*. New York: Praeger.

Donmoyer, R., and J. Yennie-Donmoyer. 1995. Data as drama: Reflections on the use of readers theater as a mode of qualitative data display. *Qualitative Inquiry* 1 (4): 402–428.

Douglas, J. 1976. *Investigative social research: Individual and team field research*. Beverly Hills, CA: Sage Publications.

————. 1985. *Creative interviewing*. Beverly Hills, CA: Sage Publications.

Ebbutt, D. 1985. "Educational action research: Some general concerns and specific quibbles." In *Issues in educational research: Qualitative methods*, edited by R. Burgess, 152–174. Philadelphia: Falmer Press.

Eisner, E. 1981. On the differences between scientific and artistic approaches to qualitative research. *Educational Researcher* 10(4):5–9.

————. 1990. Objectivity in education research. Paper presented at the annual meeting of the American Educational Research Association, Boston.

————. 1997. The promise and perils of alternative forms of data representation. *Educational Researcher* 26 (6):4–10.

Eisner, E., and A. Peshkin, eds. 1990. *Qualitative inquiry in education: The continuing debate*. New York: Teachers College Press.

Ellen, R. F. 1984. *Ethnographic research: A guide to general conduct*. New York: Academic Press.

Ellis, C. 1995. The other side of the fence: Seeing black and white in a small southern town. *Qualitative Inquiry* 1 (2): 147–167.

Ellis, C., and A. Bochner, eds. 1996. *Composing ethnography: Alternative forms of qualitative writing*. Walnut Creek, CA: AltaMira Press.

English, F. 1988. The utility of the camera in qualitative research. *Educational Researcher* 17(4):8–15.

Enright, S., and J. Tammivaara. 1984. Tell me more: The elicitation of interview data in a microethnographic study of multicultural classrooms. Paper presented at the annual meeting of the American Educational Research Association, New Orleans.

Erickson, F. 1973. What makes school ethnography "ethnographic"? *Council on Anthropology and Education Newsletter* 4(2):10–19.

————. 1986. "Qualitative methods in research on teaching." In *Handbook of research on teaching*, edited by M. C. Wittrock, 119–161. New York: Macmillan.

Erickson, F., and G. Mohatt. 1982. "Cultural organization of participant structures in two classrooms of Indian students." In *Doing the ethnography of schooling: Educational anthropology in action*, edited by G. Spindler, 132–174. New York: Holt, Rinehart and Winston.

Esch, R. 1996. Conversation between intimates, an evening of chamber music: Girls friendship, self, and experience during the transition from childhood to adolescence. Unpublished doctoral dissertation proposal, University of Vermont, Burlington.

Esteva, G., and M. S. Prakash. 1998. *Grassroots post-modernism*. New York: Zed Books.

Farganis, S. 1994. Postmodernism and feminism. In *Postmodernism and social inquiry*, edited by D. Dickens and A. Fontana, 101–126. New York: The Guilford Press.

Fetterman, D. 1989. *Ethnography: Step by step*. Newbury Park, CA: Sage Publications.

Finch, J. 1984. "It's great to have someone to talk to: The ethics and politics of interviewing women." In *Social researching: Politics, problems and practice*, edited by C. Bell and H. Roberts, 70–88. London: Routledge & Kegan Paul.

Fine, G., and K. Sandstrom. 1988. *Knowing children: Participant observation with minors*. Newbury Park, CA: Sage.

Fine, G. A. 1980. "Cracking diamonds: Observer role in Little League baseball settings and the acquisition of social competence." In *Fieldwork experiences: Qualitative approaches to social research*, edited by W. Shiffir, R. Stebbins, and A. Turowetz, 117–132. New York: St. Martin's Press.

Finley, S., and G. Knowles. 1995. Researcher as artist/artist as researcher. *Qualitative Inquiry* 1 (1): 110–142.

Firestone, W. 1987. Meaning in method: The rhetoric of quantitative and qualitative research. *Educational Researcher* 16(7):16–21.

Flinders, D. 1987. What teachers learn from teaching: Educational criticisms of instructional adaptation. Unpublished doctoral dissertation, Stanford University, Stanford, CA.

———. 1992. In search of ethical guidance: Constructing a basis for dialogue. *Qualitative Studies in Education* 5 (2): 101–115.

Flinders, D., and G. Mills, eds. 1993. *Theory and concepts in qualitative research: Perspectives from the field*. New York: Teachers College Press.

Fonow, M., and J. Cook, eds. 1991. *Beyond methodology: Feminist scholarship as lived research*. Bloomington: Indiana University Press.

Fontana, A. 1994. Ethnographic trends in the postmodern era. In *Postmodernism and social inquiry*, edited by D. Dickens and A. Fontana, 203–223. New York: The Guilford Press.

Fontana, A., and J. Frey. 1994. "Interviewing: The art of science." In *Handbook of qualitative research*, edited by N. Denzin and Y. Lincoln, 361–376. Thousand Oaks, CA: Sage.

Freilich, M. 1977. *Marginal natives: Anthropologists at work*. New York: Harper & Row.

Freire, P. 1988. *Pedagogy of the oppressed*. New York: Continuum. (Orig. published 1970)

Fulwiler, T. 1985. Writing is everybody's business. *National Forum: Phi Kappa Phi Journal* 65(4):21–24.

Furney, K. 1997. Caring as the cornerstone of change: A cross-case analysis of three schools' experience in implementing general and special education reform. Unpublished doctoral dissertation, University of Vermont, Burlington.

Gall, M., W. Borg, and J. Gall. 1996. *Educational research*, 6th ed. New York: Longman.

Galliher, J. F. 1982. "The protection of human subjects: A reexamination of the professional code of ethics." In *Social research ethics*, edited by M. Bulmer, 152–165. London: Macmillan.

Gans, H. 1962. *The urban villagers: Group and class in the life of Italian-Americans*. New York: Free Press.

———. 1982. "The participant-observer as a human being: Observations on the personal aspects of fieldwork." In *Field research: A sourcebook and field manual*, edited by R. Burgess, 53–61. London: George Allen & Unwin.

Geertz, C. 1973. *The interpretation of cultures*. New York: Basic Books.

———. 1988. *Work and lives: The anthropologist as author*. Stanford: Stanford University Press.

———. 1995. *After the fact: Two countries four decades one anthropologist*. Cambridge, MA: Harvard University Press.

Gilligan, C. 1982. *In a different voice*. Cambridge, MA: Harvard University Press.

Gitlin, Andrew, ed. 1994. *Power and method: Political activism and educational research*. New York: Routledge.

Glaser, B. 1978. *Theoretical sensitivity*. Mill Valley, CA: Sociology Press.

Glaser, B., and A. Strauss. 1967. *The discovery of grounded theory: Strategies for qualitative research*. Chicago: Aldine.

Glazer, M. 1972. *The research adventure: Promise and problems of fieldwork*. New York: Random House.

———. 1982. "The threat of the stranger: Vulnerability, reciprocity, and fieldwork." In *Ethics of social research: Fieldwork, regulation, and publication*, edited by J. Sieber, 49–70. New York: Springer-Verlag.

Glesne, C. 1985. Strugglin', but no slavin': Agriculture, education, and rural young Vincentians. Unpublished doctoral dissertation, University of Illinois, Urbana.

———. 1989. Rapport and friendship in ethnographic research. *International Journal of Qualitative Studies in Education* 2(1):45–54.

———. 1997. That rare feeling: Re-presenting research through poetic transcription. *Qualitative Inquiry* 3 (2): 202–221.

Glesne, C., and A. Peshkin. 1992. *Becoming qualitative researchers*. NY: Longman.

Gold, R. 1969. "Roles in sociological field observations." In *Issues in participant observation: A text and reader,* edited by G. McCall and J. L. Simmons, 30–39. Menlo Park, CA: Addison-Wesley.

Gonzalez, N. 1986. "The anthropologist as female head of household." In *Self, sex. and gender in cross-cultural fieldwork*, edited by T. L. Whitehead and M. E. Conaway, 84–100. Urbana: University of Illinois Press.

Gorden, R. 1975. *Interviewing: Strategy, technique, and tactics*. Homewood, IL: Dorsey Press. (Orig. published 1969)

Goswami, D., and P. Stillman, eds. 1987. *Reclaiming the classroom: Teacher research as an agency for change*. Upper Montclair, NJ: Boynton Cook.

Gould, S. 1990. *Wonderful life: The Burgess Shale*. New York: W. W. Norton.

Griffiths, G. 1985. "Doubts, dilemmas and diary-keeping: Some reflections on teacher-based research." In *Issues in educational research*, edited by R. Burgess, 197–215. Philadelphia: Falmer Press.

Guba, E., 1990. "The alternative paradigm dialog." In *The paradigm dialog*, edited by E. Guba, 17–27. Newbury Park, CA: Sage.

———, ed. 1990. *The paradigm dialog*. Newbury Park, CA: Sage Publications.

Guba, E., and Y. Lincoln. 1994. "Competing paradigms in qualitative research." In *Handbook of qualitative research*, edited by N. Denzin and Y. Lincoln, 105–117. Thousand Oaks, CA: Sage.

Hagedorn, M. 1994. Hermeneutic photography: An innovative esthetic technique for generating data in nursing research. *Advances in Nursing Science* 17(1):44–50.

Hammersley, M., and P. Atkinson. 1983. *Ethnography: Principles in practice*. New York: Tavistock.

Hamnett, M., and D. Porter. 1983. "Problems and prospects in Western approaches to cross-national social science research." In *Handbook of intercultural training*, edited by D. Landis and R. Breslin, 61–81. New York: Pergamon Press.

Hansen, J. P. 1976. "The anthropologist in the field: Scientist, friend, voyeur." In *Ethics and anthropology: Dilemmas in field work*, edited by M. A. Rynkiewich and J. P. Spradley, 123–134. New York: Wiley.

Harding, S., ed. 1987. *Feminism and methodology*. London: Routledge.

Harker, R. 1993. Searching for trees in the postmodern forest: Tales of an educational dog. Paper presented at the NZARE Annual Conference, University of Waikato, New Zealand.

Heath, S. B. 1983. *Ways with words: Language, life, and work in communities and classrooms*. Cambridge: Cambridge University Press.

Hersey, J. 1988. Agee. *New Yorker,* 18 July, 72–82.

Hollingsworth, S. ed. 1997. *International action research: A casebook for educational reform*. Washington DC: The Falmer Press.

Holstein, J., and J. Gubrium. 1994. "Phenomenology, ethnomethodology, and interpretive practice." In *Handbook of qualitative research*, edited by N. Denzin and Y. Lincoln, 262–272. Thousand Oaks, CA: Sage.

Homan, R., and M. Bulmer. 1982. "On the merits of covert methods: A dialogue." In *Social research ethics*, edited by M. Bulmer, 105–124. London: Macmillan.

hooks, b. 1984. *Feminist theory from margin to center*. Boston: South End Press.

Horowitz, R. 1986. Remaining an outsider: Membership as a threat to the research report. *Urban Life* 14:409–430.

Howe, K. 1988. Against the quantitative-qualitative incompatibility thesis, or dogmas die hard. *Educational Researcher* 17(8):10–16.

Humphreys, L. 1970. *Tearoom trade: Impersonal sex in public places*. Chicago: Aldine.

Hunt, J. 1984. The development of rapport through the negotiation of gender in field work among police. *Human Organization* 43:283–296.

Hustler, E., A. Cassidy, and E. C. Cuff, eds. 1986. *Action research in classrooms and schools*. Boston: Allen & Unwin.

Hyman, H. 1975. *Interviewing in social research*. Chicago: University of Chicago Press. (Orig. published 1954)

Hymes, D. H. 1982. "What is ethnography?" In *Children in and out of school*, edited by P. Gilmore and A. Glatthorn, 21–32. Washington, DC: Center for Applied Linguistics.

Jacob, E. 1988. Clarifying qualitative research. *Educational Researcher* 17(1):16–24.

Jacobs, S. E. 1987. "Cases and solutions." In *Handbook on ethical issues in anthropology*, edited by J. Cassell and S. E. Jacobs, 20–36. Washington, DC: American Anthropological Association.

Jansen, G., and A. Peshkin. 1992. "Subjectivity in qualitative research." In *The handbook of qualitative research in education*, edited by M. LeCompte, W. Millroy, and J. Preissle, 681–725. New York: Academic Press.

Jeske, J. 1984. Demystifying the dissertation. Los Angeles: University of California (ERIC document Reproduction Service no. ED 268 529; CS 209 648).

Johnson, C. 1982. "Risks in the publication of fieldwork." In *Ethics of social research: Fieldwork, regulation, and publication*, edited by J. Sieber, 71–92. New York: Springer-Verlag.

Jorgensen, D. 1989. *Participant observation: A methodology for human studies*. Newbury Park, CA: Sage Publications.

Kay, P. 1997. Whose child is this? Reader's Theater exploring the sociocultural tensions experienced by a parent and a teacher around a child's emotional and behavioral issues. Paper presented at the American Educational Research Association meetings, Chicago, Illinois.

Kelly, A. 1985. "Action research: What is it and what can it do?" In *Issues of educational research*, edited by R. Burgess, 129–151. Philadelphia: Falmer Press.

Kemmis, S., and R. McTaggart, eds. 1988. *The action planner*, 3rd ed. Geelong: Deakin University Press.

Kinchelow, J., and P. McLaren. 1994. Rethinking critical theory and qualitative research. In *Handbook of qualitative research*, edited by N. Denzin and Y. Lincoln, 138–157. Thousand Oaks, CA: Sage.

Kleinman, S., and M. Copp. 1993. *Emotions and fieldwork*. Newbury Park, CA: Sage.

Krieger, S. 1985. Beyond "subjectivity": The use of the self in social science. *Qualitative Sociology* 8:309–324.

———. 1991. *Social science and the self: Personal essays on an art form*. New Brunswick, NJ: Rutgers.

Kulick, D. 1995. "The sexual life of anthropologists: Erotic subjectivity and ethnographic work." In *Taboo: Sex, identity and erotic subjectivity in anthropological fieldwork*, edited by D. Kulick and M. Willson, 1–28. New York: Routledge.

Kulick, D., and M. Willson, eds. 1995. *Taboo: Sex, identity and erotic subjectivity in anthropological fieldwork*. New York: Routledge.

Kvale, S. 1996. *InterViews: An introduction to qualitative research interviewing.* Thousand Oaks, CA: Sage.

Lamott, A. 1994. *Bird by bird: Some instructions on writing and life.* New York: Pantheon Books.

Lareau, A., and J. Shultz, eds. 1996. *Journeys through ethnography: Realistic accounts of fieldwork.* Boulder, CO: Westview Press.

Lather, P. 1991. *Getting smart: Feminist research and pedagogy with/in the postmodern.* New York: Routledge and Kegan Paul.

———. 1995. The validity of angels: Interpretive and textual strategies in researching the lives of women with HIV/AIDS. *Qualitative Inquiry* 1 (1): 41–68.

———. 1996. Troubling clarity: The politics of accessible language. *Harvard Educational Review* 66 (3): 525–545.

Lather, P., and C. Smithies. 1997. *Troubling the angels: Women living with HIV/AIDS.* Boulder, CO: Westview Press.

Lawless, R., V. Sutlive, and M. Zamora, eds. 1983. *Fieldwork: The human experience.* New York: Gordon & Breach Science Publications.

LeCompte, M. 1987. Bias in the biography: Bias and subjectivity in ethnographic research. *Anthropology and Education Quarterly* 18:43–52.

LeCompte, M., and J. Preissle, with R. Tesch. 1993. *Ethnography and qualitative design in educational research,* 2nd ed. New York: Academic Press.

Lewin, E., and W. Leap, eds. 1996. *Out in the field: Reflections of lesbian and gay anthropologists.* Chicago: University of Illinois Press.

Lewis, O. 1979. *Children of Sanchez.* New York: Random House.

Liebow, E. 1967. *Tally's Corner.* Boston: Little, Brown.

Liggett, A., C. Glesne, A. P. Johnson, S. Hasazi, and R. Schattman. 1994. Teaming in qualitative research: Lessons learned. *The International Journal of Qualitative Studies in Education* 7(1):77–88.

Lightfoot, S. 1983. *The good high school.* New York: Basic Books.

Lincoln, Y., and N. Denzin. 1994. "The fifth moment." In *Handbook of qualitative research,* edited by N. Denzin and Y. Lincoln, 575–586. Thousand Oaks, CA: Sage.

Lincoln, Y. 1990. "Toward a categorical imperative for qualitative research." In *Qualitative inquiry in education: The continuing debate,* edited by E. Eisner and A. Peshkin, 277–295. New York: Teachers College Press.

Lincoln, Y., and E. Guba. 1985. *Naturalistic inquiry.* Beverly Hills: Sage Publications.

Linden, R. 1993. *Making stories, making selves: Feminist reflections on the Holocaust.* Columbus: Ohio State University Press.

Lipson, J. 1994. "Ethical issues in ethnography." In *Critical issues in qualitative research methods,* edited by J. Morse, 333–354. Thousand Oaks, CA: Sage.

Lofland, J. 1971. *Analyzing social settings: A guide to qualitative observation and analysis.* Belmont, CA: Wadsworth.

Loving, C. 1997. From the summit of truth to its slippery slopes. *American Education Research Journal* 34 (3):421–452.

Luke, C. and J. Gore, eds. 1992. *Feminisms and critical pedagogy.* New York: Routledge.

Macleod, J. 1987. *Ain't no makin' it: Leveled aspirations in a low-income neighborhood.* Boulder, CO: Westview Press.

Maguire, P. 1987. *Doing participatory research: A feminist approach.* Amherst: The Center for International Education, University of Massachusetts.

———. 1996. Considering more feminist participatory research: What's congruency got to do with it? *Qualitative Inquiry* 2 (1): 106–118.

Malcolm, J. 1987. Reflections. *New Yorker,* 20 April, 84–102.

Malinowski, B. 1967. *A diary in the strict sense of the term.* New York: Harcourt, Brace & World.

Marcus, G., and M. Fischer. 1986. *Anthropology as cultural critique: An experimental moment in the human sciences.* Chicago: University of Chicago Press.

Markham, B. 1983. *West with the night.* San Francisco: North Point Press. (Orig. published 1942)

Marris, P. 1974. *Loss and change.* London: Routledge & Kegan Paul.

Marshall, C., and G. Rossman. 1995. *Designing qualitative research,* 2d ed. Thousand Oaks, CA: Sage.

Maxwell, J. 1996. *Qualitative research design: An interactive approach.* Thousand Oaks, CA: Sage.

McCall, G., and J. L. Simmons, eds. 1969. *Issues in participant observation: A text and reader.* Reading, MA: Addison-Wesley.

McDermott, R. 1987. "Achieving school failure: An anthropological approach to illiteracy and social stratification." In *Education and cultural process,* 2d ed., edited by G. Spindler, 173–209. Prospect Heights, IL: Waveland Press.

McMillan, J. 1989. Focus group interviews: Implications for educational research. Paper presented at the annual meeting of the American Educational Research Association, San Francisco.

McTaggart, R., ed. 1997. *Participatory action research: International contexts and consequences.* Albany: State University of New York.

Mead, M. 1949. *Coming of age in Samoa.* New York: Mentor Books.

Measor, L. 1985. "Interviewing: A strategy in qualitative research." In *Strategies of educational research: Qualitative methods,* edited by R. Burgess, 55–77. Philadelphia: Falmer Press.

Merriam, S. 1988. *Case study research in education: A qualitative approach.* San Francisco: Jossey-Bass.

Metz, M. H. 1978. *Classrooms and corridors: The crisis of authority in desegregated secondary schools.* Berkeley: University of California Press.

Mienczakowski, J. 1995. The theater of ethnography: The reconstruction of ethnography into theater with emancipatory potential. *Qualitative Inquiry* 1 (3): 360–375.

Mies, M. 1983. "Towards a methodology for feminist research." In *Theories of women's studies,* edited by G. Bowles and R. Duelli Klein, 117–139. Boston: Routledge & Kegan Paul.

Miles, M., and A. M. Huberman. 1994. *Qualitative data analysis,* 2d ed. Thousand Oaks, CA: Sage.

Miller, J. 1990. *Creating spaces and finding voices: Teachers collaborating for empowerment.* Albany: State University of New York Press.

Miller, S. M. 1952. The participant observer and "overrapport." *American Sociological Review* 17:97–99.

Mills, C. W. 1951. *White collar.* New York: Oxford University Press.

Mitchell, R. Jr. 1993. *Secrecy and fieldwork.* Newbury Park, CA: Sage.

Mohr, M., and M. Maclean. 1987. *Working together: A guide for teacher researchers.* Urbana, IL: National Center of Teachers of English.

Moorehead, A. 1959. *No room in the ark.* New York: Harper & Brothers.

Moreno, E. 1995. "Rape in the field: Reflections from a survivor." In *Taboo: Sex, identity, and erotic subjectivity in anthropological fieldwork,* edited by D. Kulick and M. Willson, 219–250. New York: Routledge.

Morgan, D. 1997. *Focus groups as qualitative research,* 2nd ed. Newbury Park, CA: Sage.

Munoz, V. 1995. *"Where something catches": Work, love, and identity in youth.* Albany: State University of New York Press.

Murray, D. 1986. One writer's secrets. *College Composition and Communication* 37:146–153.

Myerhoff, B. 1979. *Number our days: Culture and community among elderly Jews in an American ghetto.* New York: Meridian.

Myrdal, J. 1965. *Report from a Chinese village.* New York: Pantheon Books.

Nagel, P. 1988. "The Adams women." In *Extraordinary lives: The art and craft of American Biography,* edited by W. Zinsser, 91–120. Boston: Houghton Mifflin.

Naples, N., ed. 1998. *Community activism and feminist politics: Organizing across race, class, and gender.* New York: Routledge.

Nielsen, J., ed. 1990. *Feminist research methods.* San Francisco: Westview Press.

Nisbet, R. 1976. *Sociology as an art form.* New York: Oxford University Press.

Noffke, S., and R. Stevenson, eds. 1995. *Educational action research: Becoming practically critical.* New York: Teachers College Press.

Oboler, R. S. 1986. "For better or worse: Anthropologists and husbands in the field." In *Self, sex, and gender in cross-cultural fieldwork,* edited by T. Whitehead and M. Conaway, 28–51. Chicago: University of Illinois Press.

Olesen, V. 1994. "Feminisms and models of qualitative research." In *Handbook of qualitative research,* edited by N. Denzin and Y. Lincoln, 158–174. Thousand Oaks, CA: Sage.

Pachter, M., ed. 1981. *Telling lives: The biographer's art.* Philadelphia: University of Pennsylvania Press.

Patton, M. 1990. *Qualitative evaluation and research methods,* 2d ed. Newbury Park, CA: Sage Publications.

Pelto, P. J., and G. H. Pelto. 1978. *Anthropological research: The structure of inquiry,* 2d ed. Cambridge: Cambridge University Press.

Perreault, J. 1995. *Writing selves: Contemporary feminist autography.* Minneapolis: University of Minnesota Press.

Peshkin, A. 1972. *Kanuri schoolchildren: Education and social mobilization in Bornu.* New York: Holt, Rinehart & Winston.

———. 1978. *Growing up American: Schooling and the survival of community.* Chicago: University of Chicago Press.

———. 1982a. *The imperfect union: School consolidation and community conflict.* Chicago: University of Chicago Press.

———. 1982b. "The researcher and subjectivity: Reflections on ethnography of school and community." In *Doing the ethnography of schooling,* edited by G. Spindler, 20–47. New York: Holt, Rinehart & Winston.

———. 1985. From title to title: The evolution of perspective in naturalistic inquiry. *Anthropology and Education Quarterly* 16:214–224.

———. 1986. *God's choice: The total world of a fundamentalist Christian school.* Chicago: University of Chicago Press.

———. 1988a. In search of subjectivity—one's own. *Educational Researcher* 17(7):17–22.

———. 1988b. "Virtuous subjectivity: In the participant-observer's I's." In *The self in social inquiry,* edited by D. Berg and K. Smith, 267–282. Newbury Park, CA: Sage Publications.

———. 1991. *The color of strangers, the color of friends: The play of ethnicity in school and community.* Chicago: University of Chicago Press.

Pettigrew, J. 1981. "Reminiscences of fieldwork among the Sikhs." In *Doing feminist research,* edited by H. Roberts, 62–82. Boston: Routledge & Kegan Paul.

Pfaffenberger, B. 1988. *Microcomputer applications in qualitative research.* Newbury Park, CA: Sage Publications.

Pigeon, Y. 1998. Among Adults: An Exploration of Adult-Student Learning Groups. Unpublished dissertation, University of Vermont, Burlington. Manuscript in preparation.

Plante, D. 1986. Profiles: Sir Steven Runciman. *New Yorker,* 3 Nov., 53–80.

Plummer, K. 1983. *Documents of life.* Boston: Allen & Unwin.

Popkewitz, T. 1984. *Paradigm and ideology in educational research: The social functions of the intellectual.* New York: Falmer Press.

Potter, W. J. 1996. *An analysis of thinking and research about qualitative methods.* Mahway, NJ: Lawrence Erlbaum.

Pritchett, V. S. 1987. Books: One of nature's Balkans. *New Yorker,* 21 Dec., 132–154.

Pugach, M. 1998. *On the border of opportunity: Education, community and language at the U.S.-Mexico line.* Mahwah, NJ: Lawrence Erlbaum.

Punch, M. 1986. *The politics and ethics of fieldwork.* Beverly Hills, CA: Sage Publications.

———. 1994. "Politics and ethics in qualitative research." In *Handbook of qualitative research,* edited by N. Denzin and Y. Lincoln, 83–97. Thousand Oaks, CA: Sage.

Purvis, J. 1985. "Reflections upon doing historical documentary research from a feminist perspective." In *Strategies of educational research: Qualitative methods,* edited by R. Burgess, 179–205. Philadelphia: Falmer Press.

Quantz, R. 1992. "On critical ethnography." In *The handbook of qualitative research in education,* edited by M. LeCompte, W. Millroy, and J. Preissle, 447–505. San Diego, CA: Academic Press.

Rajchman, J. 1988. Foucault's art of seeing. *October* 44 (Spring): 89–117.

Rawlings, M. 1942. *Cross creek.* New York: Charles Scribner.

Reason, P., ed. 1988. *Human inquiry in action: Developments in new paradigm research.* Newbury Park, CA: Sage.

Reed-Danahay, D., ed. 1997. *Auto/Ethnography: Rewriting the self and the social.* New York: Berg.

Reichardt, C. S., and T. D. Cook, eds. 1979. "Beyond qualitative versus quantitative methods." In *Qualitative and quantitative methods in evaluation research,* 7–32. Beverly Hills: Sage Publications.

Reinharz, S. 1992. *Feminist methods in social research.* New York: Oxford University Press.

Richardson, L. 1990. *Writing strategies: Reaching diverse audiences.* Newbury Park, CA: Sage.

———. 1992. "The consequences of poetic representation." In *Investigating subjectivity: Research on lived experience,* edited by C. Ellis and M.G. Flaherty, 125–137. Newbury Park, CA: Sage.

———. 1994a. Nine poems. *Journal of Contemporary Ethnography* 23 (1): 3–13.

———. 1994b. "Writing: A method of inquiry." In *Handbook of qualitative research,* edited by N. Denzin and Y. Lincoln, 516–529. Thousand Oaks, CA: Sage.

———. 1997. *Fields of play: Constructing an academic life.* New Brunswick, NJ: Rutgers.

Riley, G., ed. 1974. *Values, objectivity, and the social sciences.* Reading, MA: Addison-Wesley.

Rist, R. 1977. On the relations among educational research paradigms: From disdain to detente. *Anthropology and Education Quarterly* 8:42–49.

Robbins, T., D. Anthony, and T. Curtis. 1973. The limits of symbolic realism: Problems of empathic field observation in a sectarian context. *Journal for the Scientific Study of Religion* 12:259–271.

Rogers, C. 1942. The non-directive method as a technique for social research. *American Journal of Sociology* 50:279–283.

Ronai, C. 1995. Multiple reflections of child sex abuse: An argument for a layered account. *Journal of Contemporary Ethnography* 23 (4): 395–426.

Rose, D. 1993. "Ethnography as a form of life: The written word and the work of the world." In *Anthropology and Literature,* edited by P. Benson, 192–224. Urbana: University of Illinois Press.

Rosengarten, T. 1985. "Stepping over cockleburs: Conversations with Ned Cobb." In *Telling lives: The biographer's art,* edited by M. Pachter, 105–131. Philadelphia: University of Pennsylvania Press.

Rubin, H., and I. Rubin. 1995. *Qualitative interviewing: The art of hearing data.* Thousand Oaks, CA: Sage.

Rynkiewich, M. A., and J. P. Spradley, eds. 1976. *Ethics and anthropology: Dilemmas in field work.* New York: Wiley.

Sandelowski, M. 1994. "The proof is in the pottery: Toward a poetic for qualitative inquiry." In *Critical issues in qualitative research methods,* edited by J. Morse, 46–63. Thousand Oaks, CA: Sage.

Sanjek, R., ed. 1990. *Fieldnotes: The makings of anthropology.* Ithaca, NY: Cornell University Press.

Scheper-Hughes, N. 1992. *Death without weeping: The violence of everyday life in Brazil.* Berkeley: University of California Press.

Schofield, J. 1989. *Black and white in school: Trust, tension, or tolerance?* New York: Teachers College Press.

Schuman, H. 1970. "The random probe: A technique for evaluating the validity of closed questions." In *Stages of social research*, edited by D. P. Forcese and S. Rocher, 240–245. Englewood Cliffs, NJ: Prentice-Hall.

Schwandt, T. 1989. Solutions to the paradigm conflict: Coping with uncertainty. *Journal of Contemporary Ethnography* 17:379–407.

———. 1990. "Paths to inquiry in the social disciplines: Scientific, constructivist, and critical theory methodologies." In *The paradigm dialog*, edited by E. Guba, 258–276. Newbury Park, CA: Sage.

Scott, D. 1996. "Methods and data in educational research." In *Understanding educational research*, edited by D. Scott and R. Usher, 52–73. New York: Routledge.

Scott, D., and R. Usher, eds. 1996. *Understanding educational research.* New York: Routledge.

Seidman, I. E. 1991. *Interviewing as qualitative research.* New York: Teachers College Press.

Shaffir, W. G., R. A. Stebbins, and A. Turowetz. 1980. *Fieldwork experience.* New York: St. Martin's Press.

Shaw, C. 1930. *The jack roller.* Chicago: University of Chicago Press.

Shweder, R. 1986. Storytelling among the anthropologists. *New York Times Book Review*, 21 Sept., 1, 38.

Sieber, J., ed. 1982. *Ethics of social research: Fieldwork, regulation and publication.* New York: Springer-Verlag.

Silverman, D. 1993. *Interpreting qualitative data: Methods for analyzing talk, text, and interaction.* Thousand Oaks, CA: Sage.

Sindell, P. 1987. "Some discontinuities in the enculturation of Mistassini Cree children." In *Education and cultural process*, 2d ed., edited by G. Spindler, 378–386. Prospect Heights, IL: Waveland Press.

Smith, M. 1954. *Baba of Karo.* London: Faber.

Soltis, J. 1990. "The ethics of qualitative research." In *Qualitative inquiry in education*, edited by E. Eisner and A. Peshkin, 247–257. New York: Teachers College Press.

Spradley, J. 1970. *You owe yourself a drunk: An ethnography of urban nomads.* Boston: Little, Brown.

———. 1979. *The ethnographic interview.* New York: Holt, Rinehart & Winston.

Spradley, J., and B. Mann. 1975. *The cocktail waitress: Woman's work in a man's world.* New York: Wiley.

Spradley, J., and D. McCurdy. 1972. *The cultural experience: Ethnography in complex society.* Chicago: Science Research Associates.

Stewart, J. 1989. *Drinkers, drummers, and decent folk: Ethnographic narratives of village Trinidad.* Albany: State University of New York Press.

Stoller, P. 1989. *The taste of ethnographic things: The senses in anthropology.* Philadelphia: University of Pennsylvania Press.

Strauss, A. 1987. *Qualitative analysis for social scientists.* Cambridge: Cambridge University Press.

Stringer, E. 1996. *Action research: A handbook for practitioners.* Thousand Oaks, CA: Sage.

Strouse, J. 1988. "The real reasons." In *Extraordinary lives: The art and craft of American biography*, edited by W. Zinsser, 163–195. Boston: Houghton Mifflin.

Strunk, W., and E. B. White. 1979. *The elements of style*, 3d ed. New York: Macmillan.

Sullivan, M. A., S. A. Queen, and R. C. Patrick. 1958. Participant observation as employed in the study of a military training program. *American Sociological Review* 23:610–667.

Sze, M.-M., and K. Wang. 1963. *The Tao of painting.* New York: Pantheon Books. (Orig. published 1701)

Tesch, R. 1990. *Qualitative research: Analysis types and software tools.* New York: Falmer Press.

Thomas, J. 1993. *Doing critical ethnography.* Newbury Park, CA: Sage.

Tierney, W., and Y. Lincoln, eds. 1997. *Representation and the text: Re-framing the narrative voice.* Albany: State University of New York Press.

Tierney, W. 1995. (Re) presentation and voice. *Qualitative Inquiry* 1 (4): 379–390.

Tolkien, J. R. R. 1965. *The lord of the rings.* Boston: Houghton Mifflin.

Tsing, A. L. 1993. *In the realm of the diamond queen: Marginality in an out-of-way place.* Princeton, NJ: Princeton University Press.

Turner, J. 1985. In defense of positivism. *Sociological Theory* 3:24–31.

Ueland, B. 1987. *If you want to write,* 2nd ed. St. Paul, MN: Graywolf Press.

Usher, P. 1996. "Feminist approaches to research." In *Understanding educational research,* edited by D. Scott and R. Usher, 120–142. New York: Routledge.

Usher, R. 1996. "A critique of the neglected epistemological assumptions of educational research." In *Understanding educational research,* edited by D. Scott and R. Usher, 9–32. New York: Routledge.

Van Galen, J., G. Noblit, and D. Hare. 1988–1989. The art and science of interviewing kids: The group interview in evaluation research. *National Forum of Applied Educational Research Journal* 1(2):74–81.

Van Maanen, J. 1983. "The moral fix: On the ethics of fieldwork." In *Contemporary field research,* edited by R. Emerson, 269–287. Boston: Little, Brown.

———. 1988. *Tales of the field: On writing ethnography.* Chicago: University of Chicago Press.

———. 1995. "An end to innocence: The ethnography of ethnography." In *Representation in ethnography,* edited by J. Van Maanen, 1–35. Thousand Oaks, CA: Sage.

———, ed. 1995. *Representation in ethnography.* Thousand Oaks, CA: Sage.

Vidich, A., and J. Bensman. 1968. *Small town in mass society,* rev. ed. Princeton, NJ: Princeton University Press.

Vidich, A., and S. Lyman. 1994. "Qualitative methods: Their history in sociology and anthropology." In *Handbook of qualitative research,* edited by N. Denzin and Y. Lincoln, 23–59. Thousand Oaks, CA: Sage.

Wang, J. 1995. Comparisons of research methods in China and United States from personal experience. Unpublished manuscript. University of Vermont, Burlington.

Warren, C. 1988. *Gender issues in field research.* Newbury Park, CA: Sage.

Wax, M. 1982. "Research reciprocity rather than informed consent in fieldwork." In *Ethics of social research: Fieldwork, regulation, and publication,* edited by J. Sieber, 33–48. New York: Springer-Verlag.

Wax, R. 1971. *Doing fieldwork: Warnings and advice.* Chicago: University of Chicago Press.

Webster's Third International Dictionary. 1986. Springfield, MA: Meriam & Webster.

Wehlage, G. 1981. "The purpose of generalization in field-study research." In *The study of schooling,* edited by T. Popkewitz and R. Tabachnick, 211–226. Westport, CT: Greenwood Press.

Welch, D. D. 1994. *Conflicting agendas: Personal morality in institutional settings.* Cleveland, OH: Pilgrim Press.

Weitzman, E., and M. Miles. 1995. *Computer programs for qualitative data analysis.* Thousand Oaks, CA: Sage.

West, J. 1945. *Plainville, U.S.A.* New York: Columbia University Press.

West, W. G. 1980. "Access to adolescent deviants and deviance." In *Fieldwork experience,* edited by W. B. Shaffir, R. A. Stebbins, and A. Turowetz, 31–44. New York: St. Martin's Press.

White, C., D. Andino-Demyan, D. Primer, and M. Storz. 1996. Constructing a scholarly community of jazz freedom fighters: (Re)writing the university classroom for the postmodern world. *Planning and Changing* 27 (1/2): 58–73.

Whitehead, T., and M. Conaway, eds. 1986. *Self, sex, and gender in cross-cultural fieldwork.* Chicago: University of Illinois Press.

Whyte, W. 1981. *Streetcorner society*. Chicago: University of Chicago Press. (Orig. published 1943)

———. 1984. *Learning from the field: A guide from experience*. Beverly Hills: Sage Publications.

———. ed. 1991. *Participatory action research*. Newbury Park, CA: Sage Publications.

Wildavsky, A. 1989. *Craftways: On the organization of scholarly work*. New Brunswick, NJ: Transaction.

Wilkins, L. T. 1979. "Human subjects—whose subject?" In *Deviance and decency*, edited by C. B. Klockars and F. W. O'Connor, 99–123. Beverly Hills: Sage Publications.

Willis, P. 1977. *Learning to labor*. New York: Columbia University Press.

Wilson, S. May 1989. Alaskan journal. *Vermont Quarterly*, 13–18.

Wolcott, H. 1973. *The man in the principal's office: An ethnography*. New York: Holt, Rinehart & Winston.

———. 1975. Criteria for an ethnographic approach to research in schools. *Human Organization* 34:111–127.

———. 1981. "Confessions of a trained observer." In *The study of schooling*, edited by T. S. Popkewitz and B. R. Tabachnick, New York: Praeger.

———. 1990. *Writing up qualitative research*. Newbury Park, CA: Sage Publications.

———. 1992. "Posturing in qualitative research." In *The handbook of qualitative research in education*, edited by M. LeCompte, W. Millroy, and J. Preissle, 3–52. San Diego, CA: Academic Press.

———. 1994. *Transforming qualitative data: Description, analysis, and interpretation*. Thousand Oaks, CA: Sage.

———. 1995. *The art of fieldwork*. Walnut Creek, CA: AltaMira Press.

Woods, P. 1985. "New songs played skillfully: Creativity and technique in writing up research." In *Issues in educational research*, edited by R. Burgess, 86–106. Philadelphia: Falmer Press.

———. 1986. *Inside schools: Ethnography in educational research*. New York: Routledge & Kegan Paul.

Woolfson, P. 1988. Non-verbal interaction of Anglo-Canadian, Jewish-Canadian, and French-Canadian physicians with their young, middle-aged, and elderly patients. *Visual Anthropology* 1:404–414.

Wright, R., and S. Decker. 1997. *Armed robbers in action: Stickups and street culture*. Boston: Northeastern University Press.

Yoors, J. 1967. *The gypsies*. New York: Simon & Schuster.

Young, B., and C. Tardif. 1988. Interviewing: Two sides of the story. Paper presented at the annual meeting of the American Educational Research Association, New Orleans.

Zigarmi, D., and P. Zigarmi. 1978. The psychological stresses of ethnographic research. Paper presented at the annual meeting of the American Educational Research Association, Toronto.

Zinsser, W., ed. 1988a. *Extraordinary lives: The art and craft of American biography*. Boston: Houghton Mifflin.

———. 1988b. *Writing to learn: How to write and think clearly about any subject at all*. New York: Harper & Row.

Zuber-Skerritt, O., ed. 1996. *New directions in action research*. Washington, DC: The Falmer Press.

Name Index

Subject Index